Personality and Ideology

Critical Texts in Social Work and the
Welfare State

General Editor: Peter Leonard

Published

Pete Alcock and Phil Harris
WELFARE LAW AND ORDER

Steve Bolger, Paul Corrigan, Jan Docking and Nick Frost
TOWARDS SOCIALIST WELFARE WORK:
WORKING IN THE STATE

Paul Corrigan and Peter Leonard
SOCIAL WORK PRACTICE UNDER CAPITALISM:
A MARXIST APPROACH

Norman Ginsburg
CLASS, CAPITAL AND SOCIAL POLICY

Ian Gough
THE POLITICAL ECONOMY OF THE WELFARE STATE

Chris Jones
STATE SOCIAL WORK AND THE WORKING CLASS

Peter Leonard
PERSONALITY AND IDEOLOGY: TOWARDS
A MATERIALIST UNDERSTANDING
OF THE INDIVIDUAL

Chris Phillipson
CAPITALISM AND THE CONSTRUCTION OF OLD AGE

Forthcoming

Paul Clifford, Stephen Frosh, Ragnhild Banton, Julian
Lousada, Jo Rosenthal
THE POLITICS OF MENTAL HEALTH

Lena Dominelli and Eileen McLeod
FEMINISM AND WELFARE: SOCIAL ACTION AND SOCIAL
WORK

Personality and Ideology

Towards a Materialist Understanding of the Individual

Peter Leonard

MACMILLAN PRESS
LONDON

First published 1984 by
THE MACMILLAN PRESS LTD
London and Basingstoke
Companies and representatives
throughout the world

ISBN 0 333 34725 0 (hard cover)
ISBN 0 333 34726 9 (paper cover)

Typeset by
Wessex Typesetters Ltd
Frome, Somerset

Printed in Hong Kong

This book is for **Lynne** with my love

Contents

Preface   x

1 Introduction: The Need for a Materialist Understanding of the Individual   1
A question of practical necessity   1
The gap in Marxism   5
The purpose and plan of the book   7

PART I   MATERIALISM AND PSYCHOLOGICAL THEORY

2 The Limitations of Psychology   11
Major trends in psychology   12
Enter historical materialism   19
Intellectual production and material structure   20
Materialism and the individual   23
Psychology and 'human nature'   29
Psychoanalysis and ideology   32

3 Materialism, Instinct and Intention   39
Freudianism as a response to Marxism's 'failure'   40
Sexual repression and class struggle   42
Women's psychology and patriarchal relations   47
Production, consumption and class relations   56
Social being and biological being   64
Human intention and the self   70

4 Personality Theory from within Historical Materialism   76
Humanism and alienation theory   77
Personality development and social labour   83

Acts, capacities and needs   87
The structure of personality and use-time   90
A general topology of personalities   92
Psychological superstructures   96
Production, ideology and gender   99

5 **Key Concepts in a Materialist Analysis**   **102**
Problems of theory   102
Omissions   105
Summary of key concepts   109

**PART II   PERSONALITY DEVELOPMENT
              WITHIN CAPITALISM**

6 **Entering the Social Order**   **121**
The triumph of the bourgeois family form   122
The penetration of ideology   129
The dialectic relationship between parent and child   135
Material determinants and use-time   138
Instinctual repression and redirection   141
Problems and deprivations   145
State intervention in childhood   147
The older child and the young adult   150

7 **Working in the Social Order**   **153**
Performing socially necessary labour   154
The experience of wage labour   160
Parental roles and familial ideology   165
Contradictions in family and sexual relations   170
The state and the parent   174
Contradictory consciousness and adult personality   178

8 **Marginality in the Social Order**   **180**
Poverty and the absence of wage labour   182
The ideological context of marginality   187
The self, identification and repression   191

9 **Personality Development and Collective Action**   **202**
Pessimism and the incorporation of dominant ideology   203
Revolutionary *praxis*   206
Consciousness-raising   208

Varieties of political practice 209
Psychological benefits of collective action 211
Conclusion · 217

References 218

Index 225

Preface

The origins of this book could be traced to a time, nearly twenty-five years ago, when, like most social workers, I lived in a professional culture dominated by social reformism and Freudian theory. It was after an education in sociology and social administration that I gained my introduction to psychoanalytic theory and the practice of psychiatric casework. Some time later I contributed to the teaching of subjects called 'Human Growth and Development' and 'Social Influences on Behaviour', subjects which were based on a psychoanalytic conception of the human life cycle injected with a mild dose of structural-functional sociology.

All of this took place before I became disillusioned with the social reformism which was the explicit political culture in which I had worked. As I gradually became committed to Marxism as a politics, a theory and a method of historical analysis, I re-evaluated all my previous intellectual allegiances. Apart from rejecting much of the mainstream sociology and social administration of which I had previously been part, I felt impelled to turn aside from the psychoanalytic-based insights and skills which I had developed over many years of professional practice. I wished to avoid the reductionism and liberal pessimism with which such insights and skills were often associated.

In more recent years, partly under the strong impact of feminism, I have been forced, like many others, to return to Freud once more. Despite its obvious limitations as a view of human beings and the reactionary purposes to which it has often been put, perhaps it still has, I thought, some possibilities when it is interrogated from the perspectives of Marxism and feminism. At the same time, I have been introduced to the beginnings of a theory of the individual in Marx's work, and to the potentials which lie in symbolic interactionism, first revealed to me as a possibly progressive approach at the National Deviancy Conferences of the early 1970s. It is from immersion in this heady mixture of frequently conflicting approaches to the individual that this book breaks to the surface.

Apart from the more obvious theoretical and technical problems posed by writing this book comes a specifically political one. A book which attempts to give some account of the material existence and psychological experiences of others, even at a very general level and from what attempts to be a socialist perspective, runs the danger of appearing both to *psychologise* their situations and *appropriate* their experiences for purposes outside their particular interests. Feminists have rightly resisted the attempts of men to colonise their work, from a similar standpoint to that of people with disabilities who are beginning to resist the definitions of their situation produced by able-bodied 'experts'. I hope that in this book I have been able to avoid these particular dangers: the reader must judge.

As this book represents, for me, a settling of accounts with my professional and academic past, attempting to acknowledge all the influences on my writing would be a major task. Instead, I shall mention just one name from over twenty years ago – Donald Winnicott, paediatrician and psychoanalyst, who taught me how a theory could be integrated into a practice that was supremely sensitive, imaginative and reflective. More recently influential was the impact on me of the students who participated in my postgraduate seminars on Marxism and psychoanalysis and on personality development and social structure at Warwick University. My colleagues in the Department of Applied Social Studies have been immensely encouraging in their support, Lena Dominelli, Eileen McLeod and Janet Read in particular contributing helpful criticisms of drafts of the book. A former fellow-student of many years ago, like me exposed then to a powerful psychoanalytic influence, Elizabeth Wilson, also provided me with valuable comments. My special thanks must go to Janet Sayer of the University of Kent and Mike Seltzer of Norges Kommunal-Og Sosialhøgskole, Oslo, for their unstinting and detailed criti-

cisms and comments on the book, a combination of scholarship
and commitment which I found inspiring. Without Lydia
Thorpe, who so faultlessly typed from the handwritten manu-
script, my task would have been much harder. Finally, I must
express my appreciation to my wife, Lynne, for providing so
much encouragement and support, especially during the final
weeks of rewriting when we were not sure which would be
produced first, the book or our second child.

University of Warwick
September 1983   Peter Leonard

1
Introduction: The Need for a Materialist Understanding of the Individual

For socialists to attempt to develop their understanding of the individual, her development as a person, her attitudes, motivations and experiences, and the ways these are historically constructed within particular societies, may seem to some a self-evidently worthwhile task. It would be mistaken, however, to assume the validity of such an enterprise: rather, it must be *argued*. More particularly, if one starts, as this book does, from the standpoint that Marx's materialist theory of history must be a major foundation upon which a socialist understanding of the individual rests, then the absence of a developed theory of the individual within Marxism might be taken to indicate that Marxists, at least, have not always accorded the enterprise the priority which we suggest. Later in this chapter, and more fully in the book as a whole, we will be arguing for the theoretical (and by implication or directly the wider political) justification for working towards a materialist understanding of the individual. At this point we wish to start by emphasising its *practical necessity* in the present historical context.

A QUESTION OF PRACTICAL NECESSITY

Although the political resurgence of the Right characterises the present period within many capitalist countries, and often sows despondency and discord amongst those who oppose it, it is a resurgence which also brings a contradiction: it makes clearer issues which were previously confused and it compels those of us who consider ourselves part of the Left to re-evaluate the ways in which we understand our society and ourselves. The ideological victories of the Right and the present failure to develop socialist alternatives which resonate with the experiences and beliefs of the mass of the population must lead us to explore more fully the nature of human consciousness, how it is constructed within specific historical conditions, how it is manipulated in the interests of particular class, gender and ethnic groups, and how such manipulation might be more effectively resisted.

Amongst those who are experiencing the full onslaught of right-wing ideology and policies and their penetrating effect upon individuals are socialists who work within the broad fields of health, welfare and education, both State employees and community and pressure group activists. Under the impact of cuts in public services, of the restructuring of the services that remain in the direction of greater central control, and of the privatisation of services, all within a context of mass unemployment, many workers within these fields are being forced to reconsider the role of the State in every aspect of people's lives. Part of this reconsideration centres on the problem of whether it is possible for socialists to act 'in and against the State' (London–Edinburgh Weekend Return Group, 1980) as social workers, teachers, health workers and others. Although acting within a capitalist state apparatus in a progressive, socialist way is recognised as highly problematic and difficult, there is wide agreement that one of the major aims of such action is to restructure the various services in order to ensure the widest possible democratic participation of individuals, groups, communities and organisations in defining problems and issues, in determining the kinds of interventions which should take place and in evaluating the results of service provision. Such objectives of struggle within the state apparatus have emerged as a result of practical community action and of sustained critiques of the social democratic 'Welfare State', dominant since the end of World War II until the political triumph of the radical Right at the end of the 1970s (see Leonard, 1979). This attack by the Left on the nature and the oppressive characteristics of state welfare institutions was rejected by the mainstream leaders of the Labour movement, but utilised by the Right as part of its broad ideological offensive against welfare and in favour of the private market economy (see Corrigan, 1979; Hall, 1979).

If attention to the social democratic State apparatus has been one focus of criticism by both Left and Right, the other major focus has been on 'the family'. Sustained feminist criticism of the ideology of the nuclear family as a crucial factor in women's oppression (see Barrett and McIntosh, 1982) has left socialist practitioners and community activists in the health, education and welfare fields uncertain about how to respond to families and households in a manner which does not reinforce gender oppression (of both females and males, adults and children) but which might even contribute to the development of a wider critical consciousness of this oppression. Against this, the radical Right seeks to re-emphasise the crucial positive role which the family performs in the reproduction of the social order and in the defence of society against individual deviancy and more widespread civil disorder. State policy is once more directed to ensuring that women remain at home to be the carers of children, the elderly and the handicapped as state-provided services decline or are entirely eliminated.

But if socialists are to give increased attention to the State and the family as 'arenas of struggle' and to counteract the dominant ideologies which permeate policies, practices and experiences within these arenas, then we must give more emphasis to understanding how the individual person's consciousness of the State, the family, the economy and herself is formed. During the long post-war period of social democratic hegemony, most socialist state workers and activists incorporated mainstream psychological theories, such as psychoanalysis, into their conceptions of the individual, though often in vulgarised form, and attempted to practise progressively on the basis of such theories. The resulting disjuncture between their conceptions of the social order and of the individual was experienced as one major block to progressive work with individuals and families. Others overtly rejected psychological theorising as such, considering it reductionist and inevitably tainted with individual pathology models of social problems; they sought to concentrate analysis and action at the level of the group, community or class. The problem with this approach was that in the absence of a worked-out critical theory of the individual, the psychological assumptions embedded in dominant 'common sense' understandings, carrying with them vulgarised traces of Freudianism, behaviourism and other psychological work, remained largely unexamined in the consciousness of such workers. The result was that although they were bound to interact with individuals (co-workers, community leaders, campaign activists) they were deprived of the means by which they could reflect systematically upon such interaction in terms of understanding the motivations, attitudes and experiences of themselves and others, and so improve their interactions.

The result of the lack of integration between an understanding of the development of the individual and of the imperatives of the social order can be seen in the way social workers have responded to the problem of the relationship between individual experience and social structure (see also Cohen, 1975). The predominant response has been to emphasise the significance of individual development within the family in the understanding of 'problems', and to see the 'social environment' as a *background* which influences individual psychological and social development through general cultural norms or sub-cultural values and practices. Despite the attempt within social work education in the past to break through the disciplinary boundaries between sociology, psychology and biology by mounting courses on 'Human Growth and Development' and 'Social Influences on Behaviour', such courses have usually failed to prevent a psychologically reductionist end product. Within this approach, the individual *per se* has been heavily theorised, while the social system as constructing the individual within specific historical conditions has been relatively untheorised. The consequent perception of the individual in ahistorical terms, somehow separate from the social structure, has permeated social work practice, thus supporting that cult of individualism which is a necessary part of bourgeois ideology and of state policies and practices.

The alternative response within social work to the problem of understanding the relationship between individuals and social structure has been that often advocated by radical sociologists attempting to fight the individualism of social work education – heavy theorising about the determining effects of the social order on the individual. The analysis of class and gender relations, the central role of production and reproduction, the controlling operations of the modern state, the place of the mass media in the production of 'moral panics', have all been seen as highly determinant in relation to individual consciousness and behaviour. Within this alternative, the individual has often been relatively untheorised with the result that many social workers tend to see welfare recipients only as victims of an oppressive and monolithic social order. In this functionalist picture, the individual is seen as having little opportunity for resistance and at its extreme this leads social workers to despair of the possibilities of progressive practice with individuals. The most usual result is that social workers act upon two relatively self-contained images: one is of the individual as determined by early and current family experiences; the other is of a social order which is *generally* determinant. What is lacking is detailed attention to the dialectic between the individual and the social order, whereby the former is socially constructed, but within a context of struggle and resistance.

THE GAP IN MARXISM

In spite of the foregoing strictures, it would be an obvious mistake to lay the failure to develop an integrated understanding of the individual within the social structure simply at the door of socialist practitioners, or of teachers within professional education courses concerned with health, welfare, schooling or community work. The historic gap in Marxist theory about the individual, to which we have already referred and to which we will return later in the book, without doubt presents a massive obstacle to our understanding of how the individual is constructed under specific historical conditions. Sartre (1963, p. 56) refers to this as the problem that 'Marxism lacks any hierarchy of mediations which would permit it to grasp the process which produces the person and his product inside class and within a given society at a given historical moment'. The problem, in other words, of being unable to produce a biographical account of a specific individual from within Marxist categories. Sartre's 'solution' to this gap was to turn to existentialism (see Poster, 1979), an enterprise which could not be considered to be successful, but which highlighted the difficulties involved in developing a materialist understanding of the individual within a general theory which emphasises production rather than the family.

> To-day's Marxists are concerned only with adults; reading them, one would believe that we are born at the age when we earn our first wages. They have forgotten their own child-hoods. As we read them, everything seems to happen as if men experienced their alienation and their reification *first in their own work*, whereas in actuality each one lives it *first*, as a child, *in his parents' work*.
>
> (Sartre, 1963, p. 62; see also Poster, 1979, p. 26)

Sartre wrote *Search for a Method*, from which this quotation comes, in 1957 and much has happened within socialist thought since that time which has had an immense influence on Western Marxism. Most importantly, under the impact of feminist work, the family has now become a significant focus of attention. Because it begins by rendering an account of the oppression of women in everyday life – in child care, domestic labour and wage labour – feminism has made an historic contribution to our understanding of the social construction of individual consciousness. No materialist theory of the indi-vidual could now be developed which did not found itself, at least in part, upon the insights which feminist scholarship has established concerning the central significance of gender relations and of the family in the construction of an individual's consciousness.

But the gap in Marxism remains. Feminism and Marxism retain an uneasy relationship with one another and so the development of a general theory of the individual which would satisfy both perspectives is not yet in sight. Following a detailed critique of Marx's work in relation to the analysis and aspirations of feminists, Barrett comes to a characteristically cautious conclusion:

> To speak of 'Marxist-feminism' is not to invoke a systematic and integrated approach to the oppression of women in

[handwritten margin notes: gender different from class, loos united — difference classes, contradiction]

capitalism or in any other mode of production. The meaning that I would attach to it is that one's feminism exists alongside the recognition that Marxism provides an unrivalled explanation and analysis of the capitalist society in which we live. The task, if it be possible, of synthesising Marxism and feminism was not attempted by Marx and to suggest that it was is to belittle feminism. We would do well, however, to heed Marx's views on comparable questions and refrain from taking too sanguine a view of this integrative project.

(Barrett, 1983)

The establishment of a satisfactory materialist theory of the individual basing itself on both Marxism and feminism lies, then, in the future. In the meantime, we can review the various strands of work that are being undertaken on materialist approaches to the individual, note the convergences and divergences between different positions in such work, and identify the most central concepts which are emerging. This book may be seen as part of a wider enterprise, though focused on a particular set of concerns and primarily directed to a specific readership.

THE PURPOSE AND PLAN OF THE BOOK

The book is divided into two parts. Part I reviews some of the attempts that have been made to develop a materialist approach to personality, the structure of a person's consciousness and behaviour. It begins with a critique of mainstream psychological theories from the point of view of historical materialism (Chapter 2) and then goes on to examine two alternative approaches to developing a materialist understanding of the individual. In Chapter 3 we examine the possibility of utilising existing psychological theories as part of a materialist analysis, using psychoanalysis and symbolic interactionism as examples. Chapter 4 is devoted to attempts that have been made to establish a materialist psychology on foundations within Marxism, specifically on the theory of human alienation and on the theory of labour. In Chapter 5, we discuss the relative influence of ideology and of the actual material relations of production in the formation of individual personality and then proceed to identify some of the key concepts which are necessary to a materialist understanding of the individual.

Part II of the book moves, on the basis of the key concepts we have identified, to an introductory exposition of some aspects of the formation of personality in the human life cycle under the specific historical conditions of late capitalism. Chapter 6 looks at the processes involved in entering the social order in childhood, whilst Chapter 7 explores the adult experience of wage and domestic labour as a determinant of personality. In Chapter 8 we consider the experience of those consigned to marginality in the social order and its psychological consequences, taking as examples the long-term unemployed, people with disabilities and the elderly. Finally, in Chapter 9 we explore the impact on individuals of engaging in collective action and see this as a *psychological* justification for a politics of mass participation both in relation to state services and more widely.

PART I

MATERIALISM AND PSYCHOLOGICAL THEORY

2
The Limitations of Psychology

Given the present condition of contemporary psychology – a battle-ground of conflicting schools and tendencies – it might seem a diversion to enter the current debates and more profitable to begin at once the central task of outlining the preconditions that need to be met if a materialist understanding of the individual is to be established. In the past, there has often been an intermittent tendency on the Left to dismiss mainstream psychology as 'bourgeois psychology' and therefore as appropriate for consignment to the dustbin of history. Of course, there is a strong case for labelling the main psychological schools as bourgeois, for they have emerged within bourgeois societies and in major respects perform significant legitimating functions on behalf of the dominant social order. But there is a danger in such labelling if it leads to an undifferentiated lumping together of conflicting perspectives, and a consequent failure to identify the contradictions inherent in the scientific ideas and practices which emerge in bourgeois societies. Such contradictions arise in part from the fact that scientific developments involve real discoveries and progressive ideas, and are not simply passive reflections of dominant ideologies and the imperatives of social and economic organisation. However, all science is deeply affected by its historical location within ideology, in that it takes place within certain 'mental frameworks – the languages, the concepts, categories, imagery of thought, and the systems of representation – which different classes and social groups deploy in order to make sense of, define, figure out and render intelligible the way society works' (Hall, 1983, p. 59).

We shall return to this issue of the relation of science to ideology later in this chapter when we set out the main critiques of contemporary psychological schools from the perspective of historical materialism. At this stage we are making the point that mainstream psychology and its internal debates deserve a serious critical attention, which may be forfeited if one is swept along by the rhetoric of an over-mechanical and over-determinist view of the status of social science ideas and practices in capitalist societies.

MAJOR TRENDS IN PSYCHOLOGY

We can make our point by showing that the main theoretical divisions within psychology are important from the perspective of historical materialism. Despite the mass of debates and perspectives which exist within contemporary psychological work, it is useful to simplify the most significant divisions concerning the formation of human personality as those existing between social learning theories, phenomenological perspectives and intrapsychic theories.

Theories of the development of the individual which emphasise the central place of *social learning* are based upon certain developments in behavioural psychology and exert a dominating influence within the whole field of British psychology. It is important to note from the very beginning, however, that there is very substantial diversity within behaviourism itself. The most important divergence is on the issue of whether, as Eysenck (1971) maintains in his discussion of the relationship between race and intelligence, genetic factors have the greatest influence on the individual's development, or whether as Skinner (1974) has argued, it is the environment which is crucially determining. Skinner has been the most important exponent of the theory of the dominating influence of the environment through its conditioning of the behaviour of the individual and it is this view which lies at the core of the social learning approach. The environment through which the individual learns or is conditioned includes other people and social institutions; it is the means by which, for example, children learn 'correct' behaviour in the family or at school. The most important mechanism of human learning is that which occurs as a consequence of an interaction between an individual and some environmental event – operant conditioning (see Blackman, 1974). Learning through the experience of negative or positive results, acting upon feedback, does not necessarily depend upon a *direct* experience of some environmental stimulus but can be achieved, it is argued, through observing what other people do. We can learn through imitating other's behaviour or, if the consequences appear to be negative or unpleasurable, be deterred from doing so.

In its original formulation and as still espoused by Skinner, social learning theory has argued that the individual is best understood as a recipient of external stimuli rather than as an active element in the individual–environment interaction, bringing with her thinking, volition, intentions and meanings. Skinner does not deny the existence of human intentions and purposes and concedes that 'we can create a vocabulary for talking about them and part of human progress has been the improvement of our description of these things' (Skinner, 1964, p. 106). He argues, however, that mental states have no place in his approach because first, our knowledge of them is not sufficiently scientific and second, because behaviour can be adequately explained without reference to human intention.

The denial of the significance of internal intentions and meanings in the explanation of the individual's behaviour has been disputed not only by other schools of psychology, but also within social learning approaches themselves. An 'identical' environmental stimulus appears, after all, to affect people's behaviour differently and this is likely to be the result of the fact that the individual attaches a particular meaning to an environmental stimulus (person or object) determined by her previous experience. The more recent work of social learning theorists has suggested in fact that the individual's cognition enters as a significant variable in the determination of behaviour, *evaluating* other persons and objects (see Mischel, 1973). This evaluation, based upon the result of the previous personal experiences of the individual, creates a unique self-concept which guides further behaviour.

But introducing the idea of meaning, or of other internal mental states, into explanations of behaviour is problematic, as we have seen in Skinner's case, for those psychologists who aspire to a natural sciences model of psychology based upon 'objective' laboratory experiments, an aspiration which has dominated behavioural psychology. It is an issue which has a long history in the development of the social sciences, a history which is of significance to us. The triumphs of the natural sciences in securing the expansion of the forces of production in nineteenth century capitalism were bound to provide a strong argument in favour of the application of such scientific objectives and techniques to the study of the social reproduction of the human beings upon whose labour capitalism is based. But such an application has always met with resistance. In nineteenth century Germany, a philosophy of science emerged which maintained that the social or *human sciences* were, and should be, distinct from the physical or *natural sciences*. This distinction lay, it was argued, in the fact of human intention, for to study human beings in a social context, rather than simply as biological beings, required an additional element. Max Weber called this element *Verstehen*, a form of understanding which took account of people's intentions, the meaning that behaviour had for the acting individual. How the individual defines the situation in which she is placed is, for Weber, an essential ingredient in the understanding of human action. Influenced by the same debates within German nineteenth century philosophy, George Herbert Mead (1962) the founder of the *symbolic interactionist* stream within phenomenology, also takes issue with behaviourism in his non-determinist stance. Mead argued that a dialectic exists between the organism and the environment, so that organisms are not simply determined by the environment within which they live, but interact with it in various ways according to their species. In the case of humans, responses to the environment include the capacity to relate to the *symbols* of objects that stand in the place of objects themselves, symbols that include language, bodily postures and cultural objects.

Current examples of this historic debate between traditional experimental behaviourism and the phenomenological emphasis on meaning can be seen in the struggles of the so-called 'new social psychology' against a weakening experimentist hegemony. Harré and Secord (1972) complain

[handwritten annotation: Theories often based on small samples — not particularly significant. Wrapped in Science must be right.]

that much of experimental psychology is based on three assumptions, all of them mistaken:

(a) that only a mechanistic model of man will satisfy the requirements for making a science, (b) that the most scientific conception of cause is one which focuses on external stimulation and which excludes from consideration any treatment of the mode of connection between cause and effect, and (c) that a methodology based on logical positivism is the best possible approach to a behavioural science.

(Harré and Secord, 1972, p. 5)

The authors argue further that, in contrast to traditional behaviourist approaches, human beings must be treated as agents with intentions and goals and that it is unscientific to treat them as anything else. Social behaviour, they maintain, must be conceived of as actions mediated by meanings, not responses caused by stimuli. Brenner (1980), editing a collection of papers by a number of European and American psychologists, maintains that social psychology is 'in turmoil' as a result of its break with traditional behaviourism. Social interaction, the various authors argue, must take account of both the structure of that interaction (its social context) and of the individual as an active agent within that structure. Meaning and interpretation, Brenner suggests, are crucial determinants of human action, and not simply the external world, as such. John Shotter maintains that 'intentionality is a fundamental and irreducible feature, a pre-supposition of all thought, all conceptual activity, and all action' (Brenner 1980, p. 5).

Whilst many contemporary psychologists struggle with the conceptual and methodological problem presented by the introduction of meaning into the explanation of human behaviour alongside the stimulus of the environment, a particular strand of psychological work, representing most fully the phenomenological tradition, places dominating emphasis on meaning and the concept of 'self'. We can take the work of Carl Rogers and George Kelly as the most influential examples of this perspective, very powerful in America and associated with a range of 'growth' therapies and individual and group counselling.

For Rogers (1951) the most significant concept for the individual is the 'self', a pattern of perceptions, meanings, feelings and values which constitute the 'I' and which, together with the 'organic' needs of the total individual, determines activity. The primary motivation for human action is 'self-actualisation', the need for increasing self-expression and independence, but the need for love, 'positive regard by others', is also highly determinant and will shape the concept of the 'self', and particularly of the 'ideal self' − what the person would like to be. The degree of distance between the 'self' and the 'ideal self' is one indication of the extent of the individual's maladjustment. Kelly (1955) in his Personal Construct theory, like Rogers, places the individual's understanding of herself and her environment at the centre of his explanation of human behaviour. Cognition, the development of mental constructs by which the individual makes sense of the environment, is decisive, for it is through these constructs or concepts that future events are predicted and the predictions acted upon, rather than on the basis of some 'objective reality'. It is constructs such as good/bad, possible/impossible, friend/enemy which constitute the individual's personality and which determine behaviour, rather than the 'actual' environmental situation.

Although sharing some of the same ground as the phenomenological perspectives in psychology, and attracting even greater opprobrium from traditional behaviourists on account of its 'unscientific' base in introspection, psychoanalysis and other intrapsychic theories have a rather different origin and trajectory. Human intentions and meanings are taken account of in psychoanalysis, but they are deeply determined by the unconscious, a reservoir of instinctual needs and mental representations which is in continuous interaction, and frequently conflict, with conscious human intention.

For Freud (1963) the environment (the family and the wider culture) certainly affects human behaviour, but the focus of attention is on the personality structure of the individual − consisting of three major aspects, the id, the ego, and the superego. The id includes the individual's innate, biological needs, especially the 'libido' − sexual energy defined very widely − which frequently conflicts with cultural norms and social institutions. When such conflict or tension occurs, the id produces a mental representation of the object of its instinctual urges (e.g. incestuous desires for the parent) – an internal fantasy which is expressed to some degree through dreams, errors and slips of the tongue.

The ego relates directly to external reality and develops in early childhood from the id as a means of managing and discharging instinctually derived tensions and directing them towards socially acceptable forms of expression. Whereas the id operates on the 'pleasure principle', the ego acts according to the 'reality principle', action which frequently requires the use of defence mechanisms, such as denial, rationalisation or projection as a means by which instinctual drives are repressed.

The superego develops, in turn, from the ego as representing the internalised moral and political imperatives, standards of behaviour, and general cultural values derived primarily from the parents. These standards, imperatives and values are often perfectionist, idealistic and even 'punishing' and so in managing the tension between id, superego and the outside world, the ego must also temper the demands of the superego with the compromises required of the reality principle.

As the individual develops, the libido is focused on different parts of the body; first the mouth, for sucking is essential to survival, then the anus as the focus of bowel training and then the genitals, the focus of the child's desire for the parent of the opposite sex. Each of these stages of psychosexual develop- ment, oral, anal and genital, is assimilated into the preceding stages and each involves new adaptations if the individual is to be adequately prepared for the later stages. 'Mature sexuality', it is argued, depends upon the successful resolution of the oedipus complex, and the love, hate and rivalry towards parents that this involves.

The historical origins of these psychoanalytic conceptions of the determinants of human action lie, significantly, not in the laboratory nor the seminar, but in the consulting room. Freudian theory begins from *practice*, the practice of medicine in the particular historical context of nineteenth century Euro- pean bourgeois society. Within this society, sexual repression generally and the sexual oppression of women in particular was a specific outcome of the dominant form of patriarchal family structure. This outcome was especially evident, Freud discovered, in the mental states and puzzling behaviour of women patients, a behaviour which was explored first by hypnosis and later through the analysis of dreams. The theory of the unconscious, the corner-stone of all the various streams within intrapsychic psychology, emerged from the attempt to understand and *treat* these mysterious symptoms. With it came the discovery of infantile sexuality and the centrality of sexual drives and relationships in the unconscious influence on human action.

Because of its origins in medicine and its continuing commitment to treatment, psychoanalysis has never laid much emphasis on the objectivity and reproducability of its 'results'. But within mainstream psychoanalysis a crisis is evident. It has lost ground to phenomenologically based therapies which concentrate on the here-and-now social situation of the person; they are above all cheaper than the traditional years of psychoanalysis. Psychoanalysis is also, in that school which studies *ego psychology*, desperate for the academic respectability which comes, Fromm (1971) argues, through emphasis on learning and adaptation (like the behaviourists) rather than the exploration of the unconscious.

> The ego psychological revision did not only start by studying the psychology of adaptation, it *is* in itself a psychology of the adaptation of psychoanalysis to twentieth century social science and to the dominant spirit in Western society. Seeking shelter in conformity is very understandable in an age of anxiety and mass conformity; however, it does not constitute progress in psychoanalytic theory, but retreat.
>
> (Fromm, 1971, p. 39)

Because of the importance of the dialogue which has existed throughout most of this century between Marxism and psychoanalysis, we shall be examining in the next chapter its claims as a possible basis for a materialist understanding of the individual, and therefore giving attention to the Left-wing revisionists within Freudian theory.

In pointing to some of the emphases, divisions and conflicts between and within the three main streams of contemporary

psychological theorisation, we have tried to show that debate
centres on two closely related issues. *First*, what are the
determinants of human action? From a base as a physiological
being, the person acts in a social world: how are we to account
for that action? In terms of external stimuli, in terms of
conscious intentions and meanings, or in terms of unconscious
drives? Does emphasis on one of these determinants preclude
consideration of the others? *Second*, by what means are we to
attempt to understand human action? Specifically, what is the
role of laboratory experimentation, of reported intentions and
meanings, and of introspection? Are these various methods
incompatible in the search for the evidence upon which to
build an understanding of human action?

ENTER HISTORICAL MATERIALISM

Historical materialism enters these debates substantially from
outside. It is undeniable, we would argue, however, that these
questions within psychology are of importance to historical
materialism; the place of individual and class purposes within
historically specific material circumstances is a central concern
of Marxism. Disagreement within the Left about the relative
importance of economic development compared with political
action, or of economic crises compared with broad ideological
struggle, testifies to the significance, for historical materialism,
of theorising about the role of human agency in history, and of
acting upon such theorisation. But from the perspective of
historical materialism we cannot simply decide to support *one* of
the three main streams of psychological theorisation. In the
first place, a materialist critique, as we shall see later, points to
the gross limitations and distortions of all mainstream
psychological theorisation in contemporary capitalist society.
Secondly, we have the problem that, at various times, Marxists
appear to have given some support to all three major streams.

We have mentioned already the long association between
some Western Marxists and psychoanalysis. In the next
chapter we shall examine this connection. At this point we can
note that amongst socialist feminists in particular, following
Mitchell (1975), there has been a recent revival of interest in

the progressive possibilities of psychoanalysis. Psychoanalysis, Mitchell suggests, 'gives us the concepts with which we can comprehend how ideology functions; closely connected with this, it further offers an analysis of the place and meaning of sexuality and of gender differences within society' (Mitchell, 1975, p. xxii). But the phenomenological stream in psychological theorisation has also received support from the Left, especially the contribution of symbolic interactionism to understanding the social construction of the person within ideology. Roberts (1977, p. 81) argues that 'for the purposes of the development of a "Marxist psychology" or "social psychology" Mead's idea of the self is significant because of his concern to produce a "socialised" conception of the individual personality'. Finally, there has also been some support from the Left for behaviourism and social learning theory. Behaviourist psychology is, it is argued, a materialist psychology, free of the idealist illusions of the other streams of psychology. It has, in Pavlov, a common ancestor with Soviet psychology, and the latter's principles, McLeish (1975) suggests, would 'when divorced from their special terminology and polemical context [be] acceptable to a large body of non-communist psychological opinion'. In other words, behaviourist opinion.

Faced with the diversity of opinions amongst Marxists themselves, what are we to do? How are we to evaluate the claims of the various streams of psychological theorisation and the debates between them? Earlier we suggested that historical materialism enters these debates from outside; it should, indeed transform these debates by locating them within an historical-theoretical analysis which renders a more profound critique than is possible within mainstream psychology itself. We will begin this process in the remainder of the chapter and in so doing attempt to set the stage for the rest of the book.

INTELLECTUAL PRODUCTION AND MATERIAL STRUCTURE

Before entering into historical materialist criticism of specific psychological theories, however, it is necessary to provide more general comments on how historical materialism approaches the problem of the relationship between intellectual work, such as psychological theorising, and the material circumstances governing the historical period within which that work takes place. We can say immediately that within Marxism this relationship is both complex and controversial and that it is probably wise to approach the relationship with some caution.

Marx states the relationship between material circumstances and ideas in the following terms:

In the social production which men carry on they enter into definite relations that are indispensable and independent of their will: these relations of production correspond to a definite stage of development of their material powers of production. The sum total of these relations of production constitutes the economic structure of society – the real foundation, on which rise legal and political superstructures and to which correspond definite forms of social consciousness. The mode of production in material life determines the general character of the social, political and spiritual processes of life. It is not the consciousness of men that determines their consciousness. . . . With the change of the economic foundation the entire immense superstructure is more or less rapidly transformed. In considering such transformations the distinction should always be made between the material transformation of the economic conditions of production which can be determined with the precision of natural science, and the legal, political, religious, aesthetic, or philosophic – in short, ideological forms in which men become conscious of this conflict and fight it out.

(Marx and Engels, 1968, p. 182)

Although Marx indicates that the superstructure of ideas, of consciousness and its institutional forms, is problematic so far as investigation is concerned, nevertheless he is clear that the economic structure determines the *general* character of consciousness, including scientific activity. Following this line of thought, some Marxist critics have pursued the question of how the economic system of capitalism determines both psychological theorisation and practice. Schneider (1975), for example, shows how the demands of capitalist production and consumption have a definite effect on the direction of psychological work – the maintenance and rehabilitation of the worker/consumer.

Before we take ourselves too far along this path, however, we need to acknowledge the dangers of a mechanical and one-sided conception of the relation between economic structure and intellectual activity. Engels recognised this danger:

> According to the materialist conception of history, the determining element in history is ultimately the production and reproduction in real life. More than this neither Marx nor I have ever asserted. If therefore somebody twists this into the statement that the economic element is the only determining one, he transforms it into a meaningless, abstract and absurd phrase. The economic situation is the basis, but the various elements of the superstructure – political forms of the class struggle and its consequences, constitutions established by the victorious class after a successful battle, etc. – forms of law – and then even the reflexes of all these actual struggles in the brains of the combatants: political, legal, and philosophical theories, religious ideas and their further development into systems of dogma – also exercise their influence upon the course of the historical struggles and in many cases preponderate in determining their form. There is an interaction of all these elements, in which, amid all the endless host of accidents (i.e., of things and events whose inner connection is so remote or so impossible to prove that we regard it as absent and can neglect it) the economic element finally asserts itself as necessary. Otherwise the application of the theory to any period of history one chose would be easier than the solution of a simple equation of the first degree.
>
> (Marx and Engels, 1968, p. 694)

Engels is here emphasising *interaction*, and showing us that a simple formula which argued that contemporary psychology could be 'read off' the economic infrastructure or even the commanding ideologies of advanced capitalism is likely to miss the real complexities and even to underestimate the semi-autonomy of institutions and ideas. So although we may refer to 'bourgeois psychology' if we wish, and explore, as we shall do later, the immersion of psychological thinking in ideology, we must remain cautious of overstating the case. Specifically, it is important to recognise that psychological theorisation is not simply an element in the ideology of the ruling class, as the early hostile reception of Freud's work clearly shows. In so far as ideas and explanations about human action reflect, in however complex a way, material interests and experiences, it might be best to acknowledge that these interests and experiences are contradictory and, as Engels suggests, exist in a context of class struggle. It is this context, after all, which justifies the Marxist belief that it is possible to develop *alternative* revolutionary ideas and practices, even within the social sciences themselves.

With these cautionary comments in mind, we can now proceed to identify the main elements of a materialist critique of dominant psychological theorisation. We undertake this critique in three stages: *first*, by suggesting that historical materialism points to certain ways of understanding the individual which mainstream psychologies cannot grasp; *second*, by examining the general limitations of contemporary psychological theorising which are a result of their being outside historical materialism; and *third*, by taking one example, psychoanalysis, and subjecting it to a more detailed historical/theoretical critique.

MATERIALISM AND THE INDIVIDUAL

Although, as we emphasised in Chapter 1, a great gap exists in historical materialism in its analysis of individual action and personality, we have nevertheless some general guidelines as to how understanding the individual should be approached. Most importantly, we know that the person should not be understood as a separate, atomised entity, although she may experience the world in such a way, but as part of the social processes which constitute society. In his most famous statement of this position, Marx writes that the human essence 'is not an abstraction inherent in each single individual [but] in its reality . . . is the ensemble of social relations' (Marx and Engels, 1968,

p. 29). It follows that an understanding of these social relations is basic to developing a conception of the individual. It is this understanding which mainstream psychology lacks. Furthermore, we are able to recognise, with Engels, the crucial role of the family in the social reproduction of the individual:

> According to the materialist conception, the determining factor in history is, in the last resort, the production and reproduction of immediate life. But this itself is of a two-fold character. On the one hand the production of the means of subsistence, of food, clothing and shelter and the tools requisite thereof; on the other, the production of human beings themselves, the propagation of the species. The social institutions under which men of a definite historical epoch and of a definite country live are conditioned by both kinds of production; by the stage of development of labour on the one hand and of the family on the other.
>
> (Marx and Engels, 1968, p. 455)

Finally, the association of Marxism with third world liberation movements has brought into focus the relationship between racism, colonial exploitation and personality development from a materialist perspective (see Fanon, 1967). The self-identity of oppressed colonial, immigrant or ethnic minorities, it is argued, is directly affected by the economic imperatives and ideology of the oppressing class and in particular the need for a readily exploitable source of labour. Furthermore, the personality development of both the oppressed and the oppressors is stunted and distorted by the exploitive relationship (see Memmi, 1965). In the context of the racism and exploitation which is a consequence of the imperialist stage of international capitalist development, the emergence of a black identity which is not subordinate but a source of pride is clearly an uncertain process. It depends upon the struggle to overthrow domination, including its attempts to control the politicisation of black populations.

In order to understand the ensemble of social relations which constitute the essence of the human being in any particular historical period we must take a step further back and at this point suggest what are the fundamentals of the historical materialist account of these social relations. We can do this most simply and briefly by identifying four propositions; the rest of this book could be seen as largely devoted to working through the implications of these propositions in detail.

I. *Consciousness is determined by existence*

We have already suggested that the relationship between ideas (including scientific theories) and material, particularly economic, conditions is a complex one. None the less, this basic *materialist* proposition directs our attention to their material conditions of existence in approaching human beings, rather than, initially, their states of mind. So if we are trying to understand an individual person, trying to make sense of or explain attitudes or actions, we are drawn first to examine the material conditions of the individual's existence. Of course, we cannot simply 'read off' attitudes, intentions, or behaviour by studying material circumstances – we cannot expect a direct correspondence between them and states of mind – but we cannot *begin* to understand without considering the individual's material existence. Although material life determines the *general* character of consciousness historically, there is at any given point a dialectical relationship between them. States of mind, intentions, can also change material circumstances, though always within certain historically determined limits such as the availability of resources and the level of scientific development. At the individual level, we might say that access to the means by which intentions can influence one's material conditions of existence is limited or enhanced by one's class, gender and ethnic minority status within the general economic structure.

Any psychology which fails to grasp the dialectical relationship between consciousness and existence will, according to historical materialism, be deeply flawed. Intrapsychic theories, such as traditional psychoanalysis, which tend to give overwhelming attention to the influence of consciousness and the unconscious over a person's existence, are to be considered just as defective as those behaviourist theories which give attention to immediate material stimuli and do not consider the reciprocal influence of consciousness.

II. *Existence demands the continuing necessity for production and reproduction*

Material existence cannot be sustained, however, without what Marx and Engels refer to as 'the first historical act', namely production.

> Men must be in a position to live in order to 'make history' but life involves before anything else eating and drinking, a habitation, clothing and many other things. The first historical act is the production of the means to satisfy these needs, the production of material life itself.
>
> (Marx and Engels, 1970, p. 48)

Production is essential to existence: *how* that production is carried out, what social relations exist in order for that production to proceed and how the human labour involved is itself socially reproduced in order to engage in productive activity – these, from an historical materialist perspective, are the dominant concerns. Under capitalism, production involves the expropriation by the capitalist of the products which men and women create through their labour and also – primarily through the exploitation of women's domestic labour – the social reproduction, through the family and other institutions, of a relatively disciplined and subordinate labour force. The structure of productive and reproductive activity and the social relations associated with them penetrates the life of every individual according to his or her place within this structure. Consequently an understanding of the individual person cannot begin, we argue, in the absence of a grasp of the centrality of these activities and relations and how the individual experiences and reflects upon them.

Mainstream psychological theories, although they may give attention to the significance of the family, or even of work, in the experience, ideas and activities of the individual, suffer from the fact that their non-materialist conception of society prevents them from understanding its necessarily exploitive character and therefore how this exploitative structure constructs the individual's inner experience of class, gender and ethnic status.

III. *The necessity for production and reproduction gives rise to contradictions*

The most fundamental contradiction within the capitalist mode of production is that capitalism has to create and continually reproduce, or at least contribute to the creation and reproduction of, the working class which provides the labour upon which production is based. Capitalism requires that workers shall be brought together in a co-operative way to engage in collective production. But these co-operative social relations in the work place provide one of the foundations for the experience of common collective interests among those who sell their labour. In turn, this collective experience may give rise to a collective consciousness amongst workers which stands ultimately in conflict with the interests of capital. For the study of the individual, the importance of recognising contradictions lies in the support it provides for a conception of individual and group resistance to the imperatives of capitalist production and reproduction. Not only in the work place, but also in the family and in a range of State structures such as the educational system, contradictions arise as a consequence of the fact that working class and other subordinate interests are reflected, though in a minor way, in these institutions and systems. Recognising contradictions enables us to avoid an over-socialised view of human beings and to give our attention not only to how the individual is 'moulded' to fit the requirements of the social structure, but also how she resists and subverts that structure in daily life.

Although the major streams of psychology are anxious to account for individual deviance, predominantly for the purpose of learning how to control it (because these accounts cannot comprehend *structured* contradictions), they are unable to place individual resistance or deviance within a systematic analysis of class, gender and ethnic relations. Only where they have attempted to connect with Marxist and feminist theory have some phenomenological and psychoanalytic approaches to deviance, resistance and contradiction begun to render a more effective account.

IV. *Contradictions in production and reproduction are experienced in ideology*

Here, Marx's work on *commodity fetishism* is of central importance to us. In the first chapter of *Capital* he writes:

> A commodity is therefore a mysterious thing, simply because in it the social character of men's labour appears to them as an objective character stamped upon the product of that labour; because the relation of the producers to the sum total of their own labour is presented to them as a social relation, existing not between themselves, but between the products of their labour.
>
> (Marx, 1974, p. 77)

So people experience themselves as totally separate individuals and the relation between persons is perceived as a relation between *things*, the commodities which people produce. But the mystification goes further, for although these social relations between producers (workers), between men and women, and between workers and capitalists are socially constructed within specific historical periods, they are nevertheless seen predominantly by those who experience them as *natural*, as part of an unchanging order. That these social relations are seen as natural is the fundamental result of exploitive class relations, for in these relations people are actually reduced to the status of things. The lack of awareness of the essential nature of these relations is an 'objective illusion' which can only be completely abolished along with the relations themselves. But this ideological illusion, embedded in the actual material relations and practices of society, is accompanied by another strand of ideology: the legitimation of these exploitive relations through the creation and propagation of ruling class ideas. It is clear that understanding the nature of our own and other people's material existence is extremely difficult, because this 'understanding' reflects ideologies. Mainstream psychology and Marxism both exist within ideologies, both are subject to illusion; with historical materialism, however, we are able at least to recognise that we act within ideologies, and therefore begin to take them into account and struggle against them.

Because we experience ourselves and others within ideologies we must, in understanding the individual, attempt to compare the consciousness that people have of their existence against their 'objective' social relations. It is pointing to this contrast which forms the basis of 'consciousness-raising' in the Women's Movement and elsewhere, although the experience of the personal (consciousness) cannot be the only base for political action.

Whereas a materialist approach to the individual would not, because of its recognition of the permeation of ideology, maintain that its perspective was neutral (unlike the natural science perspective of behaviourism) neither would it suggest, as some strands of phenomenology do, that the subjective consciousness of the individual should be treated as sovereign. Against psychoanalysis, historical materialism argues that the individual's illusions, her 'false consciousness', does not refer back primarily to childhood or to internal instincts, but stems from the powerlessness of the individual in the face of exploitive social relations.

Having outlined some of the basic ideas which underlie the historical materialist approach to the individual, and suggested that these ideas are generally lacking in mainstream psychology, we are in a position to take our critique one step further.

PSYCHOLOGY AND 'HUMAN NATURE'

In approaching mainstream psychology from the terrain of historical materialism we are not obliged necessarily to reject many of the concrete findings of psychological work, but we must *contextualise* these findings. When we examine psychoanalysis later in this chapter we will see that this contextualisation must include detailed historical ideological analysis. But at this stage our critique concentrates on a particular use of the concept of 'human nature'.

The idea of human nature is of course used predominantly in political/ideological discourse in the sense of some basic, unalterable characteristic of human beings which lie outside history and culture: aggressiveness, competitiveness, the nurturing roles of women, the long dependency of children. Although the idea of human nature can be progressive (see Ch. 3), it is often used to suggest that social changes cannot take place because they would be 'contrary to human nature'. We could trace one aspect of this idea of unalterable human nature in the growth of the cult of individualism coincident with the demands of a free market for labour as capitalism develops its productive forces. Mészáros (1972) suggests that Aristotle's idea of the essentially *social* nature of human beings gives way to another concept as capitalism emerges.

> As a result of capitalistic developments the notion of a social instinct 'implanted in all men by nature' disappears completely. Now *individual* liberties appear to belong to the realm of 'nature' and *social* links, by contrast, seem to be artificial and imposed, as it were, 'from outside' upon the self-sufficient individual.
>
> (Mészáros, 1972, p. 254)

The point that Mészáros makes most strongly is that social relations are seen simply as moral or political considerations; one ought to relate socially to others in certain ways. The *essentially* social nature of the human being as an inescapable fact, so prominent an idea in pre-capitalist societies, is superseded under capitalism:

> In such an ethical theory the concept of 'human nature' – a mystified, desocialised reflection of the 'natural law' of capitalism in the human relations of privatised, fragmented, isolated, self-seeking, 'autonomous individuality' – serves to absolutise, as a metaphysical inescapability, a social order which 'keeps men in their crude solitariness', antagonistically opposed to each other.
>
> (Mészáros, 1972, p. 259)

Now it would be inconceivable that psychology could escape entirely the profound influence of dominant ideologies of human nature. What is basic to human beings, historical materialism maintains, is primarily their *animal nature*, a nature appropriately studied by the natural sciences, including biology and physiology. Thus the physiological work of behaviourist psychologists is important in understanding our animal nature – important, necessary, but not sufficient to understand us as human beings, because human-ness is not simply given, naturally present in each isolated individual, but becomes such through social relations with others. The contradiction which most psychology faces is that whilst the social construction of the human being is evident to it, its conception of a basic human being, outside history, remains to haunt it and to drive it to search for an 'objective' timeless science of the individual. Sève (1975) argues this point forcibly:

> Almost all current concepts of the human personality are based on the belief that the individual personality is a particular example of the general personality, in other words, the concrete individual is understood as a singular example of the human genus . . . This logical monstrosity, the abstract 'general individual', is the skeleton in the cupboard of the psychology of personality.
>
> (Sève, 1975, p. 12)

Although Sève makes a forceful case, we must note that he is referring to *almost* all current concepts of human personality, and that there are important exceptions. These exceptions arise from the contradictions to which we referred earlier, where the influence of dominant ideologies is *resisted* as well as incorporated. One example of this resistance can be seen in the work of the liberal reformist founder of symbolic interactionism, Mead, who argued that the individual must be seen as a social being. He maintained that the individual 'constitutes society as genuinely as society constitutes the individual' (Mead, 1964, p. xxv) and that 'selves must be accounted for in terms of the social process' (Mead, 1964, p. 49). Mead also distinguishes human being from animal being when he sees the *self* emerging as a social entity distinct from but on the basis of the physical organism. Even so, the nature of this social entity, the social process about which symbolic interactionism is so concerned, remains obscured: only historical materialism, perhaps, could utilise effectively the work which Mead and his successors have undertaken, a possibility we will explore in the next chapter.

This second stage in our critique of mainstream psychology, then, centres on its tendency to see the individual as *prior* to the social relations of which the individual is constituted, including, within some behaviourist-influenced approaches, conceiving of human psychology as essentially predetermined by biological inheritance. The frequently inappropriate use of animal experimentation as a basis for conclusions about human behaviour stems from failure fully to understand that animals are psychologically animals from birth, being overwhelmingly predetermined biologically, whereas humans *become* human through 'the ensemble of social relations'. This does not mean, Sève points out, that 'social relations are "human relations" in the ordinarily ideological meaning of the expression, that is, relations between persons essentially considered as *existing prior to these relations'*. Rather, Sève suggests 'human beings, in as far as they are developed personalities, are in the last analysis *produced* by social relations' (Sève, 1975, p. 39).

PSYCHOANALYSIS AND IDEOLOGY

In concluding our critique of mainstream psychologies, we are now selecting one, psychoanalysis, for specific attention. We do this because we need an example to underline the general criticisms that have already been made. We choose psychoanalysis because in the next chapter we will examine the claims made by some Marxists that, notwithstanding its limitations, psychoanalytic theory has a valuable contribution to make to a materialist understanding of the individual.

It would not be difficult in criticising psychoanalysis from the terrain of historical materialism to cite the damning condemnation which it has evoked from the Left and to leave it there. Two examples will suffice to illustrate the ferocity of these attacks. From the United States, some Left-wing writers, overwhelmed by the dominance of psychoanalytic theory and practice in their own country, accuse Freud of actively and consciously aiding the capitalist system. In Freud's theory, Brown (1974) argues,

The id represented the basic activities of human beings which so frightened the ruling classes, the superego represented the social restrictions against the id, and the ego maintained the proper balance for the reality principle. Providing industrial discipline for the working class and moral training for the middle class, psychoanalysis recreated bourgeois social relations in the human and personal realm.

(Brown, 1974, p. 57)

In a similar vein, Brooks (1973) sees Freudian theory and practice as wholly repressive. He maintains that the concept of the unconscious involves the idealist separation of the person from the material world, reinforces passivity in the face of 'irrationality', and teaches people that they cannot control their own lives. Such critics often acknowledge that Freud revealed how, in certain respects, people acted in capitalist society, but they go on to condemn him in the following terms:

What [Freud] did with these [capitalist] realities, however, was to mystify them, to psychologise them into a system that told people that they could never alter their world.

(Brown, 1974, pp. 59, 60)

Coinciding with this kind of criticism is that which, until very recently, was strongly expressed within the Women's Movement and which produced a hostile reception to Mitchell's (1975) spirited defence of Freud from a feminist perspective. Some feminist critics of Freud believe that his theory of sexuality not only reflects the fact of women's oppression, but actively supports it. In an influential pamphlet much discussed in the Women's Movement in Britain in the 1970s the Red Collective maintained that

Freudian theory represents, in a transformed version, many of the assumptions that are built into the lived experience of capitalist sexual relations: there is a definite relation between the ideological consciousness, the ways we think and feel capitalist sexual relations when within them, and the ideological theory which we think Freudian theory is.

(Red Collection, 1978, p. 102)

Many of the specific criticisms which these and similar authors antagonistic towards psychoanalytic theory make, we would support. Freudian theory must be understood as being historically limited by its origins and its subsequent exploitation within capitalist society. But some of Freud's Left-wing critics hold, we would suggest, too monolithic and functionalist a model of capitalist society. It is a model of a society where psychological theorists and practitioners like Freud are creatures of ruling class ideology, and it fails to acknowledge deep contradictions. It may be that Freudian theory turns out to have little to offer a materialist understanding of the individual; nevertheless any assessment of the possible contributions of psychoanalysis must begin not from wholesale condemnation but from an acknowledgement that, as a set of ideas and practices, what it represents in relation to ruling class interests is at the very least ambiguous. Nevertheless, our comments on psychoanalytic theory in the remainder of this chapter will concentrate entirely on its limitations and distortions – its progressive claims we will consider later.

We can say immediately that from the terrain of historical materialism the major limitations of Freudian theory and practice stem from its failure to *understand itself* as a specific historical product. Freud's unmasking of the psychic reality behind the appearance of bourgeois morality, and its accounts of childhood and the family, certainly makes it progressive in its own time. One might say that Freud's work was an unremitting battle against a consciousness which falsifies, distorts and represses thoughts and feelings which are considered as dangerous deviations from the dominant culture. It is even possible to argue that Freud's theory of the unconscious was revolutionary within its own field. But this progressiveness of Freud is essentially a *bourgeois* progressiveness – a nineteenth century rationality which was struggling against pre-capitalist religious and mystical ideas and maintaining that scientific knowledge of human experience was both possible and necessary. Although Freud is rightly seen as predominantly a liberal pessimist (see Foreman, 1977), traces of the more optimistic side to progressive bourgeois thought occasionally break through, as when he suggests that people must learn to give up fantasy in the face of the suffering which society creates:

By withdrawing his expectations from the other world and concentrating all his liberated energies on this earthly life, [man] will probably attain to a state of things in which life will be tolerable for all and no one will be oppressed by culture any more.

(Freud, 1927, p. 89)

The problem for progressive bourgeois liberals like Freud was that they saw that the advance of capitalism, which in his ahistorical way Freud equated with advancing 'civilisation', was a development which was both progressive, compared with earlier epochs, and also oppressive. With no notion of the contradictions involved in the development of capitalism, the progressive and oppressive elements could not, as they were in Marx, be brought together in a comprehensive understanding of the dynamic of its expansion.

Whilst Freud emphasised, in his theory of instincts, the struggle of the individual against social constraints, these constraints are essentially outside history. It is 'civilisation' in general, not a specific historical social and economic structure, which in Freud's view is based upon the subjugation of human instincts, especially those involving sexuality and aggression. The repression of the person's innate needs and their deflection in the interests of 'society', means a renunciation or delay of instinctual satisfactions and their subordination to the discipline of work, the discipline of monogamous sexual relationships and the discipline of established law and order. There can be little doubt that Freud was deeply ambivalent about this subjugation: on the one hand it appeared to him necessary to the progress of society, whilst on the other hand it was paid for at a terrible price so far as the individual was concerned. So traditional psychoanalytic theory fails to locate the unconscious within an historically specific social context which can account for the antagonisms which exist between human beings. 'The ideological obtuseness of psychoanalysis', argues Schneider (1975, p. 115) 'consists of its invariable mistaking of the *bourgeois* for *man as such.*' Freud sees the basic antagonism between individuals and society as deriving from biologically determined instructual drives, rather than as historically constructed by human beings themselves. Freud's ahistorical

Darwinian

biology-dominated account is therefore severely *reductionist* in that it fails to connect to the reality of class relations; it is *overdeterminist* in that no fundamental changes in social relations are envisaged as possible; and it is therefore *pessimistic* in that human beings' understanding of their own history, whilst it can be utilised for adjustment and small-scale change, cannot be a key to the transformation of their lives.

Because of its inability to understand the bourgeois society in which it is situated, the impact of that specific society on the development of the individual is mistaken for characteristics which exist in some fundamental 'human nature'. For example, in arguing that in infancy the female vagina is never discovered and that therefore it is proper to talk of the infantile genital organisation as phallic, Freud neglects to take account of the cultural suppression of female sexuality. From the point of view of historical materialism, on the other hand, the structure of psycho-sexual instinctual development, Schneider (1975) argues, with its temporary end result in the oedipus complex and the exclusive claim of ownership of the mother and rivalry with the father, carries the imprint of bourgeois relationships within production – commodities, owning, alienation and competition. So the non-reflexive stance of psychoanalysis so far as its own ideological and structural location is concerned is, we would argue, its overwhelming deficiency, one from which other limitations flow. Because it does not understand itself ideologically, it shares with other psychological systems the idealist fallacy that it is possible to develop a science of the psychology of human beings *as such*, rather than in a specific historical context of 'the ensemble of social relations'.

It is because of the ideological blindness of Freudianism that the body of Freud's work, despite its emphasis on conflict between the individual and an oppressive social structure and its unmasking of patriarchal bourgeois morality, could serve oppressive ends. It directs attention to individual pathology and the need for individual adjustment, and in vulgarised forms acts as a justification, in liberal welfarism, for treating 'deviant' people as if they had no conscious intentions. Whether the basic elements of psychoanalytic theory can be held responsible for all of these oppressive consequences, as the most ferocious critics argue, is a matter of debate. Marxism, after all, has also been utilised for immensely oppressive purposes. Against the oppression of bourgeois therapy must be placed the Gulag Archipelago.

But once we have appreciated the deepest flaw in psychoanalytic theory – its lack of historical contextualisation – we can begin to understand why it gives primary attention to instructual repression, rather than to the central elements of the individual's social experience – productive and reproductive labour. We have noted already that for historical materialism the 'first historical act' is production and reproduction. But, as Sève maintains, in psychoanalysis the individual does everything *except* engage in labour:

> How could a science which *in principle* neglects labour and therefore the determinant role of the *relations of production*, be the general science of that being who is defined in his very essence by his labour, who is produced in his very essence by these relations of production?
>
> (Sève, 1978, p. 149)

The fact that people engage in labour is in no way central to Freud's model of human beings; on the contrary, it is built upon considering the human being outside the sphere of labour, which is why theorising about *childhood* is so important to psychoanalysis. Now Sève is not arguing that childhood is without significance, for he also suggests that psychoanalysis 'is perhaps destined to be integrated into general theory [of historical materialism] as a theory of the initial stages of the making of man and of its effects on the later stages' (Sève, 1975, p. 56). The point, however, is that the earlier stages must be seen in the light of later involvement in social and domestic labour. We may wish to consider, despite its over-functional implications, the argument of Schneider (1975, p. 116) that in capitalist society psychosexual development acts as a means of anchoring, early in the instructual life of the child, 'anal retentive' and aggressive responses to possessions and of fostering a disposition towards wage labour or domestic labour, depending on the child's gender. In any case, we can say in general terms that the failure of psychoanalysis lies, to a major extent, in its failure to direct attention towards human labour:

to do so it would need to enter the realm of political economy.

In the next chapter we will see whether, despite its major limitations, psychoanalytic theory together with symbolic interactionism retains a potential which can be used as part of an account of the individual within capitalist social relations.

3
Materialism, Instinct and Intention

The attempt to develop a materialist understanding of the individual demanded that we should first subject the dominant psychological accounts to fundamental criticism. All Marxists agree that these accounts are unsatisfactory, at the very least in their failure to contextualise the person within 'the ensemble of social relations'. But we have seen that Marxists differ on whether and to what extent, notwithstanding their limitations, certain psychological theories can be utilised within a materialist analysis.

At this juncture, two alternative ways forward are presented to us. One of these alternatives consists of beginning to build, on the basis of the principal concepts of historical materialism, an entirely new psychology of the individual. This new psychology-in-the-making may refer to psychological work elsewhere, but only in a relatively minor way: it will not connect itself to or draw upon any of the dominant trends in psychological theory and practice. In Chapter 4 we will examine the possibilities of this approach, mainly through an exposition and critique of the work of Lucien Sève. The other alternative, which we consider now, is to approach a major stream in psychological theory from the standpoint of historical materialism and so transform it that it becomes possible to draw upon it substantially as part of a materialist account of the individual. This alternative, we might argue, follows Marx's example in his approach to nineteenth century English political economy and to Hegelian philosophy.

In the past twenty years, two main currents in psychological work have been especially important in contributing to the efforts of Marxists to develop a satisfactory account of the individual's experience of capitalist society: psychoanalysis and the phenomenological perspective, particularly symbolic interactionism. Psychoanalysis is by far the most important of these contributors, has the longest history and will be given most attention here. Later in the chapter we will turn to consider those theoretical strands which influenced the anti-psychiatry movement and the 'radical' study of deviance.

FREUDIANISM AS A RESPONSE TO MARXISM'S 'FAILURE'

The dialogue between Marxism and psychoanalysis has now lasted for over fifty years and may be characterised as resulting primarily from dissatisfactions with orthodox Marxism both as a theory and a practice. The failure of working class socialist revolutions in Europe in the 1920s, the rise of Fascism and its attraction to the working class, and the growth of Stalinist oppression, all produced a crisis for the Western European and American Left. The question that was posed was how these events could have occurred when orthodox Marxism would have suggested very different outcomes. Marxism had developed as *political economy* and its lack of an adequate understanding of the psychology of the individual, it was suggested, accounted for its failure to give sufficient weight to the complexities of human motivation and especially the role of the irrational in people's false consciousness. Fascism, above all, was a celebration of irrationality and destruction; alongside Stalinism it appeared to demonstrate how completely Marxism had underestimated people's 'need for authority' and their willingness to submit themselves to new manifestations of power. Later, the 'economism' and 'workerism' of orthodox Marxism came under attack, too, from the feminist Left for its over-emphasis on production and its neglect of the oppressive power of the family on the lives of women, reflecting as it did the broader patriarchal structures of all societies, including those which called themselves socialist.

It was in the context of this turmoil and disenchantment on the Left that Freudianism entered as an already existing theory which was most likely to offer the insights which Marxism lacked and, perhaps, complement it. Our critique of psychoanalytic theory so far suggests that the chances of a complementary relationship between psychoanalysis and Marxism, let alone an integrating marriage, look far from promising, as Lasch suggests:

> What brought about this improbable alliance . . .? We seem to have here a remarkable instance of the attraction of opposites. Freud puts more stress on human limitations than on human potential, he has no faith in social progress and he insists that civilisation is founded on repression. There isn't much here, at first glance, that would commend itself to reformers or revolutionaries – and in the last analysis, the theorists of the Freudian left in one way or another have had to get around or explain away the deterministic, tragic side of Freud's thought, which has more in common with St. Augustine and Calvin than with Marx.
>
> (Lasch, 1981, p. 23)

The Freudian Left have indeed made continuous efforts to overcome the serious limitations of psychoanalysis in the interests of grasping hold of some of its most significant central ideas. These ideas, especially the theory of the unconscious as a means of explaining how psychic repression takes place, appear as an answer to the failures of orthodox Marxism. Freudian theory can be used to suggest that the means by which patriarchal and capitalist social relations are legitimated and reproduced is a complex matter involving the deep penetration, at an unconscious level, of the dominant modes of patriarchal and bourgeois authority, and the repression of those instinctual needs which might otherwise prove challenging to the social order. Despite its internal differences and conflicts, the Freudian Left has been united in maintaining that we must understand capitalist society not only in terms of economic and political oppression, but also as involving the psychic oppression and emotional impoverishment of the individual who, through the inculcation of guilt, is an active participant in her or his own subordination to the imperatives of the social system as a whole.

It is not appropriate here to enter into an account of the

history of the Freudian left (see, for example, Jay, 1973; Foreman, 1977; Mitchell, 1975; Brown, 1974, for different interpretations of this history). Instead, we shall concentrate our attention on three basic questions which, from the point of view of historical materialism, must be asked of psychoanalysis, given the latter's claims concerning the psychic origins of human personality. The first is whether a connection can be established between sexual repression at the level of the individual, and the imperatives of class struggle; in other words, does sexual repression serve the interests of the bourgeoisie? The second question is whether the reproduction of women's oppression can be explained, at the level of the individual, through the insights of psychoanalysis. The third question is whether psychoanalysis can be utilised to explain the way in which men and women are psychologically prepared for and affected by the social relations of production and consumption. In exploring these questions we shall interrogate a number of writers and assess how satisfactory their answers appear to be.

SEXUAL REPRESSION AND CLASS STRUGGLE

If, despite their evident incompatibilities, the aim of many left Freudians is to produce a *synthesis* of psychoanalysis and historical materialism, then, one could argue, it is necessary to grasp hold of both libido theory and the theory of class struggle. For Freud, libido, instinctual sexual energy, its sublimation and repression, is the central force in human life. For Marx and Engels (1968, p. 35) 'all recorded history is the history of class struggle'. Is it possible, then, to locate particular forms of sexual sublimation and repression within specific historic conditions of class struggle and thus bring Freudianism out of its false idealist universalism and into a materialist analysis?

Reich (1970; 1972) writing in the 1920s and 1930s maintained that the neuroses of working class patients were a direct result of the material conditions of working class life, namely poverty and exploitation. These conditions gave rise to sexual repression, the damning-up of a sexuality which would otherwise have expressed itself in enjoyment, comradeship, and mutuality. In contrast to Freud, who saw sexual repression as necessary for all 'civilisation', Reich argued that sexual repression, particularly the repression of genital sexuality, was simply an historic necessity for capitalist society and would no longer be required in a communist one. The unconscious, which for Freud is something fearful, full of lust and hatred, is for Reich that which must eventually become conscious, for it is the source of people's spontaneous capacity for love and sociability. But his emphasis on sexual repression also brought Reich into conflict with orthodox Marxism, which he accused of failing to understand the mechanism by which ideology is anchored in the character structure of the individual. Marxism was too exclusively concerned with economic factors, he maintained, sexuality was an element of the superstructure of capitalism which must not be neglected.

Reich seems to have arrived eventually at a position totally incompatible with historical materialism, namely his belief that the development of working class genital sexuality was itself a prime revolutionary force, the actual *form* that class struggle should take, rather than a consequence of the success of the working class in its broader political and ideological battles with the ruling order.

There is, however, a major aspect of Reich's work through which he contributed in a significant way to that study of patriarchal relations which was to be the focus of subsequent left-wing Freudian feminists, namely his analysis of *the family* as a vehicle of ideological oppression. His political concern with the psychological basis of the apparent attractions of Fascism led him to explore the ways in which the reproduction of authoritarianism takes place within the family. In one of his most influential works, *The Mass Psychology of Fascism*, Reich makes his famous claim:

> The interlacing of the socio-economic structure with the sexual structure of society and the structural reproduction of society takes place in the first four or five years and in the authoritarian family. The church only continues this function later. Thus, the State gains an enormous interest in the authoritarian family: it becomes the factory in which the State's structure and ideology are moulded.
>
> (Reich, 1970, p. 30)

Sexual repression of children in the family induces in them a respect for authority, a docile, guilty submission to those 'above' them, Reich argues, which perfectly suits them for their future roles as disciplined labour serving the interests of capital and the State. Authority in the family is essentially the authority of the father, based upon women's domestic labour and their role as mothers. In this analysis of women's position, Reich builds upon the earlier work of Engels's *The Origins of the Family, Private Property and the State* but goes on to relate it directly to the growing ideology of Nazi Germany with its emphasis on the male leader/father (Hitler) and on the function of German women as the breeders of the pure Aryan race. For Reich, Fascism only demonstrates in extreme form the psychological foundations of all capitalist societies. The internalised repression upon which such societies are based is exceptionally difficult to combat because it is embedded in the daily activities and rituals of individual and family life in the working class: the socially created 'need' to 'behave properly', to 'show respect', to be a 'dutiful daughter', a 'providing' husband and father, or a 'good mother'.

Reich's view of the role of the family as the *necessary* vehicle for the reproduction of bourgeois morality and of submission to capitalism appears now to be, perhaps, overfunctional and determinist, but it contributes a significant step in the attempt to transform Freud's ahistorical analysis of sexual repression into a historically located materialist understanding.

Marcuse (1968; 1969) can also be interrogated at this point because he was concerned to contextualise sexual repression and show that it served the interests of capitalist society, but through keeping closer to Freud's original notion of repression by distinguishing between different kinds of repression and by taking care not simply to equate all instinctual repression with oppression.

We have shown already that Freud's liberal pessimism arose in essence from his conclusion that a basic antagonism existed between the instinctual needs of the individual and the requirements of civilisation. The organic needs of the id operated on the *pleasure principle*, but these needs had to be repressed and sublimated into social activity in accordance with the *reality principle*. In Marcuse's view it was unsatisfactory, however, to maintain, as Reich had done, that *all* instinctual repression was a function of specific class societies: such a position gave too much emphasis to the conscious reflection and action of the ego and insufficient attention to unconscious impulses which would always be in tension with social structures. In *Eros and Civilization* (1969) Marcuse attempts to historicise the phenomenon of instinctual repression by maintaining that the irreconcilability of pleasure and reality principles must be understood in the context of the organised domination upon which all civilisations have developed. Thus, Marcuse (1969, p. 32) suggests, 'repression is a historical phenomenon . . . [for] the primal father, as the archetype of domination, initiates a chain reaction of enslavement, rebellion, and reinforced domination which marks the history of civilisation'. But this external repression is supported by internal repression: 'the unfree individual introjects his masters and their commands into his own mental apparatus'.

Marcuse proceeds to locate repression historically a stage further by introducing two new concepts into his analysis. The first is the notion of *surplus repression*, which signifies the restrictions upon the individual's instinctual impulses required by social domination, to be distinguished from those restrictions necessary for human survival and perpetuation as such. The second concept is the *performance principle*, which is the specific historical form of the reality principle required by the capitalist mode of production. Using these two concepts, Marcuse returns to Marx's basic proposition that production is 'the first historical necessity': human labour is necessary for existence, but such labour requires some modification and renunciation of instincts, particularly delayed gratification. This is the repression which would be necessary for production and reproduction in any conceivable society, including a communist one based on co-operation and mutuality. But historically, this necessary repression has been overlaid with the surplus repression required of alienated labour based upon the exploitation and domination of the labourer. In class societies, women and men labour to perform pre-established functions over which they have no control, abstract labour for the purpose of exchange in the interests of the dominant class. The emphasis on performance, on control over nature and on technological advance, which is the hallmark especially of capitalist society, requires the repression of the pleasure principle in the interests of a form of progress, in the face of material scarcity characterised by domination. 'In attacking, splitting, changing, pulverizing things and animals (and, periodically, also men)' Marcuse (1969, p. 55) contends, 'man extends his dominion over the world and advances to ever richer stages of civilization.' The cost of this advance is paid by alienated labour based upon exploitation. It requires sexual repression which enables the body to be used as an instrument of labour and restricts the libido to genital sexuality in those short periods of recreation allowed to the labourer and which perform the function of physical and psychological preparation for further labour.

Although surplus sexual repression, in Marcuse's analysis, has been usefully located historically in the forms of domination through which societies have made their progress, the conclusion that one might draw from this analysis could be as pessimistic as that of Freud's. How is this history of domination to be ended and sexual repression reduced to the basic level necessary only for survival? *Eros and Civilization* (1969) was first published in the USA in 1955 and it is perhaps the context of the Cold War which partly explains Marcuse's reluctance to give the answer one might expect of a Marxist, namely that domination can only be overcome by the revolutionary struggle of the working class. In a later book *One Dimensional Man* (1968) Marcuse suggests, in fact, that the organised working class, certainly in America, has been so conditioned to accept domination that it is no longer a possible instrument for revolution. In the earlier work, Marcuse places his faith in what he sees as two important developments in advanced capitalism. Firstly, technological progress has gone so far that the problem of basic material scarcity has been removed and only *organised* scarcity remains. This means that the imperative of the performance principle has been weakened and with it the necessity for extensive sexual repression. Second, the institution of the family, upon which both Reich and Marcuse placed so much emphasis, is actually in decline as its functions are progressively taken over by the State. With the decline in the family would come, Marcuse suggested, a decline in its conditioning power over the individual presently exercised through the inculcation of guilt and subordination of the authority of the father.

There are a number of objections that could be made to Marcuse's solution to the problem of the elimination of surplus repression. Technological progress, especially where it involves the depletion of finite natural resources, is a two-edged sword still in the hands of the exploiting classes. The family shows no sign of decline and even its newer, more open, forms are not necessarily less repressive. These are points which could be debated more fully: the major problem with Marcuse's analysis lies at a deeper level. Whilst it may be within the spirit of a progressive psychoanalysis to see social change occurring as a result of the interaction between material forces (for example, changes in the forces of production) and unconscious forces within human beings (libido), such an approach to change appears to relegate human consciousness to the periphery of history. Conscious human intention is, for Marx, a central feature of change, for people make their own history within the limits of the material forces surrounding them. It is from this conception of history that Marx places class struggle as the central mechanism of change. So Marcuse, like Reich, ends – despite some useful conceptual advances – in an essentially un-Marxist position. Foreman (1977, p. 61) suggests that this end was inevitable because 'from the very beginning the Freudian theory of the libido and the sexual instincts was irreconcilable with the Marxist analysis of revolutionary change'. This is an important point especially relevant to the work of feminist Left Freudians.

WOMEN'S PSYCHOLOGY AND PATRIARCHAL RELATIONS

If attempts to connect psychoanalysis to Marxism appear fraught with problems, those accompanying the project of utilising Freudianism to explain and confront women's oppression seem even more daunting. In the most general terms, the project can be described as the analysis of the relationship between biological sexual differences and the social construction and reproduction of gender oppression. The problems which Marxist feminists must confront in Freud include not only those which any Marxist faces – his ahistorical pessimism – but also his particular theories about female sexuality and his view of the moral and intellectual inferiority of women. It may be that these latter views can be separated out from Freud's scientific work, and even submitted to a psychoanalytic interpretation of his own problematic relationships with women: the result of his own personal, cultural and class position. Left-wing Freudian feminists, Lasch (1981, p. 29) argues, 'correctly sensing that Freud's ideas are more important than his personal prejudices, have seen him as the first theorist of patriarchal psychodynamics, even an unwitting critic of patriarchy'. Other feminists take the view expressed by Barrett (1980, p. 57) that 'Freud's perceptions of the female personality are integral to his account of psychosexual development'.

We can explore our question of whether it is possible to use psychoanalytic theory in the understanding of women's oppression at the level of the individual by considering two strands of contemporary feminist work. Both of these strands are concerned with the ideological construction of masculine and feminine subjects in capitalist society, the first through a re-thinking of the Freudian theory of the oedipus complex, and the second through emphasis on the pre-oedipal interaction between mother and child.

Juliet Mitchell can be taken as representative of this first strand. 'Advocacy of Freud is the theme of this book', Mitchell writes in her introduction to *Psychoanalysis and Feminism* (1975) and in taking this uncompromising position sets herself a major task of synthesis with feminism and Marxism. This attempted synthesis is based upon the argument that it is possible, following the work of Althusser (1971), to separate out as relatively autonomous the economic, political and ideological levels of a social formation such as capitalism. In particular, ideological practices have a continually determining influence in their own right, in such a way that individuals experience their world through the mental representations of ideology. Thus, Mitchell maintains, Freud's account of masculinity and femininity is not an account of the real differences and similarities between men and women, but of their mental representation within a particular society. The construction of gender takes place, according to Mitchell, at the level of ideology and this construction is relatively autonomous in relation to the imperatives of economic production; at least it cannot be viewed as simply functional to the interests of capitalism. This is a formulation which certainly avoids the trap of seeing women's oppression in the simplistic terms of being *directly* related to the needs of capital: however the separation of ideology from economic imperatives leads, as we shall see later, to other problems.

In discussing the work of Reich and Marcuse, we have seen that there are substantial difficulties in the way of utilising libido theory in a materialist account of the individual, because the term *instinct* emphasises the biological base of sexuality and – coupled with the concept of the unconscious – implies that people's actions are determined by an unknowable biology. Mitchell's response to this problem is, in effect, to demystify the unconscious by emphasising its accessibility. The unconscious, she suggests,

> is not a deep mysterious place, whose presence, in mystical fashion, accounts for all the unknown; *it is knowable and it is normal*. What it contains is normal thought utterly transformed by its own laws (which Freud called the primary process), but nevertheless only transformed and hence still recognisable if one can deduce the manner of the transformation, that is, decipher the laws of primary process to which the thought is subjected.
>
> (Mitchell, 1975, p. 6)

Here Mitchell is making the point that the unconscious consists of mental representations within ideology and that psychoanalysis as a practice is concerned with attempting to make conscious that which is unconscious. Furthermore, she suggests that libido is related to particular social structures and that Freud recognised this in distinguishing between the sexual instincts of animals and those of humans. In an effort to avoid the biological associations of the term 'instinct', Mitchell prefers the word *drive* and argues that Freud 'humanised (sexuality) seeing that because of its ideational mental character, as it manifested itself, it existed only within the context of human culture' (Mitchell, 1975, p. 21). Whether these interpretations of libido theory are consistent with Freud's own thinking is certainly debatable (see Foreman, 1977, pp. 48ff, and Barrett, 1980, pp. 53ff) but only ultimately important if one sees Freud's theoretical system as so complete and internally consistent that it has to be accepted or rejected in its entirety, rather than be drawn upon and continually revised.

Mitchell's emphasis on the ideological character of the unconscious underpins her discussion of the oedipus complex. She pours scorn on Reich's over-simple view of the oedipus complex as a more or less superfluous outcome of an original repression of sexuality and gives it, instead, a crucial importance. She emphasises the *mythical* origins of the story of Oedipus and argues that it became a central, dynamic element in mental development, signifying, within Freudian theory, the repressed unconscious ideas surrounding the triangular relationship of child, mother and father: love, hate and rivalry. The universal taboo on incest shows, Mitchell maintains, that exogamy is essential to the development of human society, whilst the oedipus complex marks the complicated and difficult entry of the child into human society.

The entry of the child into the social order takes place, for Mitchell, in the context of a triangular sexual relationship of parents and child, of the constitutional bisexuality of each individual (Freud's 'polymorph perverse' infant) and of the authority and power of the father. This entry into society has always involved the oppression of women and so the oedipus complex is resolved differently by boys and girls and leads to the different patterns of personality development of men and women. For example, the 'passivity' of women compared with men can be explained in the following terms. In the pre-oedipal, bisexual phase of their development, boys and girls are both active and passive, but with the oedipus complex girls are structurally led to devoting themselves to 'being loved', to being acted upon rather than acting. Mitchell describes the resolutions of the oedipus complex and the entry into society thus:

With the end of the pre-oedipal attachment of the mother for the girl and the end of the oedipus complex for the boy, the psychological recognition of the sexual differences consists of, on the one hand, being 'castrated' and on the other of fearing castration. In order to enter into the oedipal desire for her father the girl has to salvage what is left of her sexual drive and devote it most actively to this passive aim of being loved.

(Mitchell, 1975, p. 115)

It is important to emphasise here that, for Mitchell, the child's experience of the oedipal phase of development is an experience *within ideology*. Thus the girl's envy of the penis is not primarily an envy of the physical organ itself, but *what it represents* in terms of male power, authority and privilege. Likewise, 'castration anxiety' in the boy is the mental representation of being cut off from that male privilege. The very terms 'masculine' and 'feminine' also, of course, have a strong ideological significance as Freud appeared to recognise when he suggested that such terms were 'among the most confused to occur in science' and that 'in human beings pure masculinity or femininity are not to be found either in a psychological or a biological sense' (Freud, 1977, p. 142).

But to understand how women, throughout history, have been oppressed, Mitchell draws upon Lévi-Strauss' structural anthropology to show that the incest taboo and the consequent forms of entry into the social order have always involved the exchange of women as objects. Social development in human society demands exogamy – one family giving up one of its members to another family – in 'primitive' societies an exchange relationship. Because of the existence of the rule of the father it is women who have been exchanged in order to ensure exogamy. Exploited for their role in reproduction, women as 'exchange objects' acquire their socially constructed feminine identification. On a biological base of bisexuality they 'become women'. The biological sexual differences between men and women are thus transformed by the social order into the construction of gender differences involving women's oppression. In order continuously to legitimate and reproduce gender differences based upon patriarchy, their social construction *within history* is fetishised, in Marx's terms, to give the appearance that they are based exclusively on innate, unchangeable biological differences.

There are numerous problems with Mitchell's analysis despite the fact that its account of the oedipus complex is undoubtedly a useful one. There are a number of issues upon which she is unclear. For example, if the unconscious is the means by which ideology is transmitted and if the unconscious, in some form, is a 'permanent' feature of human development, then are we doomed always to live within ideology? If so, what are the 'new structures' which 'will gradually come to be represented in the unconscious' (Mitchell, 1975, p. 415) when patriarchy and capitalism is overthrown? Although her emphasis on ideology brings out some significant features of the social construction of male and female personalities, Mitchell's insistence on separating ideological from economic levels of analysis means that some of the interpenetrations between them are lost, such as the ideological character of the sexual division of labour under capitalism. Exclusive concentration on the *ideology* of femininity and masculinity, Sayers (1982) rightly argues, tends to reproduce as unproblematic these ideologies – they are simply 'given'. More useful would be to explore the contradictions involved in these ideologies, contradictions which may be seen to reflect changes in the economic functions performed in practice by men and women. We will turn to a psychoanalytic understanding of these functions later in the chapter.

Whilst the oedipus complex is the centre of attention in Mitchell's analysis, for another strand of feminist psychoanalytic work it is the period *before* the oedipus complex that is significant – the period characterised by the close relationship between mother and child. Drawing on the post-Freudian work of Melanie Klein and her followers, including Donald Winnicott (1958, 1965) feminist analysis of the pre-oedipal stage of development concentrates on the differences in the very early relationships of male and female children with their mothers. Nancy Chodorow (1978) has written most impressively and influentially within this area and it is represented also more recently in the work of Luise Eichenbaum and Susie Orbach (1982) of the Women's Therapy Centre in London.

Chodorow contends that mothers identify with their daughters, not only in the way they do with their sons, because effective mothering demands a fusing or merging of mother and baby, but also because mother and daughter are of the same sex. For when 'a woman gives birth to a daughter she is in a sense reproducing herself', Eichenbaum and Orbach (1982, p. 32) write, 'When she looks at her daughter she sees herself.' Furthermore, the mother also projects on to her daughter some of the feelings she has about herself, feelings which are unconscious. 'In this projection', Eichenbaum and Orbach continue, 'she is seeing her daughter not as another person but as an extension of herself.' Chodorow sees this early mother–daughter relationship as one of over-identification which psychologically conditions the daughter to need similar merging and fusing relationships throughout later life. The psychological trajectory of boys is a different one, for they are soon experienced by the mother as separate and distinct persons because of the difference of sex. In order to identify with the masculine gender, the boy in turn has to reject his earlier identification with his mother and move towards the father. In the context of a family structure where the mother provides most of the child care, separation from mother and identification with the father is difficult for the boy but is made possible by the mother's own need to separate from her son, and by the father's role being different from mother and like himself. But this identification of the boy with the masculine gender has, according to Chodorow, an 'abstract' quality about it stemming from a lack of intimacy with the father.

It is upon these differing experiences of boys and girls in early childhood that the characteristically different personality traits of men and women are based. The early individuation of boys and their rather abstract identifications develop in them impersonal and instrumental psychological characteristics, whereas the continued symbiotic relationship with the mother develops in girls a continuing need for such relationships and prepares them for having and caring for children with whom they can identify in turn. Rituals and practices within the family and within the general culture continually reinforce these psychological differences – which are functional to a patriarchal capitalist, social order which requires from men the capacity to undertake alienated wage labour and from women a caring, nurturing role so that this labour can be reproduced.

We can see at once that this account of the psychological and social origins of gender relations has much to commend it. Concentration on the earliest mother–child relationships shows us how powerful and all-pervading are the dominant ideological constructions of personality. But there are two critical points we can make at this stage. Firstly, it appears an essentially biologically determinist and pessimistic account. 'The father–daughter relationship', Eichenbaum and Orbach (1982, p. 47) contend, 'illustrates one of the tragedies of patriarchy. A man's position in the family and the significance of gender in his early psychological development mean that men are both ill-prepared to give nurturance and at the same time scared of women.' Although Chodorow argues for a conscious break in the present reproduction of 'mothering' and thus of masculine and feminine identity, her analytic emphasis on unconscious identification does not seem to hold out much hope for the transformation of child care responsibilities and practices. This problem is connected to our second criticism which once again points to the limitations of a purely ideological analysis of mothering. Accounts which emphasise pre-oedipal experiences tend also to underplay the class differences of such experiences. Sayers (1982) has shown this in her questioning of the significance, in the socialisation of working class children, of mother–child identification, because in this case the mother may not be seeking so strongly to inculcate the child with the dominant values of the social order. Failure to relate the ideological construction of mother–child relationships and their psychological consequences to the *actual* and contradictory demands of the economy, and the contradictory consciousness of the working class, leads to an idealist and over-functional account: the typical male and female psychological traits described are surely not without problems for a late capitalism in recession.

The left Freudian work we have considered so far has been characterised by three interrelated emphases. First, its starting point has been that of Freud himself, namely libido – unconscious sexual drives – although the significance and construction of libido has been re-interpreted in a number of ways.

Second, in the psychological reproduction of the social order, concentration has been given to the relatively autonomous role of ideology. Third, and following in part from its dissatisfaction with orthodox Marxism's economic determinism, has been the powerful significance given to the patriarchal family form in the reproduction of the social relations of capitalism.

We do not believe that any of these elements in an understanding of the social construction of the individual can be dismissed or minimised in a materialist account. But are they sufficient? We have suggested already that analyses based on the supposed relative autonomy of ideology fail to reveal the interconnections between mental representations and actual economic practices. A feminist critic, sympathetic to psychoanalysis, has argued that

> only by taking account of variations between societies and classes in their economic conditions, and only by taking account of the development and changes that have taken place and that continue to take place within the forces and relations of production, can one begin to account for the divisions that exist between women, and the changes that have and can take place within sexual division in society.
> (Sayer, 1982, p. 10)

Whilst feminist work rightly concentrates its analyses on the role of the family in its account of the making of an individual, other influences are also of considerable importance. These influences, flowing from capital and the state, are not all mediated through the rituals and practices within the patriarchal family form, but have a direct impact upon the individual. These influences, such as 'youth culture' consumerism, state responses to unemployment, the interventions of welfare services and the activities of the police, often operate in a context of *resistance* by families. The current role of the patriarchal family within the working class with respect to these external influences is at the very least contradictory. We would not go as far as Christopher Lasch in seeing patriarchy as a 'pseudo-problem' when he suggests that the Freudian left

has deflected criticism from the real problem to a

pseudo-problem, from the corporation and the state to the family. The worst features of our society derive not from the despotism of the authoritarian father, much eroded in any case, but from the regressive psychology of industrialism, which reduces the citizen to a consumer and bombards him [sic] with images of immediate and total gratification.

(Lasch, 1981, p. 33)

Whilst Lasch overstates his case, he makes an important plea for other priorities. Perhaps, we could utilise psychoanalytic theory not from a starting point of libido, but by beginning where Marx himself begins, with *labour*?

PRODUCTION, CONSUMPTION AND CLASS RELATIONS

In posing our third question, namely whether psychoanalysis can be utilised to explain the way men and women are psychologically prepared for and affected by the relations of production and consumption, we can usefully turn to Michael Schneider's *Neurosis and Civilization* (1975). Schneider's analysis begins from a standpoint of criticism of both 'vulgar' Marxism and Freudianism. The former he sees as deformed by econom-ism and a mechanical materialism, whilst the latter is embed-ded in bourgeois ideology. His criticism of psychoanalysis is especially powerful in its condemnation of the typical Freudian pursuit of an ahistorical human nature. Unlike Mitchell, he is not an 'advocate of Freud', but wants to transform psychoanalytic insights so that they can be used within an historical materialist account. He argues, in essence, that a Marxist psychology can be developed through two sources. First, by picking up the beginnings of a materialist psychology and psychopathology from Marx's *Capital* and developing them further. Second, by deriving Freud's description of the 'bourgeois soul', especially as a theory of illness and neurosis, from the laws of economic movement of bourgeois society. Schneider proposes, from these two sources, to begin to show how human instinctual structures have become modified in the course of the production and reproduction of societies.

We start with Marx's contention that the nature of commodity production under capitalism involves the 'repression of use-values'. Like Marcuse, Schneider uses the term *repression* 'to designate both conscious and unconscious, external and internal processes of restraint, constraint and repression' (Marcuse, 1969, p. 8). He is able to justify this wide use of the term because the processes he describes involve, as we shall see, the removal of something from awareness as well as external oppression.

Marx shows us that in commodity production and exchange there occurs what he refers to as a 'mysterious' transformation whereby the products of labour turn into commodities: the person produces things not for his or her own *use*, but for *exchange* via money in the market place. 'When they assume this money-shape', Marx (1974, p. 90) maintains, 'commodities strip off every trace of their natural use-value, and of the particular kind of labour to which they owe their creation, in order to transform themselves into a uniform, socially recognised incarnation of homogeneous human labour.' Parallel to this transformation of useful commodities into money there appears at the psychological level an exchange value consciousness, where the human being becomes indifferent to or unaware of the original use-value of that which he or she produces. This psychological transformation in the individual in commodity production involves *instinctual renunciation* in so far as the individual's 'needs' become relatively detached from concrete sensuous satisfactions and become, instead, attached to what Marx would have called *abstract* satisfactions, namely money.

Initially, it is the personality of the capitalist that has to undergo the transformation which effectively orients itself to that pursuit of money which is especially crucial to the early stages of capital accumulation. We know from previous work in this field that protestantism played a significant ideological role in the cultural moulding of the rising bourgeoisie towards suppression of sensuality and immediate gratification in favour of order, accumulation and calculation. The sacrifice of short-term sensual enjoyment in the interests of long-term profit was not experienced, however, by the capitalist, and the bourgeois class as a whole, without some internal conflict, as Marx suggests when he refers to a 'Faustian conflict between passion for accumulation and the desire for enjoyment'.

Despite the internal conflicts it produces, this instinctual renunciation has, for the bourgeoisie, definite material benefits. For the working class, however, the situation is different. In the early stages of the development of capitalism at least, workers lived at subsistence level and therefore had nothing either to accumulate or abstain from. In the absence of a 'work morality', they would often only work long enough to earn a subsistence. By the nineteenth century, however, the situation had changed. Schneider argues that by this time the bourgeoisie were able to impose a six-day working week on the working class and, through a family socialisation which increasingly emphasised uniformity and regularity, prepare the labour force for 'barracks discipline'. Zaretsky (1976) considering the same period of history places more emphasis on the material necessity which faced nineteenth century working class families when he writes:

> capital was accumulated by restricting domestic consumption and diverting any surplus into industry. The bourgeois ethic of repression and abstinence was extended to the proletariat through the force of material circumstances. The family's internal life was dominated by the struggle of its members for their basic material needs.
>
> (Zaretsky, 1976, p. 62)

Whatever may be the balance between the force of material circumstances and the effects of the ideological offensive of the bourgeoisie through patriarchal family, church and later, schooling, the effect was to impose upon the whole of society, including the working class, bourgeois notions of necessity and rationality.

Of what does this idea of 'rationality' consist in bourgeois society? Schneider comments that Freud was quite wrong in seeing the ego as 'reason and prudence', whilst the id contained 'the passions'. Rationality, in bourgeois terms, is not an achievement of the ego, as Freud thought, but is essentially a reflection of the abstract relation of exchange and money. Because of this, as Marx continually demonstrates, relations between individuals come to assume the abstract form of their economic relations in capitalist society. In psychoanalytic

terms, when under capitalism labour power becomes a commodity, then id looks, from the perspective of ego, like a
disturbance in the process of production. Consequently
neurosis, which is a result of conflict between ego and id, comes
into existence, Schneider proposes, only as capitalism develops
and so requires the repression of instinct in the interests of a
'rationality' hell bent on accumulation. At the psychological
level, the internalisation of this 'exchange rationality' is
achieved, in part, through putting childhood erotic and other
pleasurable wishes 'through the wringer of abstract reason'.

The instinctual repression required of capitalist production,
moreover, has particular detrimental effects upon the individual, in direct relation to his or her class position. It is upon
this contention that Schneider begins to formulate a materialist
theory of mental illness. Unlike many other Marxists who draw
upon psychoanalysis, Schneider begins his approach to mental
illness not with libido, but with *work*. Thus mental illness does
not, for Schneider, emerge from an unresolved oedipus complex, but from the organisation of work itself. The capitalist
division of labour leads to a division of the individual – the
separation from the worker of labour power which is then
transformed into an object for sale in return for wages. In an
argument similar to Mitchell's concerning castration anxiety
as a 'mental representation', Schneider maintains that wage
labour is 'castrating' in that it alienates, cuts off the worker
from himself/herself. Castration anxiety is not, then, a 'biological' fear but a socially constructed reflex in the face of the
capitalist organisation of work.

In an argument which parallels that of Braverman (1974) in
his analysis of the deskilling of work in advanced capitalism,
Schneider suggests that whilst work processes themselves
become more complex and technical, the work tasks of the
majority of people become simpler, more automatic and
repetitive. Braverman shows us that lower, less intellectual
functions gradually, for the worker, replace the higher ones,
and that these latter functions are appropriated by capital in
the planning, designing and organising of increasingly fragmented work processes. This means, Schneider maintains, that
'the permanent withdrawal of mental "attention" and cathexic
energy by half-automated work processes drives the libido back

to regressive levels. Day-dreaming or dozing during work is an expression of enforced "regression" ' (Schneider, 1975, p. 175). All kinds of illness, both physical and mental, occur in workers as a result of the power of alienating labour, including heart, circulatory and stomach troubles, sleeplessness and depression.

The psychoanalytic distinction between neuroses and psychoses is the starting-point of Schneider's attempt to identify the relationship between instinctual drives and class-specific forms of psychological defence. In *neurosis*, the id is in conflict with ego and superego which represses the instinctual desire in the name of 'reality'. The repressed desire reappears in consciousness in a substitute form, namely the neurotic symptom. In *psychosis*, on the other hand, id dominates ego. External 'reality' is renounced and replaced by a delusionary reality constructed in accordance with id's wishes. In both forms of mental disturbance, there is a battle between id and superego: but which side 'wins', id or superego, depends largely on the class position of the individual. Members of the bourgeoisie or petit-bourgeoisie are more likely to fall ill with neuroses, whilst the working class person is more likely to suffer from psychosis.

There is good evidence, from Hollingshead and Redlich (1958) onwards, on the class-related incidence of mental illnesses which supports Schneider's contention, despite reservations one must hold about the bias that exists within psychiatric diagnoses. But why, when there is a mental disturbance, should superego tend to dominate the outcome for middle-class people and id for working class people? Schneider's answer lies in maintaining that people's consciousness and their characteristic internal conflicts are class-related.

The petit-bourgeoisie and the non-capital-owning bourgeois middle strata seek to maintain self-confidence. Schneider contends, through compulsively clinging to a dominant bourgeois ideology which urges personal achievement and upward social mobility. This ideology necessitates very individualistic and competitive practices at work and depends upon a strong superego which *internalises* the rules of bourgeois morality. In the face of crisis or stress, the superego remains dominant and the repressed instinctual wishes reappear as a neurosis: anxiety, obsessional-compulsive behaviour, and other forms. The working class, however, is socialised to obedience to rules and norms *external* to the self, in preparation for the alienated labour of the factory where discipline is central. In the working class family, power-oriented physical child-rearing practices tend to dominate, reproducing at home the daily experiences of the parents in the production process. In her criticism of Nancy Chodorow's failure to examine the possibility of class differences in mother–child relations already mentioned, Sayers (1982) suggests that Schneider's views about class-related child care practices gain some empirical support from the work of Zegiob and Forehand (1975) and the evidence cited by Benjamin (1978), which suggests that working class mothers make more use of direct commands and are less individualistically identified with their children, compared with middle-class mothers. The explanation for these differences, Schneider suggests (1975. p. 192), lies partly in the fact that the exploiting class always has a greater need for 'morality' than the exploited class. The bourgeoisie must legitimate and rationalise its status as an exploitive 'parasitical' class and try to compensate for it morally: this is why 'superego morality' is better internalised than in the working class.

The most important reason for the higher incidence of psychosis within the working class compared with the various bourgeois strata, however, lies in the more oppressive social reality facing the working class, a reality demanding greater instinctual renunciation. The living conditions of the working class, Schneider maintains, involves the domination of capital over every aspect of the individual's life; indeed 'paranoia becomes an excessive rationality' (1975, p. 195) because the working class *is* persecuted. Although the worker has greatest objective interest in the destruction of capitalist 'reality', because he or she cannot immediately change that reality, there occurs, given sufficient stress, a regression in which an alternative, delusionary reality is created, clinically diagnosed as psychosis. Taking the example of the diagnosis of *schizophrenia*, Schneider suggests that Laing (1959; 1971) and Laing and Cooper (1964), seeing the family as an isolated social system and schizophrenia as a product of disturbances in primary socialisation within the family, fail to trace the phenomenon back to contradictions in capitalist society. Behaviour which is clinically identified as 'schizophrenic', including identity diffusion, excessive ambivalence, thought blockage and stereotyped behaviour patterns, are all, Schneider points out, extreme variations of injured identity widespread within capitalism. The 'double-bind' situations identified by Laing and others reflect the contradictions between the forces and relations of production: the worker cannot either work fully *collectively* (reflecting his or her objective interests) or orient himself or herself fully to the bourgeois *individualistic* morality. A profoundly critical account of Laing from a rather different Left perspective can be found in Sedgewick (1982).

If Schneider's account of the effect of capitalist productive processes and of the imperatives of accumulation on personality development carries with it the scarcely veiled pessimism of much left-wing Freudian writing, his descriptions of the effects of commodity *consumption* paint an even darker picture.

Whereas in the earlier stages of capitalist development, emphasis had to be placed on the necessity for accumulation and delayed gratification, consumption as well as production becomes, in late capitalism, a significant determinant of individual personality. The symptoms which are produced by the lifelong compulsion to perform wage labour are masked, Schneider maintains, by 'a ˙perverted capitalistic pleasure principle' of a totally unfettered mania for buying. Writing from his experience of the West German 'economic miracle', now passed, with its relative affluence for the working class, Schneider gloomily suggests that whereas working class unconscious resistance through illness to capitalist work pressures can be identified, resistance appears to have vanished completely in the face of compulsive consumption. The packaging of commodities is an important factor in developing the 'consumer society' of late capitalism. Packaging can be seen as the 'appearance of use-value', an appearance which becomes increasingly detached from its *actual* use-value to the buyer. Indeed, a new mystification of the commodity emerges in late capitalism as the appearance of the commodity assumes overwhelming importance, especially through advertising.

Alongside this, however, there is a tendency for the real value of commodities to decrease through 'planned obsolescence and deterioration'.

Such an account of compulsive consumption to satisfy manufactured 'needs' is commonplace on the Left: Schneider goes on to suggest that the effects on the individual psyche are profound. In late capitalism a re-moulding of personality is necessary, away from retention and accumulation and towards the compulsive buyer, the 'highly variable commodity fetishist'. Although Schneider does not make the point, women carry an especially vital role here as consumer for the family unit. Though both men and women are socialised to consumption, women's roles as dependent 'housewives' and sexual objects play a part which deserves special attention.

How far have we come, through drawing on Schneider's work, in answering our question about the contribution of psychoanalysis to an understanding of the psychological effects of production and consumption? Because of his failure to include in his analysis the maintenance and reproduction of *gender* relations, Schneider's explanations suffer severe limitations. For example, attention is (rightly) given to the centrality of wage labour in the genesis of mental illness, but not to the significance of the domestic labour primarily carried out by women, documented through the accumulating evidence, from Brown and Harris (1978) onwards, about the particular position of working class women as the most likely victims of depression. In a discussion of the response of psychiatry to women patients, Dorothy Smith writes:

The declarations women make about themselves are specifically invalidated. In one study of schizophrenic women (Sampton, Messinger and Towne, 1964) a patient is recorded as having said that she would go crazy if she was stuck with her household routines. And she was stuck with them. And she did go crazy. Her statement is included among an inventory of her symptoms. By implication it is something she will no longer say when she is better. It certainly cannot be treated as an account of what is wrong and what might be changed.

(Smith and David, 1976, p. 14)

Failure to acknowledge gender as a significant dimension of oppression alongside class leads to a neglect of the family except in so far as it connects to the demands of the economy. Poster, a theorist of the family, criticises Schneider, alongside other left-wing Freudians, for this neglect:

> The family becomes even less significant than it was for the earlier theorists as Schneider finds contemporary psychic structure to be a product of secondary socialisation outside family networks. His interesting and important insights into the mental damage of work activity and consumption patterns still lack an adequate account of family structure not only regarding socialisation, but also as a sphere of life itself.
>
> (Poster, 1978, p. 63)

In Schneider's defence, we can point to his analysis of the socialisation role of the family not only in encouraging in the child retentive and aggressive relationships to possessions and a disposition towards wage labour, but also in identifying bourgeois power and class hierarchies with the authority of the father. But overall Poster's evaluation is well made.

Great theoretical and empirical problems confront the use of psychoanalytic theory in a materialist account of the individual and no single perspective within the left-wing Freudian position appears to be entirely satisfactory. This does not necessarily mean that alongside other approaches Freudianism does not have a contribution to make, but it suggests that the attempt to produce a *synthesis* between Marx and Freud is unlikely, in the end, to be very productive.

SOCIAL BEING AND BIOLOGICAL BEING

In seeking to explore the possible foundations in psychoanalysis of a materialist account of the individual, we have been faced at every turn with a major issue: that of the role of conscious individual intention. In many of the accounts of the individual we have considered so far, the influence of conscious intention appears to be either peripheral or nonexistent. From Marx we gain a view of human beings as *actively* relating to the world and changing it. But in much Marxist writing great emphasis is placed on *collective* intentions and purposes expressed in class struggle, whereas the individual is frequently seen as so determined by external economic and ideological practices, which are then internalised, that there seems little scope for individual resistance. Freudianism rests, as we have seen, on a libido theory which places most emphasis on the power of the unconscious, and when allied to Marxism appears to render an account of the individual as overwhelmingly acted upon by economic, ideological and psychic determinants. Some feminist work aims to counteract the fatalism and pessimism which certain approaches to women's oppression seem to engender, especially those which emphasise the significance of biological differences. Barrett (1980) is especially concerned to challenge the biologistic assumptions of some other feminists within a *general* rejection of political arguments based upon the existence of biological differences.

> Biologistic arguments can be challenged on a number of different grounds. In philosophical terms they tend to be reductionist, in that they subsume complex socially and historically constructed phenomena under the simple category of biological difference, and empiricist, in that they assume that differences in social behaviour are caused by the observed biological differences with which they correlate. The history of social science provides us with examples of the various attempts to explain social behaviour with reference to biological determinants – two notorious instances being the alleged connections between criminality and body-type and between intelligence-test scores and racial differences. All such attempts have subsequently been discredited, and psychological findings concerning supposedly innate sex differences have now been subjected to a stringent critique.
>
> (Barrett, 1980, pp. 12, 13)

These general sentiments concerning biological factors or explanations gain widespread support amongst socialists. Generally we would prefer, in explaining any social phenomenon, to maximise the significance of environmental factors and minimise the importance of biological determinants. There is sometimes a tendency, in other words, to conflate and confuse two different issues, namely that of biological reductionism which is invariably politically reactionary, and that of the contribution which biology plays in human life, alongside social forces, and which may be quite consistent with socialist theory and practice.

Given the need to ensure that issues upon which biology impinges, such as contraception, abortion and euthanasia, should be settled on political and social grounds rather than medicalised, it is perhaps understandable that biology should be kept at arms length in left-wing political debate. The growth of socio-biology in recent years suggests that it is possible to explain human behaviour in genetic terms as determined by the biological need to ensure that the necessary conditions of reproduction and survival are met. Such explanations are bound to lead to reactionary ideologies, the biologisation of human history and the denial of the overwhelming significance of the social relations of production and reproduction, class and gender structure and the importance of political struggle (see Barker, 1981). Socialists must obviously avoid beginning to go down a road which leads to such dangerous simplicities. But in resisting the current varieties of biologism we may lose sight of the ultimate material basis of all life – biological being. The relationship between biological being and social being deserves close attention.

In work which has been variously attacked as both mechanically materialist and idealist, Timpanaro (1980) has argued that Western Marxism is in danger of reducing the biological to the social and thus avoiding a basic fact: that the human being is also a biological being. He acknowledges from the start the danger of *reactionary biologism*, and the rebirth of racist theories reflected, for example, in the work of Eysenck (1971), but maintains that Marxists must find a way of describing physical illness, deterioration and change in the individual person. In a socialist future, Timpanaro suggests,

> extraordinary progress is to be expected so far as man's physical and psychic health is concerned, not just as a result of the invention of new therapies, but above all through the

establishment of a new environment in which physical ills
are prevented before they need to be cured. Yet it remains
very doubtful whether a radical elimination of the biological
limits of the individual – and potentially of the human
species as a whole – is in fact possible.

(Timpanaro, 1980, p. 18)

At the broadest theoretical level, Timpanaro argues that
materialism involves the acknowledgement of the priority of
'nature' over 'mind', and of the biological level over the
economic and ideological levels. He means by this priority
both *chronological priority*, in the sense that a long time elapsed
before life appeared on earth and a further long time elapsed
before humans appeared; and also *conditioning priority*, in the
sense that nature still conditions men and women in fundamental ways. At another level, he points to the frailty of men
and women in the face of inevitable biological processes. In an
important critical response to Timpanaro, Raymond Williams
(1978) welcomes his stand against arrogant conceptions of the
never-ending 'conquest of nature', a perspective more appropriate to the ideology of imperialism and capitalism than to
Marxism. But Williams rejects the materialist pessimism of
Timpanaro's view that nature 'oppresses' the human species: a
more hopeful, interactive, and non-dominating relationship
with nature, including our own biological inheritance, is surely
possible.

Michèle Barrett (1980) draws her own, non-pessimistic,
conclusions from Timpanaro's work when she approves of his
argument that biology is the infrastructure on which human
social relations must necessarily be built and that we must, in
'humanist' fashion, specify the qualities of purposiveness,
reflection and planning which separate human behaviour from
the behaviour of animals. At the same time, Barrett argues
strongly against the biological reductionism of some feminist
writing, particularly Firestone's (1979) thesis that women need
to be freed from the burdens of their *biologically determined*
oppression. Firestone proposes a causal role for procreative
biology: the family is a reproductive unit and there are certain
'biological facts' which determine women's oppression. She
argues that women are dependent on men for their survival

because of their reproductive biology, that human infants are dependent on adults for a long period, that mother–child interdependence is universal and that the natural reproductive division between the sexes is the origin of all divisions of labour. Barrett's answer to this biological determinism is to acknowledge the basic importance of biological differences but, with Mitchell (1975), to distinguish these differences sharply from the legitimation of the social arrangements which are supposedly based upon them. Biological differences cannot *explain* many social relations, including the oppression of women, and it is useful, Barrett suggests, to distinguish between gender differences, which are socially constructed, and sexual differences, which are biologically determined. The *fact* of biological reproduction, for example, does not necessarily require the social arrangement of 'motherhood'.

But behind these discussions of the connection between biology and social relations in the construction of the individual lurks the problem of 'human nature'. We have already referred (Chapter 2, pp. 29–32) to the way in which certain ideas about the unalterable or basic character of human nature permeate much of mainstream psychological theory. In recent years, we have also witnessed a resurrection of Social Darwinism, where 'human nature' is universally characterised as controlled by fundamental biological forces of a kind shared by other species, especially primates. These forces result moreover in an 'aggressive instinct' and the 'territorial imperative' which is stronger and more destructive in humans than in other species.

One response to such reductionist conceptions of human beings is to deny the very notion of the existence of universal characteristics of human nature, whatever they might be, and to claim for this denial the authority of Marx himself. Geras (1983) has argued, however, that the view that there is no place within historical materialism for the concept of human nature is entirely mistaken. He contends that certain ideas about basic human characteristics and basic human needs are essential to Marxism. The moral case against capitalism which fuels Marx's work rests upon showing that human needs cannot be met by the capitalist system, particularly the all-round development of the individual and the creative engagement in labour, 'man's normal life-activity'.

A belief in human nature, with its basic characteristics and needs mediated through the rich variety of human cultures, is not necessarily a reactionary conception, for ideas about human nature need not be used to prevent change but may provide a basis for social progress. Like Raymond Williams (1978) in his argument against the 'triumphalism' of the notion of 'man's [sic] conquest of nature'. Geras points to dangers which follow from making an absolute distinction between human beings or human societies and 'nature'. It is a distinction which is leading, one could say, to the danger of the destruction of much of the natural world and many of the other species that live in it. As against this distinction we should, Geras maintains,

> insist rather that human beings, for all that is distinctive about them as a species, and for all of their traits, activities and relationships which can only be explained by specification of society and history, are nevertheless, like all other species, material and natural beings: 'irredeemably' rooted in a given biological constitution; *absolutely continuous* with the rest of the natural world.
>
> (Geras, 1983, p. 54)

Certain characteristics of human beings are universal, the 'physical' needs for food, water, shelter and sexual gratification (always penetrated by social meanings) and the capacity for language, for reasoning and for productive labour – needs and capacities, Geras argues, that have made possible the purposeful transformation of the environment.

Geras is surely right in maintaining that Marx had a conception of human nature, in terms of potentialities, needs and capacities which are characteristic of all people, however mediated in specific social and historical contexts and also right that such a conception of human nature – 'an abstraction but a valid one, denoting some common, natural characteristics of humankind' (Geras, 1983, p. 60) – plays a significant role in historical materialism. Recognition of our common biological and other characteristics should enable us to appreciate the immense variety in human culture as the outcome of the impact of these characteristics within different historical and social contexts. Clearly, then, the universal characteristics of the human species are always expressed in their historical specificity – the ensemble of social relations. But does the existence of wide variations in human behaviour and social organisation suggest that there is space in our account of the individual for *personal* intentions and motives, for individual resistance? We must now turn to this question.

HUMAN INTENTION AND THE SELF

The search for an alternative to functionalist and over-determinist accounts of human behaviour characterised the liberal and radical theorists of the 1960s. In the field of psychiatry, Laing was foremost in challenging organic models of mental illness and in seeking to discover a meaning in the 'mad' talk and gestures of psychiatric patients. In the study on deviance generally, 'mainstream criminology', with its emphasis on the individual pathology of the deviant, was rejected in favour of accounts which gave attention not only to the social construction of deviance itself, but to the choices which people make in a deviant 'career'. Mainstream sociology tended to see the individual simply as a collection of roles, rather than as a reflective being able to make decisions, and, coupled with psychology, supported a 'welfarist' approach to social problems which regarded deviance as due to lack of socialisation or psychological abnormality. Rather than being seen as the result of intentions, deviant acts were often described as the 'meaningless' outcome of social and psychological conditioning.

In restoring meaning and intention to human actions, the phenomenological perspective generally proved to be a useful theoretical starting point, though for the more leftist theorists the perspective carried with it the obvious limitation that it failed to conceptualise the broader social order within which human intentions were carried out. The theorising that was most significant to this enterprise was that based upon Mead's social psychology of symbolic interactionism (see Mead, 1962; 1964) and it is this approach which we now discuss.

In the previous chapter we commented on the idea, basic to

Mead's work, that a dialectic existed between organisms and the environment involving not a one-sided determinism, but *interaction*. With human beings, this interaction is not simply in terms of concrete objects or particular events, as is the case with animals and other non-human organisms, but includes the capacity to relate to *symbols*. These symbols (language, gestures) are essentially social, constructed through human interaction within definite historical periods. Symbols make possible the transferring of mental states from one person to another and are not only external to the individual but also internal, in that they provide a code for condensing and manipulating the experience of the environment. Individuals, then, live in a world of objects that they interpret, give meaning to. Through language, humans can designate as objects non-material things, ideas which operate powerfully at individual and collective levels: love, happiness, class, obedience, the fatherland, the national interest. These objects already exist in the social world into which each individual is born: they are part of the culture of pre-existing objects. But the individual is not simply imprisoned in this culture, for these objects not only create the individual as a social being, but also are created by the individual as part of the process of interaction with others. It is through interaction with others that common understandings emerge, including the individual's understanding of himself or herself. These various understandings become condensed through the ability to generalise from them, so that the individual develops, Mead (1962, p. 90) suggests, 'all these particular attitudes into a single attitude or standpoint which may be called that of the generalised other'. The important point here is that because of the capacity that human beings have for generalisation, they can envisage alternative actions before they undertake them. Because of this, *consequences*, the future, can be a determinant of action as well as the past.

The symbolic interactionist conception of *the self* deserves particular attention. It is a conception of the self as socially constructed, as an outcome of internalising interactions with others, for the self is designated with a symbol and so the individual becomes an object in his/her own world, controlling his or her acts and anticipating the outcomes of alternative acts. This *objective self* develops before the *subjective self* because the child's first experiences of himself or herself are indirect, seen from the standpoint of significant others, especially parents. The possible connection between Marx's view of the human essence as 'the ensemble of social relations' and Mead's conception of self is evident in the following passage:

> The self is something which has a development; it is not initially there at birth, but arises in the process of social experience and activity, that is, develops in the given individual as a result of his relations to that process as a whole and to other individuals within that process . . . The individual experiences himself as such, not directly, but only indirectly, from the particular standpoints of other individual members of the same social group or from the generalised standpoint of the social group as a whole to which he belongs.
>
> (Strauss, 1956, p. 199)

Mead's analysis of the self as a 'social structure' and a process which achieves a certain autonomy emphasises its dynamic character. Because the self emerges from interaction with others, it takes account of *specific* others and so in one sense many selves develop, depending on whom the individual is interacting with. Zeitlin (1974), in his commentary on Mead, underlines the dialectic character of the self, at once both consistent and changeable, unified and diverse. A further important stage in Mead's approach to the self is his distinction between the 'I' and the 'me', two phases of the self as a process. In his exposition of symbolic interactionism, Hewitt distinguishes the two phases thus:

> 'I' designates the 'subject' phase of the process, in which people respond as acting subjects to objects, or to the particular or generalised others in their situations. 'Me' labels the 'object' phase of the process, in which people respond to themselves as objects in their situation.
>
> (Hewitt, 1979)

The 'I' then, is the actual process of thinking and acting, whilst the 'me' is the reflective process. By taking the attitudes of others, one introduces the 'me' to which one reacts as an 'I'. The 'I' thus appears only in memory, an 'historical figure' in Mead's words (1962, p. 174), and by that time it has become a 'me'.

In a complex and difficult conceptualisation of the self which can only be touched on here, certain significant features emerge which are important to our examination of the scope of individual human intention. The 'I' is clearly rooted in the individual, whereas the 'me' is the organised attitudes of others. The 'I' may be seen, as Zeitlin suggests, as comprising of spontaneity, freedom and initiative, the reason why human beings can never be totally socialised, nor completely passive. The 'I' is resistant to the world, changes and acts upon it, whereas the 'me' is acted upon by the world. *But*, and here perhaps is the most important limitation on human intention, the 'I' is, for Mead, rooted in biology and is unconscious. In a formulation which clearly parallels that of Freud, the 'me' is seen as the socially constructed censor in tension with a 'naive I', for the 'me' represents the values of the group, whereas the 'I' resists the 'me' and its underlying social relationships. The self, then, is never simply passive, for the 'I' adopts both the self and its social relations and so changes, however slightly, these social relations.

How far has this discussion of the self taken us in our search for the possibilities of choice and resistance at the level of the individual? From Mead we gain a concept of an *active* relationship between the individual and the ensemble of social relations. Reflection and choice are there, and some resistance to the imperatives of the social order. But, as in Freud, the *ultimate* resistance is biological and unconscious, and this clearly limits the scope of conscious individual intentions.

At this point we arrive at the fundamental critique of symbolic interactionism from the perspective of historical materialism. It is essentially a liberal social psychology which totally lacks an effective theorisation of the social order. Without an analysis of class and gender relations, of ideology and of other features of the capitalist mode of production, the conclusion to be drawn from Mead's work, despite its emphasis on the 'insurgent character' of human beings, remains a pessimistic one. *Conscious* resistance to dominant social relations seems only possible through individual acts of deviance which reflect conflicts between the different aspects of the self. As the wider social order is conceived as essentially monolithic and unitary, the power and influence of dominant meanings and symbols seem well nigh irresistible. If, however, we locate Mead's analysis in a context of class struggle, a more optimistic picture emerges, for the individual is then in a position, given certain historical and material conditions, to choose to resist domination and exploitation consciously through participating with others in formulating alternative meanings and symbols with which to designate the world and, ultimately, change it.

If we can take account of the ideological nature of symbols, meanings, definitions and of the self in a situation of ideological struggle between dominant and subordinate social strata, we may be able to formulate a materialist reading of symbolic interactionist concepts which helps us to understand how the individual is constituted within ideology. Such a reading would suggest that individuals are born into an already constructed social world of meanings. These meanings, communicated by symbols, particularly language, reflect the arrangements of production and reproduction and also of the class struggle which is the continuing feature of the exploitation of the forces of production in capitalist societies. Through socialisation in the family, at school, in work, through the media and elsewhere, the individual learns, through language, the roles which are appropriate to his or her class, gender and ethnic position. The *social* nature of symbols ensures that behaviour is oriented to others, and especially those dominant others (the representatives of capital and the state) who have the power to define situations in relation to their class, gender and ethnic interest. At the same time, dominant symbols and definitions are always being challenged at an intensity which reflects the precise level of class, gender and ethnic conflict. In so far as the individual consciously engages in this conflict against dominant interests, then alternative definitions and meanings will be internalised into the self. Because alternative definitions reflect the balance of class forces, overall, internalised ideologies contain contradictions. Thus, the self of an individual working class person may typically reflect both elements of capitalist ideology and its contradiction, a sense of working class solidarity. It is, perhaps, in the exploration of these internalised contradictions that we are able to locate the opportunities for choice and for resistance.

Our review of the possibilities of utilising elements from mainstream psychological theories for the purposes of a materialist understanding of the individual has highlighted the fact that much work still needs to be done if some of the problems involved are to be overcome. Attempts at *synthesis* are especially open to the objection that Marxist and non-Marxist philosophical foundations are incompatible. Foreman (1977, p. 61) rejects the possibility of a synthesis between Marxism and psychoanalysis because of the irreconcilability of instinct theory and the theory of class struggle. Likewise, the liberal reformist foundations of symbolic interactionism cannot be assimilated into historical materialism. The argument against synthesis is, we have suggested, a convincing one.

For those who reject not only synthesis with, but even substantial borrowing from, non-Marxist psychologies, the alternative before them is to develop a new psychology directly from the basic categories of historical materialism. It is to this enterprise that we now turn.

4
Personality Theory from within Historical Materialism

We have seen in the previous chapter that many efforts have been made to develop a materialist understanding of the individual on the basis of some mixture of Marxism and whole theories or selected concepts borrowed from psychological work lying originally outside Marxism. In many cases this mixture has been achieved by maintaining a dualism between ideology and the psychology of the individual on the one hand, and the economic structure on the other. Mitchell's approach is a prime example of this dualism, and we have indicated some of its limitations. In particular, it is an approach which effectively restricts Marxism to political economy and places psychoanalysis *on top of it* as an explanation of the production and reproduction of ideology. Despite its serious problems, we might see Schneider's work as, in this respect, an advance in that it attempts to develop Marx's own psychological understandings through an elaboration of the theory of value – labour, commodities and money – and, only on the basis of this elaboration, uses concepts from psychoanalysis in order to examine the interaction between personality development and historic changes in the forces and relations of production.

Schneider drew upon the later work of Marx, notably from *Capital*, and so was able to suggest an understanding of the individual which was rooted in Marx's mature theorising on the economic structure of capitalism. Most of this chapter will be devoted to the examination of an attempt to go further than Schneider: to develop a theory of personality directly from Marx's theory of labour and commodities, but without using non-Marxist theories in order to provide psychological concepts (the unconscious, instinct, repression, etc.) intended to 'fill the gap' in Marx's own work. The most impressive example of this enterprise is to be found in the work of Lucien Sève.

HUMANISM AND ALIENATION THEORY

Before we move to our central discussion, however, we must acknowledge immediately that there has existed a strong current of Marxist thought which has preferred to turn to the *early* writings of Marx in its search for the foundations of a Marxist psychology. We have seen already that some of the impetus to the development of left-wing Freudianism came from its criticism of orthodox Marxism, in particular its economism and its association with Stalinism. That same impetus led many Western Marxists, from the 1960s onwards, to find in the 'young Marx' a humanistic antidote to his later work on political economy. The first English translation of the *1844 Economic and Philosophical Manuscripts* did not appear until 1959 and it was upon this work, in particular, that 'humanist' Marxists fell. The *1844 Manuscripts* constitute Marx's major early philosophical work on the concept of alienation, work which has been seen by some Marxists as separated from his later work, and by others as the forerunner of the fundamentally important ideas of his later work, in particular the theory of commodity fetishism. This latter view appears to us to have most to commend it (see Mészáros, 1972; McLellan, 1971) but, as we shall see, the crucial question to be considered is whether Marx's later work so transformed and *made scientific* his early philosophical reflections that it is from the later rather than the earlier work that we must develop the foundations of a Marxist psychology. But let us first look at Marx's theory of alienation.

In his early work, Marx was struggling with the fact that although human beings were *active* in the world and indeed created the social world through their labour, they experienced the world as one which acted upon them. The external world, including other human beings, were experienced as alien objects above and against people, even though these objects had been created by them. The idea of alienation or estrangement could be applied to religion, philosophy, politics and, most importantly for Marx, economics. 'In all these fields', McLellan (1971, p. 106) writes, 'the common idea was that man had forfeited to someone or something what was essential to his nature – principally to be in control of his own activities, to be the initiator of the historical process. In the different forms of alienation some other entity obtained what was proper to man.' It was to the situation of the worker under capitalism that Marx gave his particular attention, in the *1844 Manuscripts*. As private property and the division of labour develops, the experience of labour itself changes: from being an expression of their own creative powers, labour and its products come to assume to men and women a character totally alien and separate.

> The worker is related to the product of his labour as to an alien object. The object he produces does not belong to him, dominates him, and only serves in the long run to increase his poverty. Alienation appears not only in the result, but also in the process of production and productive activity itself . . . Species life, productive life, life creating life, turns into a mere means of sustaining the workers' individual existence, and man is alienated from his fellow men. Finally, nature itself is alienated from man, who thus loses his own inorganic body.
>
> (Marx, 1971, p. 137)

For Marx, the concept of alienation was an exceptionally complex one, but we can begin to see from the above passage that human beings are viewed as alienated from (a) *nature*, the 'sensuous external world' which is the product of human labour, (b) *themselves* because the labour process itself is an alien activity offering no satisfactions save that of selling it to someone else, (c) their '*species-being*', that is, their essential 'humanness' in having created the social world, but experiencing it as something separate, and (d) *other people*, who as similarly alienated beings all experience each other as estranged.

The centrality of the concept of alienation in its various transformations to Marx's social theory cannot be overestimated. 'The *Manuscripts of 1844*,' argues Mészáros (1972, p. 93), 'lay down the foundations of the Marxian system, centred on the concept of alienation.' Furthermore, one can read into the *1844 Manuscripts* the basic elements of a Marxist psychology – that the human being is socially and historically produced, as is human experience of the world, and that money and commodity production corrupt human personality and estrange it from itself. It seems possible, on this foundation, to explore the transformations in human consciousness which occur as a result of particular kinds of relations of production and reproduction, how men and women experience alienation *as the contradiction* of being related to and, at the same time, separated from each other at work and in the family, and how the various ideological conditioning structures of capitalism induce in the individual an acceptance of alienated labour as natural, rather than as historically constructed. Marx himself maintained, in the *1844 Manuscripts*, that only on the basis of an understanding of how the mode of production constructed the human being would a scientific psychology be possible.

> It can be seen how the history of industry and its previous objective existence is an open book of man's faculties and his psychology available to view. It was previously not conceived of in its connection with man's essence but only as the exterior aspect of utility, because man, moving inside the sphere of alienation could only apprehend . . . the generalised existence of man . . . A psychology for which this book, and therewith the most tangible and accessible part of history, remains closed cannot become a genuine science with a real content.
>
> (Marx, 1971, pp. 153–4)

We have seen in the previous chapter that attempts to establish a materialist understanding of the individual have all been based on following, in effect, Marx's proposals for psychology. Although the work we have considered so far depended also on drawing from non-Marxist psychology, much of it was based on the theory of human alienation. We can take the work of Erich Fromm, a psychoanalyst and 'humanist Marxist', as representative of this commitment to alienation theory. In 1961 an English translation of the *1844 Manuscripts* was published together with a long introductory essay by Fromm, all under the general title *Marx's Concept of Man*, and reprinted many times (see Fromm, 1973). In 1968, Fromm wrote a paper on 'Marx's Contribution to the Knowledge of Man' (Fromm, 1971) which argued that Marx's contribution to psychology had been undervalued. It was, Fromm contended, 'a humanist depth psychology' blocked by the dominant position of behaviourist experimental psychology, and superior to Freudian theory at many points. He suggested that as there existed a 'renaissance of humanist thinking', Marx's psychology would now be more acceptable, especially as an antidote to behaviourism.

> Modern academic and experimental psychology is to a large extent a science dealing with alienated man, studied by alienated investigators with alienated and alienating methods. Marx's psychology, being based on the full awareness of the fact of alienation, was able to transcend this type of psychological approach because it did not take alienated man for the natural man, for man as such.
>
> (Fromm, 1971, p. 63)

Fromm identifies a number of elements in Marx's work upon which it should be possible to build a humanist psychology. Marx distinguishes human beings from animals by their characteristic of engaging in 'free, conscious activity', involving a dynamic conception of the person as driven by passions, or drives, some of which are *fixed* and others *relative*. The fixed drives exist under all circumstances, whilst the relative drives have their origin in particular social structures and forms of productive activity. But even the fixed drives – eating, drinking, procreating – are distinctively human in their striving to *relate* to other human beings and to nature, rather than simply satisfy physical needs. Marx also enables us, Fromm argues, to distinguish between *genuine human needs* for relatedness to others and to nature and *imaginary or synthetic needs* which are socially created to consume a mass of alien products. In linking Marx's conception of the human being with what were suggested as similar concepts in Zen Buddhism and Christian mysticism, Fromm was pushing hard a view characteristic of the optimistic humanism of the late 1960s, namely that 'progressive' philosophies from a number of sources would enable a realisation of human potential to be achieved. For Fromm, it led to an under-playing or rejection of the more abrasive and uncompromising elements in Marxism, especially the theory of revolutionary class struggle. The concept of alienation eventually became debased by Fromm into social criticism of 'industrial society' and its detrimental effects on the individual: useful as a liberal critique, but hardly part of historical materialism.

The question which confronts us, then, is whether the early work of Marx, especially his first formulations of the theory of human alienation, provides a satisfactory basis for a Marxist psychology. It is clear that the hopes in the 1960s of founding a psychology on alienation theory have not been fulfilled. Sève, wishing to argue his own approach based on Marx's mature work, makes a great deal of this failure. But the point is not a decisive one, for *none* of the attempts to develop a psychology within historical materialism has been entirely successful, including Sève's own work, as we shall see later. More important is whether there is a fundamental scientific reason for *not* basing a psychology on the early versions of alienation theory. As we have seen, Marx pointed in the *1844 Manuscripts* to what was necessary for a 'real science' of psychology. But why, one might ask, did Marx himself not continue to develop a psychology? 'Ought one to believe', Sève (1978, p. 64) asks, 'that he did not have the time to elaborate this psychology just as he did not have time to give a systematic exposition of his dialectical method? Or, on the contrary, ought one to believe that, in his maturity, acknowledging it as mistaken, he knowingly abandoned a project of his youth?' Sève believes the latter interpretation to be the correct one.

As a preliminary to the exposition of his own approach, Sève argues that in the *1844 Manuscripts* a 'pre-scientific' conception of the human being is still evident. Although the 'human essence' is conceived as having an historical and social nature, it is in the form of 'species man', that is, as *inherent* in the still abstract individual. Only immediately after the *1844 Manuscripts*, during his work in 1845–6, did Marx move decisively from abstract philosophical speculation about 'man in general' to concrete analysis of human beings produced in and by their social relations. Only the development of political economy, to which Marx now turned, could enable the general philosophical term 'alienation' to be transformed into specific processes within specific modes of production. Other Marxist scholars hold a different view, namely that the concept of alienation occurs repeatedly throughout Marx's mature work. McLellan (1971, p. 108) for example, suggests that the concept of alienation 'in so far as it implies that relations between people have been replaced by relations between things . . . may be said to be one of *Capital*'s basic themes'.

It could be argued, in a spirit of impatience, that these disputes are minor matters that we can leave to those who formed their careers on Marxist exegesis. Clearly we cannot resolve the issue here, nor would it be appropriate to engage in the lengthy review of conflicting evidence which would be necessary as a basis of informed discussion. It may be that the theory of human alienation, in its early form, could still provide a foundation for a Marxist psychology. In the meantime we can acknowledge that the concept of alienation undergoes various transformations in Marx's later work, but can still be detected as the underlying idea behind what Sève would consider to be the 'scientific' theory of commodity fetishism. Indeed, Sève himself uses the term alienation at various points in his analysis. In a famous passage in the first volume of *Capital*, Marx writes about what may be considered to be the transformed theory of alienation of his mature work.

A commodity is therefore a mysterious thing, simply because in it the social character of men's labour appears to them as an objective character stamped upon the product of that labour; because the relation of the producers to the sum total of their own labour is presented to them as a social relation, existing not between themselves, but between the products of their labour. This is why the products of labour become commodities, social things whose qualities are at the same time perceptible and imperceptible to the senses . . . There is a definite social relation between men that assumes, in their eyes, the fantastic form of a relation between things.

(Marx, 1974, p. 77)

As we have seen, Schneider begins his analysis with commodity fetishism. With much the same starting-point, Sève outlines a new Marxist psychology based on the implications for human labour of the fetishism of commodities.

PERSONALITY DEVELOPMENT AND SOCIAL LABOUR

Lucien Sève is a Marxist philosopher whose work is difficult for two reasons: *first*, because as a philosopher Sève is engaged in the task of laying foundations upon which psychologists might build, and is therefore concerned with theoretical rigour rather than providing supporting empirical evidence; *second*, because he engages in dense polemic with other French philosophers and psychologists and this sometimes obscures the clarity of his arguments. None the less, Sève's work represents an impressive contribution to the development of a materialist understanding of the individual and it is for this reason that we devote the remainder of this chapter to its exposition and critique.

In the early part of his work, Sève (1978) examines the relationship between Marxism and psychology and suggests that, starting from Marxism, one can make a number of propositions. The *first* is that people are the most important of the productive forces in an economy, because as labour power they are the subjective factor in production and when they use these productive forces, such as tools and machines, they develop their individual capacities. *Second*, the relations of production into which people enter, including the division of labour, are necessary to their continued existence, and determine the general development of individuals, their labour, their leisure activities, their consumption patterns and their incomes. *Third*, because human consciousness is a social product, an individual's consciousness cannot, on the whole, go beyond the limits characteristic of his or her class or of the general degree of historical development: social institutions, in other words, determine the life processes of individuals. *Fourth*, the characteristic contradictions of a social structure, such as capitalism, produce in people basic contradictions, including between needs and their satisfaction and between labour as a means of subsistence and as self-expression.

From the starting point of psychology, Sève similarly makes a number of assertions which are already familiar to us. Because men and women are in their essence 'the ensemble of social relations', they become human through social relations. These social relations (the division of labour and the structures and contradictions of a particular society) are not therefore simply *external factors* in the development of personality, but are the very essence of personality. Furthermore, every human need is social because men and women engage in the social production of their means of subsistence, working to earn a living in order to eat, drink, clothe and house themselves. The individual needs other people for the production of what he or she wishes to consume.

It is from these propositions about the social nature of human beings as determined by productive activities that Sève proceeds to argue that a Marxist psychology must be based upon the Marxist theory of labour. The labour upon which Sève concentrates is *social labour*, that is, the labour which produces commodities. The distinction between *concrete* and *abstract* labour is central to his argument and will be elaborated later. At this stage we must simply note that people's concrete activity, when engaged in commodity production, becomes abstract labour, separated from and opposed to the person. Thus concrete and abstract labour are two sides of the same labour which is opposed to itself. Sève does not give as much attention to domestic labour as he does to abstract social labour and defends himself by maintaining that he is not trying to *reduce* personality theory to the study of social or 'productive' labour, but he is *basing* it on such a study. We will return to the implications of this emphasis on social labour later in the chapter.

Sève begins his substantive argument in a way similar to Schneider when he points to the contradiction, in the capitalist mode of production, between the *appearance* of things and their *reality*. 'On the surface of bourgeois society', Marx (1974, p. 501) writes, 'the wage of the labourer appears as the price of labour, a certain quantity of money that is paid for a certain quantity of labour.' But if this surface appearance coincided with reality, then there would be no psychological difference between acts which are part of concrete *personal activity* (such as driving as a leisure activity) and the very same acts performed as abstract *wage labour* (such as taxi driving). We know that these acts are experienced differently, despite their being identical behaviourally, because they have different status in an individual's social activities and therefore in the real life of the personality. But wages are not, as it were, a direct *result* of labour; this is a bourgeois illusion. The worker does not sell his or her labour for wages, but his or her *labour power*, namely 'the aggregate of those mental and physical capacities of a human being which he exercises whenever he produces a use-value of any description' (Marx, 1974, p. 164).

It is the fact of the selling of a person's mental and physical capacities that is crucial to an understanding of that person's personality development, Sève argues. Labour power, like any other commodity, is sold at its value, that is, the labour time necessary for its production. This production of labour power consists of the maintenance and reproduction of a person's life for which that person requires the means of subsistence – wages. The difference between the value which labour power *creates* and its own value (what is paid for it) is the basis of capitalist exploitation. The individual's labour power, the mental and physical capacities involved, is his or her essential human-ness, but under capitalism it cannot primarily be 'free self-expression', but must be sold to the capitalist and so reduced to a commodity. Labour power does not therefore create use values for the worker, but takes on an *abstract form* as an exchange value, because even personal consumption is the means of preserving the use-value of labour power for the capitalist.

In personal life the individual *appears* to be able to determine his or her activity and relate it concretely to needs. But even here the social relations of production penetrate because *the reproduction of labour power* – that is, preparing for wage labour – still takes priority. Eating, sleeping and weekend leisure centres on the necessity to be ready and able to work. The feminist perspective, indeed, maintains that women's domestic labour in the family precisely functions to perform the task of preparing and sustaining the members for wage labour. In wage labour itself the individual is more obviously confronted with specific forces and relations of production and so cannot *fully* develop individual capacities, because this is not the aim of capitalist production; capacities are only developed *incidentally* if they contribute to the creation of exchange-value for the capitalist. The training of a worker to increase his or her skills and knowledge does not take place primarily for the worker, but for the capitalist. In short, the development of capacities and the satisfaction of needs are subjected to the requirements of social labour, but as part of the illusion of bourgeois society *appear* as 'natural' needs and as developments which primarily benefit the worker.

Because of his insistence on the centrality of social labour in the individual personality, Sève gives little attention to personal relationships within the family. Like Schneider, he sees these latter relationships as secondary because social labour is the activity in which the individual is in contact with the productive forces and therefore, in orthodox Marxist analysis, with the most *decisive* social relations. Feminist critics would, in particular, see this as characteristic of a tendency among some Marxists to over-emphasise economic structure at the expense of giving adequate attention to other social relations. We shall return to this point later, but in Sève's defence we must acknowledge the importance of his contention that to understand family relationships one must begin by examining the *material exchanges* which it consists of, or which support it, namely the domestic economy.

The domestic economy is characterised by what Lenin called 'barbarously unproductive, petty nerve wracking and crushing drudgery', but technical advances which supposedly make housework easier can no more emancipate women, Sève argues, than the growth of productive forces (such as 'the micro chip revolution') emancipates the working class generally. Sève, unlike other writers on the family, gives little attention to ideology, but concentrates on the division of labour in the family as the key to understanding its psychology. On this, he raises a number of questions which need to be answered in developing a theory of the domestic economy. What kinds of material exchanges are involved in family relations and what effect do they have on individual activities? What is the relation between the domestic labour of the housewife and the social labour of the husband bringing in a wage to the family? What is the effect of directly replacing domestic labour by wage labour, that is, paying for domestic labour to be undertaken? To what extent does the time taken to perform domestic labour play a role in regulating the relationships between men and women in a family? Can we distinguish between *concrete domestic labour* as self-expression (some aspects of child care and cookery, for example) and a *'pseudo-abstract' domestic labour* (routine cleaning, washing, cooking, general household management) which cannot, however, be exchanged for an income within domestic relations? This last question posed by Sève, but not answered by him, raises wider issues concerning the status and function of domestic labour to which we must return when we consider the limitations of Sève's overwhelming emphasis on the influence of wage labour on individual personality.

ACTS, CAPACITIES AND NEEDS

On the basis of his arguments about the centrality of social labour in the development of a Marxist theory of personality, Sève formulates his framework for such a theory in terms of what he describes as *hypotheses* which psychologists are invited to elaborate and test out. The basic concepts he begins with are *acts* and *capacities*, for the concrete individual personality (not personality *in general*) is a complex system of acts.

An *act* is any behaviour of an individual, a concrete activity. Consequences flow from an act, not only immediately for the individual who undertook the act, but also for society, and later these consequences *return to the individual* as social relations; for example, a concrete act of labour returns as part of an abstract commodity. This process is a consequence of the dual nature of human acts, on the one hand the act of an individual, part of his or her personal biography, is self-expression, but on the other hand it is also the act of a social world, an aspect of social relations and thus an expression of objective historical conditions. This duality between self-expression and social relations underlies the Marxist contention that people *both* create the social world, within certain limitations, and are also created by the social world. Clearly, contradictions may arise from this duality, for the individual's act of self-expression may return as part of an exploitive social relation.

Capacities is the term used by Sève to denote the range of innate or acquired physical and mental potentialities necessary to carry out an act. A dialectical relation exists between acts and capacities in that whilst a capacity is a precondition for carrying out an act, most capacities are themselves produced or developed in the individual by sets of acts which in their turn are a precondition for their capacities. Thus, theoretically, one can distinguish what Sève refers to as two *sectors* of an individual's total activities:

Sector I: the set of acts which produce, develop or specifically determine capacities and is primarily to do with learning
Sector II: the set of acts which make use of already existing capacities and produces some *effect*.

Sève is careful to point out that, in practice, acts are often in both sectors, because many activities are both learning and the exercise of existing capacities and that therefore this is a purely *theoretical* distinction. It is a distinction however upon which a good deal of Sève's subsequent theory lies.

Sève uses the conceptualisations of Marxist political economy to suggest that an individual's capacities can be compared with the *fixed capital* of an economic formation, in that these capacities reproduce the individual. The development of this fixed capital of the individual personality, to pursue the analogy further, interacts with and is affected by the individual's personal history, its rhythms and crises, and is open to risks of social depreciations (as in long-term unemployment) together with the possibility of expanded reproduction (as when a great deal of new learning takes place) which is, in effect, investment in new capacities. Engels (1955, p. 340) writes that 'the function of society which is most important for progress [is] accumulation': the structurally related parallel for the individual, Sève contends, is that the function of the personality which is most important for its progress is the development of capacities.

But where, asks Sève, do acts start from? Is activity a response to *need*, and is the prime need for human beings, in

Marxism, activity, labour? What are we to make of this circularity? The 'problem of need' has to be tackled first by making a distinction which we referred to earlier between *biological needs* which have to be met as the basic minimal conditions for the possibility of human life and survival and *developed human needs* which are social. Whereas biological needs demand satisfaction, are internal to the organism and are limited, human needs tolerate a degree of dissatisfaction and *respond to the needs of others*. For Sève this latter response to others is very important, cannot be characterised as enlightened self-interest, but is founded on the recognition that the basis of internal needs is external. The socialist militant is an example of this *altruism* which is neither self-sacrifice nor self-interest, Sève suggests:

> Actually, the strivings of a real militant life rest precisely on becoming aware of the fact that the general satisfaction of personal needs can only take place via the carrying out of a number of social changes, the objective logic of which more or less completely subordinates the limited, immediate satisfaction of personal needs taken in isolation.
>
> (Sève, 1978, p. 318)

A further characteristic of human needs is that their reproduction appears to be *unlimited*, as the great diversification of artistic enjoyment throughout history exemplifies.

Needs connect to activities, Sève argues, in the following way. What makes a person act is a calculation of the relationship between the possible effects of an act (the *psychological product*) and the needs to be satisfied; in short, the relationship between product and need (P/N). The proposition which emerges 'as the central element of a scientific theory of motivation articulated with an overall historical materialist concept of the concrete individual' (1978, p. 321) is that *the intuitive evaluation of P/N is one of the most simple and universal regulators of human activity*.

But if the expanded reproduction of needs, and as we have seen earlier, of capacities too, *can* take place, why is it that such expanded reproduction does *not* take place in particular individuals? Sève answers the question at this stage by

reference to the general characteristics of capitalism: later, as
we shall see, he provides a more detailed answer in terms of the
experiences of individuals. The general point is that, through its
massive development of the forces of production, capitalism for
the first time in history creates the *objective conditions* for the full
realisation of human needs and capacities by individuals, but
at the same time these very conditions are achieved only
through 'the most deep-seated alienation and the deprivation
of the vast majority of individuals and their complete subordination to the social processes of creation of wealth, which is
itself subject to the interests of an increasingly parasitic social
class' (1978, p. 325). Under capitalism, labour appears as the
means for the simple reproduction of labour power, *not* the
expanded reproduction necessary to the development of
human potential, and because only simple reproduction (for
the purpose of wage labour) is often possible for most people,
the illusion becomes established that biological needs are
generally the basis of all human activity.

THE STRUCTURE OF PERSONALITY AND USE-TIME

Sève acknowledges that his 'hypotheses' about acts, capacities
and needs do not, at this stage in his argument, provide us with
an understanding of how activities are *structured*. The structur-
ing of activities is essentially what personality consists of;
activities within a temporal structure concerned with reproduction and development. Time then is the crucial factor: how
the individual uses the time available to him or her for various
kinds of activities. Sève distinguishes between three kinds of
use-time: *ideal use-time*, which is what the individual may try to
achieve in the distribution of activities; *empirical use-time*, the
distribution which the individual sees through ideological
categories; and *real use-time*, the temporal relations between the
various objective categories of an individual's activities. It is
this real use-time upon which Sève concentrates his attention:
the 'objective categories' are those understood within the
Marxist theory of labour.

Under capitalism the real use-time of the individual is
divided between the *abstract* activities of social, or productive

labour, and the *concrete* activities directly related to the individual, including the satisfaction of personal needs and the learning of new capacities unconnected with social labour. The fact that individuals must balance the use-time between concrete and abstract activity, between social labour and personal activity, and that this balance must be achieved within a context of social relations which *predetermine the general distribution of use-time* because of the necessity of social labour for existence, provides some understanding of how such individual balancing can produce crises in individual and family life. The omnipresence of the necessity of wage labour, its influence over even 'personal activities' because of the need to recuperate from the most deadening and repetitive of the activities of abstract labour, is bound to produce tensions and conflicts, especially where capacities not necessary to social labour are relatively undeveloped. The unresolvable contradiction in the lives of most people under capitalism is that whilst social labour is necessary, it is also abstract and does not, for most, allow the expanded development of capacities. On the other side, the opportunity to develop capacities within personal, concrete activities is for many also restricted, except in so far as they further the interests of capital in maintaining labour power or increasing the consumption of commodities. The link here with Schneider's analysis is clear.

The balancing of use-time is thus a central feature of adult personality. But it is absent in the child, where it is entirely imposed externally by parents and others, because children, even of school age, cannot easily structure use-time coherently by themselves. Whilst we may detect in this observation a reflection of the French school system and therefore treat it sceptically, it leads Sève to his important contention that the origin of the developed adult personality *lies outside childhood*. In his emphasis on actual, material, social relations in the development of personality, rather than on ideology, Sève decisively parts company with the left-wing Freudians we discussed in the last chapter, even with Schneider. Children, Sève argues, are not direct psychological images of their parents, but they reflect and are determined by the real use-time of the parents as between concrete and abstract activity. Parent–child hierarchical relations, in other words, are governed by the *material* infrastructures of personality and social relations – the imperatives of abstract labour and its use-time. It will be recalled that Mitchell (1975), among others, maintains that the repressive relations between parents and children (for example, in the oedipus complex) represent an essential prohibitive law, that against incest, of which the parents are, as it were, merely the 'empirical bearers'. Sève, on the contrary, argues that such an idea is thoroughly un-Marxist in that it reduces family relations, and indeed social relations generally, to their superstructural aspect, that is, to ideology, unconnected to the economic infrastructure. Family relations can only be understood, Sève reiterates, within an historical materialist analysis of the real material world of labour.

A GENERAL TOPOLOGY OF PERSONALITIES

The preceding discussion suggests that it is possible to construct a general picture of the personalities which are formed on the basis of capitalist social relations. Whilst all personalities will have a common topology because they are the product of the same social relations, each individual personality will take a particular form, dependent on the concrete conditions of each individual's life. Sève represents the general topology graphically (1978, p. 347) – see Figure 4.1. This representation summarises all the previous exposition: it divides total activity into *concrete* and *abstract* activity, and into Sector I activity (learning) and Sector II activity (other acts). It shows that an act in any of the resulting four quadrants is determined by the evaluation of the relationship between the possible effects of an act (the product) and the needs to be satisfied, i.e. P/N. The four quadrants are thus as follows:

The concrete activity of Sector I (quadrant Ic) is all the learning and training activity in which the capacities used in concrete activity form and develop

The concrete activity of Sector II (quadrant IIc) is the ensemble of acts in which capacities are used for the direct benefit of the individual.

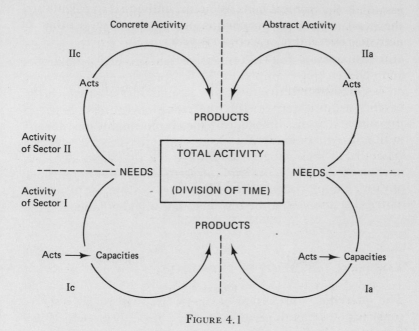

FIGURE 4.1

The abstract activity of Sector I (quadrant Ia) is the ensemble of learning and training activities which are required for social labour and for the social relations involved.
The abstract activity of Sector II (quadrant IIa) is the ensemble of acts of which social labour directly consists.

On the basis of this general topology of personalities it is possible, Sève suggests, to begin the work of constructing a picture of the real use-time of a particular individual personality. He does not mean by this a *typology* of personalities, for example, the 'typical' use-time of a child, a housewife or a factory worker, for such typification is contrary to the materialist commitment to historical specificity. But he suggests some hypothetical examples of how use-time might be distributed for particular individuals, though he acknowledges that there are many theoretical and methodological problems to be overcome before such pictures could be drawn with any precision, not least the difficulty of collecting a number of

essential biographical facts about an individual in calculating
the exact amount or proportion of time spent on a range of
activities over a day, a week or a year.

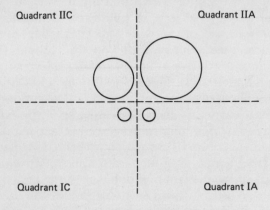

Quadrant IIC   Quadrant IIA

Quadrant IC   Quadrant IA

FIGURE 4.2

We can illustrate the possibilities of Sève's approach by
working through a hypothetical example. Let us assume that
we are able to plot the proportion of time spent by John Smith
on the concrete and abstract activity in the four quadrants as
shown in Figure 4.2. Here is a man who works on a motor car
assembly-line, where the tasks he performs have been progressively routinised and deskilled, compared with the first
generation of skilled workers in the car industry. His is an
example of what happens to workers when the process which
Marx describes takes place, namely that:

> as the division of labour increases, labour is simplified. The
> special skill of the worker becomes worthless. He becomes
> transformed into a simple, monotonous productive force that
> does not have to use intense bodily or intellectual faculties.
> His labour becomes a labour that anyone can perform . . .
> more unsatisfying, more repulsive.
>   (Marx and Engels, 1968, p. 92)

This dehumanising factory experience is represented in the abstract activity of quadrant IIa, and it clearly dominates his use-time. Furthermore, increasing automation means that the capacities required to undertake this labour is reduced and so only minimum training is required for it: very few skills are developed, as can be seen in quadrant Ia. Although John Smith's personal leisure activities (quadrant IIc) are the next most important use of his time after abstract labour, they are of a predominantly passive kind – watching television, going to the football match on a Saturday afternoon and drinking with his friends. He carries out few domestic tasks, does minimal do-it-yourself carpentry, but he reads very little and has no other activity which might develop his capacities: this is reflected in the very small use-time represented in quadrant Ic.

Some of the elements of John Smith's personality structure as represented in the distribution of his use-time are not difficult to picture. Abstract activities dominate his life, totally unbalancing it. Because he does not develop his capacities very fully either at work or outside it, he experiences life pre-dominantly as one in which he is *acted upon*: his main opportunity to exercise control lies in his family relationships, which may be characterised by petty tyranny over his wife and children. He is not, to use Sève's favourite word, a *militant*, not at all active in his trade union, in a political party, or in local community politics. Had he been active in any of these respects, the psychological picture would have been different. Although the abstract activities (quadrant IIa and Ia) would have remained the same in absolute terms, *proportionally* they would have been reduced, as the concrete activities, especially in quadrant Ic, were increased to take account of trade union, party or community activism, and of the skill development (including reading, writing and organising) which such acti-vism demands.

The importance of these preliminary attempts at mapping the use-time of individuals is that they show, Sève suggests (1978, p. 349), 'the phenomenon of capitalist exploitation inscribed in the very depths of the personality'. A retired elderly working class person, for example, might show a massive preponderance of concrete consumption activities quadrant IIc) over all other quadrants and a drastic reduction in opportunities to develop new capacities because of his or her exclusion from social labour and marginality in local community life. Once again the psychological picture would be one of great unbalance, as it might be with a long-term unemployed person.

PSYCHOLOGICAL SUPERSTRUCTURES

Having discussed the activities which contribute directly to the production and reproduction of the personality, Sève is in a position to examine what he terms *psychological superstructures*. These superstructures perform a regulating role in relation to an individual's productive and reproductive activities and consist of two kinds of controls. First, there are the *spontaneous controls* which are internal emotions which include immediate reactions when an action is completed (e.g. satisfaction or disappointment) and also the inclination or disinclination to undertake a particular act, or even passive resistance to performing it. These controls are the result of the evaluation of the outcome, in relation to need, of the activity in question (i.e. the evaluation of P/N). For example, the inclination/disinclination to get out of bed in the morning can be seen as a direct evaluation or, through anticipatory imagination that something previously not experienced is expected to happen, of the general P/N of the coming day. These spontaneous controls may, Sève admits, have connections with the psychoanalytic concept of the unconscious. Second, there are the *voluntary controls* whose aim is to control use-time through changing or maintaining the overall distribution of time given to the individual's activities. These controls include rules of conduct, the individual's self-image and his or her own norms about the distribution of use-time (i.e. ideal use-time). Here we are clearly in the realm of social construction because voluntary controls are determined by social relations exterior to the person and assimilated through the imperatives of abstract activity.

But if the voluntary controls are ultimately exterior to the person, and if the spontaneous controls, although internal, are merely immediate reactions, possibly unconscious, how far will individuals ever be able to develop a consciousness of the world which grasps its real objective social relations? Sève presents two possibilities here (1978, p. 352). Is consciousness of self and of the world necessarily rationalisation or ideology, 'a mystified interpretation of reality, the true nature of which remains misunderstood, thus enclosing man in illusion, alienation and dependence'? *Alternatively*, is it possible, and under what conditions, to reach demystified self-consciousness, a true knowledge of objective reality within the limits set by the stage of historical development achieved?

Sève's answer is the second, optimistic one – an answer derived from the experience of socialist militancy. The basic structure of personalities within capitalism are dominated by the reality of exploitive class relations which produce a *positive lack of awareness*. This lack of awareness is an objective illusion in so far as it stems from the *actual* externalisation of the human essence through the fetishism of commodities. At the same time, this lack of awareness is also *ideology* in so far as it justifies alienating social relations and the corresponding forms of use-time between concrete and abstract activities as part of the purposeful legitimating world view of the ruling class and so is resistant to attempts at demystification. So this lack of awareness, Sève argues, is essentially *historical*, in that it is related to a particular period of history, rather than part of some fundamental feature of the human species, as such. Because it does not have its roots in internal instincts, as Freud maintained, but in powerlessness, lack of awareness is a matter of practice – specifically, collective struggle. Only through such struggle can we overthrow the social relations which create the illusions in which we are immersed. These illusions Marx refers to as the 'religious reflex' when he is discussing commodity fetishism:

The religious reflex of the real world can, in any case, only then finally vanish when the practical relations of everyday life offer to man none but perfectly intelligible and reasonable relations with regard to his fellowmen and to nature. The line-process of society, which is based on the process of material production, does not strip off its mystical veil until it is treated as production by freely associated men, and is consciously regulated by them in accordance with a settled plan.

(Marx, 1974, p. 84)

It is to this understanding of the illusion of capitalist social relations, of the role of collective struggle in its overthrow, and of its implications for the personality development of the individual to which we shall return in the final chapter of this book.

Sève's final set of hypotheses are concerned with 'the laws of development of personality' within historically specific contexts. Under capitalism, for example, personal growth, or 'psychological progress', is determined as we have seen by the relation between concrete and abstract activity. A high proportion of learning activities (quadrants Ic and Ia) depends, apart from biological and general social conditions, on the individual's evaluation of the product of these learning activities in relation to need (the P/N of Sector I activities). But this evaluation of P/N in relation to the acquisition and development of capacities may, in an individual case, suggest that the *product* of a given amount of learning is falling, or that the actual amount of learning is falling. This will have the effect of reducing the motivation to continue to develop one's capacities, and so the personality will become 'stagnant and ossified'. Psychological progress falls as the acquisition of new capacities loses its appeal because of the domination of abstract activity and its limitations on self-expression. The objective social causes of this 'falling rate of psychological progress' are often *masked* by psychological and behavioural 'problems' – anxiety, depression, domestic violence, excessive drinking. As a compensation, the individual may withdraw into concrete consumption, a de-politicised 'solution', much encouraged, as Schneider pointed out, by capitalist production. Withdrawal into private life is not, therefore, the solution: it is, Sève argues, in collective struggle in the arena of production that we must seek an eventual escape from the deadening effects of abstract labour.

At the purely individual level there is, Sève concedes, some possibility of limited resistance to the onslaught on the personality of abstract labour. The best resistance is in 'militancy', as we have seen, but there is also scope for such resistance where the general P/N of the concrete aspect of abstract labour is high, that is where one has 'pride in one's work' and takes pleasure in it. This is not, of course, a consequence intended in capitalist production, but it can be experienced where there is a considerable overlap between quadrants Ia and Ic: the learning required for the abstract labour develops capacities which are especially valuable to the individual in his or her personal life. This experience is certainly possible for some workers, such as skilled craft workers, and those engaged in intellectual and professional work, but it leaves the majority of waged workers, together with women engaged full-time in domestic labour, with little hope of resistance at the level of individual personality.

PRODUCTION, IDEOLOGY AND GENDER

In attempting to evaluate Sève's contribution to a materialist understanding of the individual, we must acknowledge immediately that what has been provided in this chapter is merely a sketch of some of the leading ideas in a very complex, lengthy and scholarly work. The danger is that the simplification involved in an outline may have seriously distorted the thrust of Sève's arguments. With this in mind, we can note Sève's own admission that his work is only the *beginning* of a Marxist psychology: its philosophical foundations together with some hypotheses upon which psychologists can work. The product of his work at this stage, although it looks promising, is still very sparse in terms of its immediate application to an understanding of the individual. The analysis of the nature of labour, the development of capacities and the evaluation of P/N, may constitute an important theoretical development, provided we can follow through its implications. We must recognise that Sève assumes a profoundly difficult task when he eschews major reliance on existing psychological theory: the result is bound to appear at this stage more limited than one which is able to draw on the rich vein of psychoanalytic theory or of symbolic interactionism.

But the limitations of Sève's approach stem also, more

deeply, from its theoretical foundations. The traditional Marxist emphasis on *production* – central to Sève's thesis – profoundly affects the whole of his work. We are not suggesting that the importance of production can be denied, but rather that over-emphasis on economic production leads to as much one-sidedness in approach as does the over-emphasis on ideology which we have already criticised. In Sève, ideology is given a very subordinate role in the creation of personality so that *socialisation* to abstract labour, especially during childhood, is reduced to relative insignificance. Intent on his polemic against Althusser's (1971) contrary view, which has been influential on the Freudian Left, Sève argues that the origin of the developed personality lies outside childhood. We may agree that childhood is not the only key to personality development and that the adult experience of abstract labour is of profound importance, without then denying the crucial significance of *ideological preparation* for that labour during childhood.

The relative neglect of childhood in his account of personality development, together with his insistence on the overwhelming importance of actual material relations compared with ideology, leads Sève to undervalue the family's role. His emphasis on the study of material exchanges in the family is useful, but only if it can be linked to an analysis of the family's ideological function in the construction of gendered individuals. Sève recognises that interpersonal relations, including those within the family, can have some role in counteracting at the individual level the contradictions produced by abstract labour, because they are not, in the Marxist sense, social relations and are 'partially disalienated'. But he cannot accept that family relations and the domestic economy can be an effective arena of struggle, because economic production is the dominating centre of his vision. Feminist struggles around the patriarchal family are, by implication, to be thrust firmly into the sidelines.

This brings us to the most important problem in Sève's approach: his treatment of domestic labour and of gender. Although he acknowledges that some aspects of domestic labour may have a 'psuedo-abstract' character, he takes the orthodox Marxist position that only labour which assumes the fully abstract form functions as socially productive labour.

Domestic labour is essentially concrete labour, and although it may give rise to direct exchange or the provision of services within the family, it cannot create surplus value and therefore produce capital, and so is *bound* to be peripheral to the primary social relations. One alternative feminist view is that domestic labour is actually productive labour because it contributes to the exchange value of labour power through its servicing of current and future workers within the family. Another view, nearer to the orthodox Marxist position (Smith, 1978), suggests that we can most usefully approach domestic labour through distinguishing carefully between productive labour and socially necessary labour. Domestic labour is socially necessary in that it secures the conditions required for the reproduction of labour power and therefore for the existence of capital, but it remains external to the capitalist mode of production even though it is functional to it. This seems to be a useful approach which leads, Kuhn and Wolpe (1978) suggest, to the view either that women's struggles can only be effective when they have been fully incorporated into the capitalist relations of production; or alternatively, that women as wage workers and domestic workers are involved in two distinct modes of production, capitalist and domestic, and that the contradictions for women of occupying these dual roles is the arena within which the struggle should be fought.

It is not Sève's distinction between domestic labour and productive labour which is problematic but his failure to acknowledge sufficiently the socially necessary role of domestic labour and its importance in the development of personality, as studies of depression in women must surely suggest. This is linked to a failure to confront the particular problems of women's personality development in capitalist society and to bring into his analysis the crucial dimension of gender relations. The failure to examine gender as well as class relations enables him more easily, perhaps, to undervalue the role of the family, which is, after all, an institution central to the construction of gender hierarchies.

5
Key Concepts in a Materialist Analysis

If there is one conclusion above all that we can draw from the discussions in the previous two chapters it is that there does not yet exist any satisfactory materialist theory of the individual. All the approaches that have been reviewed suffer from certain limitations both in terms of theory and because they frequently lack the support of detailed empirical evidence. Because of the various limitations of the different approaches and the theoretical conflicts between them, it is also premature to suggest that we are yet near to achieving a *theoretical synthesis* which would take the project a stage further.

However, our review suggests that there are certain key concepts which appear at this stage to be of fundamental importance in a materialist analysis of the individual's personality development within a capitalist social structure. The purpose of this chapter is to identify these key concepts and to use them in Part II of the book as a framework within which to examine in outline certain aspects of the life cycle of individuals located within the specific historical conditions of late capitalism.

There are two issues which we must address, however, before we attempt to specify these key concepts.

PROBLEMS OF THEORY

The *first* of these issues concerns the theoretical disputes between the various approaches we have discussed. Some of these disputes can only be resolved when more empirical evidence is available upon which to choose between rival theories: the precise psychological mechanisms by which dominant class and gender ideologies are incorporated into the individual's inner experience of the world is one example. But there are other disputes which stem from differences about what constitute the most significant elements in the dynamics of a social formation: what are most important in its maintenance and reproduction. These differences are not, on the whole, simply philosophical alternatives, but reflect differences in the *politics* of the protagonists, both in terms of the objectives of revolutionary struggle and the means by which a transforming change is to be achieved. This should not surprise us of course because historical materialsim is not after all developed simply to understand the world, but to *change* it; to establish a *praxis* whereby theory and practice are no longer separated but fused together in a process of reflection and action.

The most significant of the differences we have discussed is that between perspectives which emphasise the overwhelming power of the material relations of economic production, and those which stress the determining effect and relative autonomy of ideology. Each side in this dispute has characteristic ways of describing the other. The former perspective is often abused as 'economistic', 'vulgar materialist' and even 'Stalinist', whilst the latter is condemned as 'idealist', 'revisionist', or 'reformist'. Both sides refer to each other as 'reductionist', thus implicitly acknowledging that the element, economy or ideology stressed by their opponents is *undeniably significant* but urge that it should not be over-emphasised with explanations of the dynamics of the social formation *reduced* to that one element.

If we take the work of Sève and Mitchell as examples, it is not difficult to see the way in which their approaches reflect the particular politics of the Left in which they are engaged. Sève is trying to steer an orthodox Marxist route within the French Communist Party and is engaged in disputes with both Althusser and with the 'humanists'. His emphasis on economic production, for example, suggests that women's oppression can only be overcome through their participation in the general revolutionary struggle of the working class and that feminist politics outside this main class struggle is at the minimum irrelevant, at most diversionary. Mitchell, on the contrary, emphasises, as a feminist, the massive importance of *social reproduction*, especially within the family, in which women play a crucial role. She therefore sees ideology as of fundamental significance in the dynamics of patriarchal capitalism.

Upon this issue, we would argue against *both* tendencies to reductionism; over-emphasis on either economic production or the reproduction of ideology is inconsistent with historical materialism. Feminist struggles are significant in their own right, but they also have importance in their contribution to the organisation and objectives of the socialist movement in general (see Rowbotham, Segal and Wainwright, 1979). Both economic production and ideology are key to a materialist understanding of the individual; their *relative importance* is determined by specific historical conditions which require detailed investigation. In the absence of concrete evidence, we cannot argue, *a priori*, the dominance of one over the other, except to acknowledge both that economic production is determinant 'in the last instance' (Althusser, 1971) and also that ideological struggle becomes, as Gramsci (1971, 1977) sugggests, of increasing significance in late capitalism. Whilst we do not wish to underestimate political and theoretical disputes, we intend as far as possible to see these differences not in terms of mutually exclusive alternatives, but as often complementary to each other. It is upon this basis that we will attempt to identify key concepts.

The *second*, and related issue is whether a materialist analysis requires us to draw upon non-Marxist psychologies. We have already suggested that at this stage a theory of the production of the individual formulated entirely from within Marxist categories appears to be too sparse, especially where, as in Sève's case, it gives little attention to the internalisation of ideology in childhood and later. Furthermore, we must recognise that criticisms of orthodox Marxism, especially from the feminist perspective, have suggested limitations which should lead us to be open to possible contributions from outside Marxism. Historical materialism's essentially *reflexive* character should indeed enable it to engage in a critique of itself as a science created within a particular historical conjuncture of social forces and therefore bearing, for good or ill, the marks of its origins. Historical materialism is therefore bound to be incomplete, and to need new infusions as it reflects further historical changes, such as the growth of feminist theory and practice. Beechey (1977, p. 61) puts the point succinctly when she argues that a 'correct analysis of the subordination of women cannot be provided by Marxists unless Marxism itself is transformed'.

In spite of earlier, strong opposition to psychoanalytic theory, socialist feminists have become increasingly interested in its possibilities of explaining, at the psychological level, the internalisation of gender oppression into the deepest structures of women's personalities. It has become clear to them that a theory of the unconscious is a necessary part of the explanation of women's oppression; such a theory must surely equally be a component of any adequate understanding of the internalisation of class relations generally.

But in drawing on psychoanalytic and other non-Marxist theory we are not necessarily committed to a synthesis between two complete bodies of theory. Deep criticisms of Freudianism and other theories is a prerequisite to using transformed versions of such of their concepts that can illuminate the problems we are trying to understand. We should feel free both to revise these concepts and reject those parts of non-Marxist theory which appear to us to be inadequate or incorrect. In her criticisms of Juliet Mitchell's work, Barrett (1980, p. 58) suggests that some of Mitchell's interpretations of Freud's work are open to considerable doubt, but that she is not 'sufficiently convinced of the internal coherence of Freudian psychoanalytic theory to argue that fundamental reservations on crucial stages of [Freud's] account invalidate his work entirely. On the contrary . . . some of his observations are of great interest and can be useful.' Such a detached, critical, but appreciative relationship to non-Marxist psychologies has much to recommend it.

OMISSIONS

Because the review in the previous two chapters could only encompass, in outline, a selected few amongst a much wider range of possible contributions to a materialist understanding of the individual, we are left with some obvious theoretical gaps.

First, we need to give more attention to the *internal relationships within families*. In our discussions so far, a perspective has emerged which could be taken to suggest that the contemporary family should be considered as almost entirely functional to the needs of capital. From their otherwise different approaches Reich and Sève, for example, each appear to take this view. It is more useful, however, to avoid such over-functionalist explanations and to see the family as to some degree relatively autonomous in relation to the capitalist mode of production, sometimes in conflict with its demands, though most usually accommodating to them. This will enable us, as Poster (1978) argues in his examination of the history of different family models, aristocratic, peasant, bourgeois and proletarian, to consider families both in terms of their internal psychic structures and of their ultimate subordination to the economy and the state. Different kinds of family structure, created in relation to different classes and historical periods, engage in different methods of child-rearing directed to different material and moral ends and produce individuals characterised by different kinds of consciousness. As the location within which the child incorporates age, sex and class hierarchies, an appreciation of the internal relations within the family will be crucial to our account.

Second, some of the Marxist theoretical work that has been undertaken on *the ideological constitution of the individual as a subject* is also of use to us. In our discussions so far we have given some attention to psychoanalytic work on identification (in the pre-oedipal period) and on the resolution of the oedipus complex and the formation of the superego as mechanisms for the transmission of ideology. We have also considered the symbolic interactionist approach to the construction of the self within the context of established social meanings. These insights would be deepened by drawing more fully on the work of Therborn (1980), where Althusser's distinction between the two meanings of the term 'human subject' (namely, being subjected to the social order, and being a subject of history in the sense of acting in the social world) are elaborated into a theory of ideology as a social process which 'interpellates' or speaks to us. Ideologies, Therborn argues, both subject us to the social order and prepare (or 'qualify') us for participation in it by telling us (a) what exists and what nature, society, men and women are like, (b) what is good, right, just, beautiful and enjoyable and its opposites, and (c) what is possible and impossible. Therborn goes on to discuss in detail the way in which human subjects are formed in ideology. We can utilise some of this work provided we are careful to avoid a reductionism which underestimates the direct significance of economic relations in the production of the individual.

Third, we have so far given insufficient weight to the *direct intervention of the State in the lives of individuals*. In the early nineteenth century the working class was still a long way from being effectively socialised to the imperatives of factory labour – resistance, indiscipline and 'immorality' were rife. From the middle of the century onwards, liberal bourgeois philanthropy, and increasingly the State itself, began to intervene more directly in working class family life, and later through schooling, in order to induce it to accept a version of bourgeois morality which would more effectively prepare people for the discipline of wage labour and the maintenance of domestic relationships conducive to the reproduction of labour power. A considerable body of Marxist and feminist work is relevant here, including that concerned with the history of state intervention (see, for example, Stedman Jones, 1971; Dale, 1976; Wilson, 1977; Ginsburg, 1980; Parry, Rustin and Satyamurti, 1979) and that directed to a description and analysis of present forms of intervention and control (see, for example, Jones, 1983; Hall, Critcher, Jefferson, Clarke and Roberts, 1978). What emerges from this and other work is that in late capitalism state policy and practice in the fields of education, health, welfare and law and order has both a direct material impact upon the individual and a more subtle ideological effect. In the area of child-rearing practices and the social construction of 'motherhood', for example, many working class families are subjected to close monitoring and control by a range of state welfare services aimed at directly affecting the internal relations within these families. We shall need to take such interventions into account when we consider the development of individual personalities through the life cycle.

Finally, we have not yet taken full account of the fact that contemporary capitalism is a *social formation characterised by institutionalised racism*. The history of imperialism and colonialism is, of course, relevant here because the very existence of some ethnic minorities in Britain is a direct consequence of the capitalist demand for cheap labour power coupled with the exploitation of the colonial territories themselves. International capital whilst it is expanding requires a firmly subordinate and inexpensive army of mobile labour, and immigrant labour appears to fill this requirement exactly; during an economic recession, however, such labour is likely to be the first to be shed. In many respects, the experience of being a British-born member of an oppressed ethnic minority can be analysed in class and gender terms. To be working class and female is already to suffer the combined effects of two structures of subordinancy; add to this being *black*, however, and another critical dimension enters. What should especially concern us is the impact upon the individual personality of racist ideologies and structures. Of particular interest should be the effects of racism on the self-identity of the member of an oppressed ethnic minority and its relationship to class and gender status. Also, the influence of racism within the personality structures of white working class individuals also deserves attention. In this respect, the distinction which Therborn (1980, pp. 27/8) makes between ego-ideologies and alter-ideologies may help us. Ideologies 'interpellate' the *difference* between oneself (ego) and others (alter); those in a dominant ethnic position, for example, designate both themselves (white) and the others (black) in a way which directly affects perceptions and which attempts to mould the dominated according to the image of the ruling ethnic group. Against this, the ideology of the dominated ethnic minority tends, Therborn would suggest, towards resistance because of its particular perceptions of alter and ego. If we are to draw upon such work we must, once again, beware of underestimating the significance for the individual of the direct material experiences of racism in relation to both capital and the state.

Having pointed to the more obvious omissions in our earlier account of contributions to a materialist understanding of the individual, we are now in a position to summarise where we have arrived by identifying certain key concepts.

SUMMARY OF KEY CONCEPTS

Basic propositions

The concepts most basic to a materialist understanding of the individual concern the *major determinants of the construction of human beings*. We begin by acknowledging the *biological nature* of men and women and their differences as a basic datum, but distinguish between the facts of biological influence and biological needs, and forms of domination which legitimate themselves by reference to biology. Although it is possible to identify some common characteristics of all human beings, these characteristics are never encountered as it were in *pure* form, but only as socially mediated. It is in this sense that we can say that human beings are produced by the *social relations characteristic of a specific social formation* at a particular point in history. These social relations centre on production and reproduction, contain contradictions and, within the social formation of capitalism, are based upon class, gender and ethnic domination. The individual's life experience and personality structure is determined, in short, by a unique biography situated within a specific set of class, gender and ethnic relations.

The individual connects to the social world through two kinds of interrelated experiences: of *material relations* and of *ideology*. The individual's *material activities and exchanges* at work, in the family, in community interactions, with state officials and in many other contexts are penetrated by *meanings, definitions, and 'common sense' assumptions* which reflect the ideologies through which a class, gender, ethnic group or other collectivity maintains its internal coherence, makes sense of the world, and either legitimates its dominant position in the social order or validates its resistance to domination.

Three social determinants of the individual

Although in the life of any specific individual, an examination of her or his personal history will reveal the influence of many unique factors, chance events and accidents, it is possible to identify three major social determinants which will have massive effect, and will form the most primary but not exclusive locations within which the individual's personality is constructed through specific experiences: *the economy, the family and the state*. The relative significance of these social determinants will vary according to the individual's class, gender or ethnic position, though we would maintain that in contemporary bourgeois democracies, the economy and the family are overall more important determinants than direct state intervention.

1. *The economy* is a major determinant in that capitalist productive and social reproductive activity, directed towards the accumulation of capital and the reproduction of the labour power upon which it rests, requires the performance of productive labour, *socially necessary labour* and the *consumption of commodities*. Each individual submits to and struggles against these requirements depending upon the chance effects of personal biography and the overall balance, within the social formation, of class, gender and ethnic forces. The individual's personality is affected by the economy through:

(a) *The nature of abstract wage labour*, a form of labour which, whilst it confers upon the individual a social identity and status and provides a primary means of material subsistence, at the same time subordinates individual needs and capacities to the imperatives of capital accumulation and profitability. The degree of alienation experienced in wage labour will be related to the individual's class, gender and ethnic position and its connection to the occupational structure.

(b) *The characteristics of domestic labour* which, because it is socially necessary to capitalist production in its role in the reproduction of labour power, subordinates those who perform it to essentially servicing and nurturing activities. As women are overwhelmingly the primary means by which domestic labour is carried out, it contributes to the maintenance and reproduction of women's oppression and male domination, even while being, like wage labour, a source of social identity.

(c) *The level of material subsistence* maintained as a result of selling labour-power (wages) and allocating resources within families for consumption. Low levels of material subsistence have physically and psychologically damaging effects upon the individual: nutritional deficiency, anxiety, depression, and other outcomes

(d) *The balance in use-time between concrete and abstract activity* in the individual's life, determined by the precise nature of her or his wage labour, domestic labour, consumption and leisure pursuits, and the opportunities these provide for the development of *capacities*. The growth of capacities (skills and knowledge) is the means through which the individual acts creatively upon the social world and is one way of securing the potential for resisting subordination.

(e) *The consumption of commodities* which are produced in order to meet the individual's socially mediated 'needs'. Commodity consumption, although in modern societies necessary to the maintenance and reproduction of life, is permeated with the capitalist imperative to create new 'needs' for new products in order to sustain profitability and capital accumulation. The effect upon the individual of this process is to link consumption to self-identity and social status, especially in relation to class, gender and age, on the one hand involving the compulsive buying of often rapidly deteriorating products, and on the other hand inducing feelings of guilt and worthlessness when poverty prevents the purchase of such products.

2. *The family household* is a significant determinant of individual personality in two ways: (i) it is the *actual material and ideological location* within which most people experience their childhoods and in turn become parents; (ii) it provides a basis for the *ideology of familialism*, a celebration of virtues of the nuclear family, the nurturing roles of women, the subordination of children and other requirements of the social order. In contemporary capitalist societies 'the family' in practice takes many diverse forms, despite the ideological reverence given to the model of the nuclear family. Actual families develop over time as systems having their own particular cultures – distinctive material and ideological practices which determine the specific experiences of individuals within them. The cultures of families, and their internal relationships, are *relatively autonomous* of the economy and the state, though deeply penetrated by both. Families are predominantly experienced as contradictory in that they are often the location of both subordination and self-fulfilment, depending in part on class and gender position, an arena of both love and hate. Within the family, individual experience and personality structures can be seen as formed through submission to and resistance against:

(a) *The establishment of gender and age hierarchies* involving subordinacy and control, whereby biological sexual differences and the physical and social dependency of young children on adults are used predominantly to legitimate gender oppression and parental control.

(b) *Family practices which prepare and maintain the individual for labour;* according to their gender, children tend to be prepared ideologically and psychologically within the cultures of their families for wage labour, domestic labour and nurturing roles related to their class position. Family definitions, meanings and interactions continuously present children and adults with models of behaviour considered appropriate for 'mothers', 'fathers', 'sons', 'daughters', and 'respectable families', models significantly influenced by familial ideology.

(c) *Family practices which may communicate wider ideologies appropriate to the production of class and gender subjects*, including acceptance of the existing social order and its major institutions, and the impossibility and undesirability of changing the society in the interests of the most subordinate.

3. *The state* in bourgeois democracies reflects, in its organisation and policies, the precise balance of class, gender and ethnic forces at any given historical point. Thus although within capitalism the state will overall further the long-term interests of capital, this is always in a context of struggle against subordinate classes and groups. The result of this struggle is that many of the state's activities will reflect a contradiction between the interests of the ruling classes and groups, and the concessions secured by subordinate classes and groups as the price for their continued general allegiance to the social order. The weakest groups politically (certain ethnic minorities) will have their interests least represented in state activities. An individual's experience of state intervention in her or his life will be determined then by class position, gender and ethnic group membership. A major activity of the state which directly affects individuals is its maintenance of law and order and the control of deviance. Deviancy control is also an activity of the other two major social determinants of the individual – industrial discipline and the 'work ethic' in the case of the economy, and parental authority and familial ideology in the case of the family. In capitalist societies, however, problem populations created as a result of class rule must also be controlled directly by the organs of the state: police, prisons and welfare services. Individuals' relationships to all forms of state intervention will be characterised by both submissions and resistance, the balance being determined in large measure by class, gender and ethnic position, that is, the extent to which state intervention serves their understanding of their material interests and ideology. Specifically, state interventions will affect individual experience and personality through a number of practices, including

(a) *State practices which define what is normal and what is deviant.* Ideologies of law, of the family, of mental health and of physical fitness underpin the material practices of medicine, welfare, education and the penal system. Individual deviants may be responded to by 'treatment', by containment in institutions or through segregation and ghettoisation, or by being 'rehabilitated' to become agents of control themselves.

(b) *State practices which reinforce gender, class, ethnic and age hierarchies and differentiations.* The educational system, although like other state services an arena of struggle, is dominated by practices directed towards preparing the individual for wage and domestic labour through the acquisition of capacities considered appropriate to class, gender and ethnic position and through attitudes of subordination to authority.

(c) *State practices which directly establish and enforce levels of material subsistence* through social security services. Substantial sections of (primarily) the working class population including the unemployed, the elderly, people with disabilities and single parents, are dependent on social security payments, a dependency which determines the material parameters within which individuals can develop their capacities and exercise choice. Low levels of subsistence have definite physical and psychological effects.

(d) *State practices which actively discriminate against and/or stigmatise a particular social stratum or group*, usually on the grounds of gender, ethnic origin and/or class. Examples of such practices would include immigration legislation which discriminates against coloured populations, social security regulations which discriminate against women claimants and police surveillance policies which are directed against black youth. Such practices will affect a person's self-evaluation either negatively if subordinacy has been internalised to a substantial degree, or positively if it confirms the view of the dominant social order entailed in an oppositional ideology to which the individual owes allegiance.

(e) *State practices which directly or indirectly propagate in general the world view of a dominant class, gender or ethnic group*. The rituals and practices of state institutions, including in Britain the monarchy, parliament and the legal system, condense major elements of dominant ideologies into 'common sense' understandings of the social order. These institutions are presented directly and through the media as *essentially* good, with the implication that radical change in them would therefore be impossible or undesirable. The inculcation of individuals with such understandings of state institutions is an essential part of the ideological legitimation of the social order.

In the case of subordinate people who do not engage in production and/or reproduction, who may not in other words be involved in either the economy or the nuclear family, such as the elderly or those with disabilities, a particular social position can be identified – that of *marginality*. To be outside the two major social roles of production and reproduction involves a magnified subordinacy encompassing experiences of stigma, loss of identity, a range of material handicaps and subjection to substantial state intervention.

Psychological mechanisms in the production of the subject

The major social determinants of the individual – the economy, the family and the state – penetrate everyone's personal biography to produce a gendered class subject with an internal sense of *subordinacy* or *superordinacy*. Every individual incorporates and resists this penetration to varying degrees dependent on the contradictions experienced, the general level of political struggle, and class, gender and ethnic position. The individual responds to the various social determinants through a number of psychological mechanisms including:

1. *Conscious control over use-time*. As the balance between abstract and concrete activity and the proportion of time devoted to the development of capacities is so crucial to an individual's experience, conscious control enters as the attempt to maintain or change the balance and the space available to develop capacities. These controls are not, of course, autonomous but operate within the definitions, norms and rules considered relevant by the individual in relation to her or his class, gender and ethnic position.

2. *Internalisation of the ideologically constructed self*. The individual's conception of self reflects the meanings and definitions common to the most significant others with whom interaction takes place, for example family members, co-workers, other political activists. Through these symbolic interactions based primarily on language, ideologies, dominant or subordinate, *interpellate* or speak to the individual from his or her birth in the form of expectations concerning how to behave, think, feel and what objectives to pursue. These ideological definitions and expectations become part of the individual's world view, so as to produce a gendered class subject who is required to submit to the social order and prepare for labour within it.

3. *Identification*, a significant mechanism of socialisation and the reproduction of social roles whereby the individual 'sees' herself/himself in another person. In early childhood it binds children and parents together depending on gender, and pre-

pares the child for gender-specific and class-specific adult roles.
4. *Repression*, an unconscious mechanism operating when
drives and attributes of the individual, though experienced as
pleasurable, meet a social prohibition which has been
internalised into the person's psychic structure. Repression
involves the renunciation of drives and attributes unacceptable
to dominant meanings and understandings, for example of the
parents, and their re-direction into socially accepted activities
and attitudes – towards wage and domestic labour, the
consumption of commodities, the adoption of 'appropriate'
gender roles and heterosexual preferences, and the acceptance
of discipline and authority.

Modes of avoidance, resistance and dissent

In the key concepts we have specified so far, although reference
has been made to deviance, emphasis has tended to be laid on
the individual as *moulded*, *inculcated* or *penetrated* by the institutions and activities of the social order and the ideologies which
inform and legitimate them. In any materialist understanding
of the individual, however, we need concepts which reflect the
dialectic which exists between the individual and the social
order, and the resistance which the social order encounters in
individuals. Although we identified as a basic proposition the
contention that human beings are produced by the social
relations characteristic of a specific social formation, because
these social relations contain contradictions *there is never a perfect
fit between the individual and the social order*. Contradictions within
and between the economy, the family and the state, connecting
to the highly variable experiences of specific individuals,
provide space for avoidance, resistance and dissent. Into this
space enters individuals' contradictory consciousness, their
unconscious resistance, the development of their capacities,
and their participation in collective action.

1. *Contradictory consciousness.* In so far as individual consciousness reflects material relations and ideology, it also reflects the
contradictions within ideology and the struggle between
ideologies resulting from the different material interests of
different classes and groups. Although dominant ideologies
are, by definition, generally successful in inculcating a particu-

lar world view, nevertheless because ultimately they contradict the material interests of subordinate people, their grip on the personalities of such people is always imperfect. Class, gender and ethnic struggles enter the consciousness of the subordinate individual *as a disturbance* which points to the gap between dominant definitions and meanings and the actual material experiences of everyday life. Apart from continuing to submit to the dominant order, albeit with mental reservations, the individual may *engage in individual acts of deviance* where the intention is to gain materially, to express an individual protest or to fulfil particular values and needs not acceptable to the social order. Theft, industrial sabotage or certain sexual preferences such as paedophilia, may be taken as examples of such forms of deviance.

2. *Unconscious resistance*. This form of resistance can be seen as the psychological struggle against the *repression* of drives and attributes which are unacceptable or inconvenient to dominant social forces. It may be represented as the struggle of id against ego and superego, or of 'me' against 'I'. Some forms of resistance, if only expressed through anxiety, inevitably accompany the social demand that the individual shall renounce some aspect of herself. But where internal conflict becomes most severe, the consequence is a 'mental illness' which may be class and gender linked. Neurosis tends to be the characteristic form of unconscious resistance amongst the bourgeois and the middle strata because of the necessarily strong superego development required of an oppressing and exploiting class. Psychosis tends to be a major form of resistance amongst the working class, especially women, for the construction of an 'alternative reality' provides some escape from an exceptionally oppressive social reality of subordination.

3. *The development of individual capacities* may in some respects be seen as a means of avoiding the de-humanising effects of much of abstract labour. Individuals may develop personal concrete capacities which have no direct relevance to their wage labour, such as reading literary works, engaging in artistic production or developing craft skills. Even within the context of their wage labour, individuals may develop abstract capacities, certain kinds of knowledge and skills, which, though from the perspective of capital are simply functional to the needs of productive

activity, have a benefit for the individual outside the performance of abstract labour.

4. *Participation in collective action* is a major means of resistance to
the dominant forces in the social order. Although involvement
in collective action is an experience which contains contradictions between hope and despair, optimism and depression,
depending in part on the balance of political forces at any given
time, its benefits for the individual are considerable. A major
benefit is the opportunity collective action may provide for
moving from the cult of individualism and the pressure of
competition and rivalry towards more *altruistic activity*, where
the individual recognises that personal needs cannot be met
except through a transformation of social relations undertaken
through co-operative activity with others. Collective action
also provides the opportunity for the *development of capacities*
necessary to effective struggle, such as writing, organising and
public speaking, so that the individual may benefit through a
change in the balance of use-time. Most important of all,
perhaps, involvement in collective action may, over a period of
time, lead to the *internalisation of an altered conception of the self*,
whereby subordinacy is resisted through the incorporation of
alternative meanings and definitions, including altering conceptions of what is possible in terms of change, in other words a
raising of consciousness.

This summary of key concepts provides our introduction to
Part II of the book, an indication of the general orientations
which will govern our account of some aspects of the life cycle
within contemporary capitalism.

PART II

PERSONALITY DEVELOPMENT WITHIN CAPITALISM

6
Entering the Social Order

Children are born into a social world they do not choose: they arrive with certain biological characteristics and *become human* through interaction with others and with their material environment. Entering the social order, becoming human, is not therefore an immediate consequence of birth but a process stretching over a number of years.

The purpose of this chapter is to provide a materialist understanding of this process of entry, a long preparation for the tasks of producing and reproducing the social order. Immediately we are faced with a difficulty. When speaking of childhood we are referring first to a biological condition or a stage in physical development, something material; but this condition is conceived of differently in different cultures and historical periods.

Childhood is at least as much a social construction with a history as it is a biological fact of relative helplessness and dependency in the early years. Philippe Ariès' ground-breaking study *Centuries of Childhood* (1973) showed how the idea of childhood changed in France from the eighteenth century onwards, and argued that preoccupation with childhood, its length and its degree of dependency on adults, is a function of the rise of capitalism. Whilst some of Ariès' methods and conclusions have been disputed, his general point is a vitally important one: there is no single trans-historical notion of childhood. Indeed, it is inconceivable from a materialist standpoint that there could be, for children from birth begin a process of entry into *a historically specific* social formation whose institutions, including 'the family', must ultimately contribute to its production and reproduction. Thus the demands placed upon children, their degree and length of dependency on adults, and the way they are cared for and disciplined are all to a greater or lesser degree determined by the requirements of the social order.

In very general terms, changes in the ideology of childhood, that is, how children are viewed by adults, could be related, in a functional way, to changes in the forces and relations of production. In the feudal and early capitalist period, for example, where the family was an economic unit of production, younger males and females took part (in relation to their size, strength, skills and social position) in agriculture and manufacturing. With the development of capitalism comes the establishment of factory wage labour, the demand for more skilled labour power and the evident dangers for the future reproduction of the labour force of the use of child labour. In this situation, the need to extend the period of socialisation of children and prepare them more effectively for factory and domestic labour becomes an overriding concern which leads to direct state intervention through, among other things, the Factory Acts and the provision of schooling for the working class. Thus the ideology of childhood becomes changed in the development of new practices towards children.

But such an account of changes in the ideology of childhood, though valuable, is insufficient, for it does not allow enough emphasis on the impact of the *internal relations* within the changing family form on the ideology of childhood. Indeed, before we proceed to an account of the process of entry into the contemporary capitalist social order and its relationship to class and gender, we must contextualise childhood historically in terms of changing family forms, their characteristic internal relationships and their connection to the imperatives of the wider economy.

THE TRIUMPH OF THE BOURGEOIS FAMILY FORM

The present-day ideological and material context within which children engage in the process of entering the social order has its origins, to a substantial degree, in the family form which emerged within the European bourgeoisie during the eighteenth century and grew to dominance in the nineteenth and twentieth centuries. It was a family structure based upon the considerable material wealth resulting from successful capitalist exploitation. We have already noted in Chapter 3 that Freud's work can be looked upon as a penetrating picture of the internal emotional structure of the bourgeois family: we need now to return to this picture.

Before we do so, however, we need to note that whilst all families must be understood as structurally determined material and ideological entities, *each* family has distinctive characteristics and interactions, influenced by but never wholly accounted for by the general features of the social order and historical period in which it is located. Approaching families anthropologically, Seltzer and Seltzer in their examination of family therapy conceive of the unique differences between families in terms of distinctive family cultures:

> At the material plane of family culture are found those observable patterns of behaviour exhibited by family members. In operation, these patterns are most clearly represented by the rituals of the family: the particular procedures for action and reaction to – in varying degrees – family members. The ideational plane of family culture is the focus of the non-materialised, hence non-observable, beliefs and affects shared wholly or differentially by members of the family. It is along this plane where cognitions and affects associated with family rituals are localised in such forms as myths and thematic beliefs.
>
> (Seltzer and Seltzer, 1982)

Underlying our generalisations about family forms there will be the, usually unexpressed, acknowledgement of the differences which exist between families, the result of unique individual biographies and distinctive family cultures. When we contemplate our own or others' families we take account of how the requirements and influences of the dominant social order intersect with the unique histories of each family member.

However, to return to our generalisations, we can say that from the mid-eighteenth century onwards there emerged a bourgeois family structure in many respects similar to the present family form among the bourgeoisie, petit-bourgeoisie and most of the working class, with its characteristics of low fertility, low mortality, and emphasis on privacy and emotional intensity (see Löfgren, 1982). In the nineteenth and early twentieth centuries the most significant features of the bourgeois family were the monogamous ideal of dependent wife and wage-earning husband and the *repression of sexuality*. Drawing upon Freud's work, Reich and Schneider both place considerable emphasis on sexual repression, though by the late twentieth century such repression was no longer so significant except in the case of homosexuality. During the former period, however, the child's entry into the social order through the bourgeois family was characterised by massive and systematic emphasis on delayed sexual gratification. The child was expected to internalise this denial of the senses in the earliest years, and later take a different path depending on gender. The bourgeois female ideal to which girls were trained to aspire was one of angelic asexuality, whereas boys had to acknowledge the 'lustful nature' of males and learn to express this lust, not with the bourgeois wives they would eventually marry, but with working class women, prostitutes and domestic servants. The abuse of prostitutes and the battering of wives is an important part of this story. For the child, an internalised morality was established in which a consistent set of attitudes was applied both to sexuality and to capitalist enterprise, namely calculation and caution. 'A gospel of thrift', Poster (1978, p. 169) writes, 'was applied to semen as well as to money. The act of sex, with its connotations of lust, rapture and uncontrolled passion, was the epitome of unbusinesslike behaviour.'

But by the later Victorian period, the bourgeois family became also seen as the place where it was possible to *avoid* the spirit of capitalist rational calculation, aggression and competitiveness and within its relative autonomy cultivate the virtues of tenderness and spirituality, centred on the role of the loving mother. Children experienced themselves as the prime objects of their mother's loving attentions. But this love was paid for at a price: it could be withdrawn from children who failed to control their physical, sensual needs. Thus general cleanliness and toilet training in particular became a focus of maternal attention in the earliest years, whilst the denial of sexual gratification with the taboo on masturbation became a central concern of the later years. The result of this *conditional love* of the mother was that the child internalised massive guilt in the form of a 'punishing superego': sexual repression and aggression was turned inwards and constructed a self which was able to act autonomously on the basis of the internalised rules of bourgeois morality.

Although we might see this concern for the child as to some degree progressive, the object of the concern – sexual repression – and the method of ensuring it – the inculcation of deep feelings of guilt – carried a terrible cost for the child. Freud shows us how these costs were paid for both in childhood and in later life, especially by women. Unconscious resistance resulted characteristically in neurosis. The privatisation of the bourgeois family meant that the young child had only the parents to identify with and, later, only the parent of the same sex. In the heated atmosphere of repressed sexuality and aggression the child became deeply affected by the model of parental relationships and activities, and so subject to a powerful mechanism for ensuring that he or she was fitted for entry into the social order in the appropriate class and gender position.

The material base of the bourgeois family at its height was the ownership of capital. Later, sections of the bourgeoisie became to some extent 'proletarianised' in that their material base became the wage labour of white collar (including professional) occupations. So the traditional bourgeois family form became modified – but it has none the less retained its power, as we might see by reflecting from the child's perspective on the continuities as well as the discontinuities between the traditional bourgeois family and the widespread family form of late capitalism. Indeed, Poster goes so far as to suggest that the bourgeois family form had direct political consequences in its effect upon the working class:

> The conservatism of the working class in the twentieth century can be attributed, in part, to the attraction of the bourgeois family model. Unlike the liberal bourgeoisie of an earlier day, which rose up against the aristocracy in part from disgust at its promiscuous family life, the working class,

at least important sections of it, acknowledged the moral legitimacy of the bourgeoisie by adopting its family structure.

(Poster, 1978, p. 196)

This overstates the case by giving the ideology of the family too important a role in class struggle, but it underlines for us the ability of a modified bourgeois family form to achieve hegemony despite changes in its material base.

For the child, the powerful socialising structure of the bourgeois family was the primary determinant in the construction of personality. The demands of productive and reproductive activity in relation to the economy presented themselves to the bourgeois child through the use-time of a distant powerful father concerned with capital accumulation and profits, and an omnipresent mother apparently dedicated to the gender-specific roles of nurturing and moral training.

For the first time in history the mother was not directly engaging in production, and her dependent position paralleled the long dependency of the child (see Dally, 1982).

Our third determinant of personality development, the state, hardly entered the scene of the bourgeois child, for the private authority of the partiarchal father, coupled with a non-state education, ensured that the state had no direct part to play in the child's development.

For the working class child in the nineteenth century, the situation was dramatically different not least because the mother was a wage earner. Most important was the fact that whereas the bourgeois child experienced instinctual repression in a context of material prosperity, working class children experienced almost entirely the reverse. The context of their lives was the day-to-day struggle for the basic material needs required for existence itself. This certainly led, through material necessity, to the need for abstinence but it was not, as it was with the bourgeoisie, a *moral* imperative. The bourgeoisie saw the new working class, thrown into the industrial cities, as immoral and promiscuous, a class to be protected against and later reformed. In so far as there were grounds for this bourgeois view they lay in the material conditions of the working class, especially in the case of women who found in prostitution one of the only forms of employment available to them as they were swept along by the mass exodus from rural to urban living required by capitalist industrialisation. Certainly, sexual repression of the kind practised within the bourgeoisie was not evident within the working class in the first half of the nineteenth century. Although the working class father was dominant, his authority was diminished as the family lost its productive functions to the factory and both parents engaged in wage labour. Gender roles were not yet so sharply segregated and children did not receive the constant supervision and training within the family of their bourgeois counterparts and were not so dependent on their parents. Young children worked in factories and mines and they 'lived on the streets': in such a context guilt played little part in personality structures charac-terised, we might say, by 'weak superegos'.

So in the earlier part of the nineteenth century, the working class child's personality was more directly determined by the material relations of the economy: poverty, child wage labour, and the general impact of urban life. Although the family was still significant as a determinant of personality development, its power had weakened as its material base changed from rural production to urban wage labour.

But now the state and the bourgeois class itself entered the stage as a new direct influence on the individual child within certain of the most oppressed sections of the working class. By the latter part of the nineteenth century, bourgeois condemna-tion of the 'immorality' of the working class family found material expression in philanthropic activity. The Charity Organisation Society, for example, was established in order to distinguish between the 'deserving' poor and the 'residuum'. The latter were to be consigned to the mercies of the Poor Law, whilst the former were to be subjected to moral improvement as a result of direct relationships with visiting bourgeois women who could pass on their expertise in child care and delayed gratification (see Stedman Jones, 1971; Jones, 1983; Moore-land, 1982). From this base of welfare as private enterprise, coupled with the experience of the long history of the Poor Law in the management of the destitute poor, was gradually established a new form of state intervention in working class life – social work. Although social work did not become fully established until the mid-twentieth century, its nineteenth century origins lay in a determination to affect the child care practices of the working class and bring them nearer to the ideals of bourgeois family life. It was important to improve the quality of the moral life of the working class; the 'labour aristocracy' of the most skilled workers had already achieved the morality necessary to a motivated, productive and disciplined labour force. Compulsory state education coupled with growing state welfare services were the means by which, by the end of the nineteenth century and the beginning of the twentieth century, this morality was to be extended to the most recalcitrant and resistant sections of the working class. Children were to be the target (see Platt, 1969).

By the middle of the twentieth century the working class family conformed increasingly to the bourgeois family model: a maternal domestic role for the wife, increased emotional involvement of parents with children but, by the later twentieth century, with less sexual repression. Whether there is now within the working class that complete identification with the bourgeois pattern, for example by using love and authority to inculcate guilt in the child as a means of socialisation, as Poster (1978, pp. 195–6) claims, is open to dispute. We have seen already that identification between mother and child may operate differently between classes, and the experience of increasing material hardship within the working class as a result of economic recession and state policy may have its own differential effect upon family relations and therefore the personality development of the child. But Zaretsky (1976, p. 61) is surely right to maintain that the 'proletariat itself came to share the bourgeois ideal of the family as a "utopian retreat" '. As a general model of family relationships and of the means by which a child begins the process of entering the social order, the bourgeois family undoubtedly has become dominant; deviation from it, especially within the working class, produces an immediate state response 'in the interests of the child'.

We can see from the foregoing discussion that the ideology of childhood has undergone substantial changes in the last two centuries. These have been connected to changes both in the economy and in the family structures of different classes (see

Wilson, 1980). As we turn to a more detailed discussion of entry of the contemporary child into the social formation of capitalism in its late stages, we will be able to see that the process is structured by both the material experiences of everyday life, and the meanings by which these experiences are understood.

THE PENETRATION OF IDEOLOGY

Preparation for the beginning of the child's entry into the social order start while he or she is still in the womb. The mother *anticipates* the birth of the child and, if the woman is part of a couple, so does the father. This anticipation may include a number of elements: fantasies about what the birth will be like, what personality characteristics the child will have, what its sex will be, who it will 'take after'; anxieties about whether there are sufficient material resources to care for the child effectively, and about the parents' personal capacities to be a 'good mother' or a 'good father'. Anger may be felt at an unwanted pregnancy or, in the case of the woman, at the disruption to her wage labour which the birth will necessitate and at the new demands and pressures that will be placed upon her. These anticipations take place within a material context determined by the parents' class and ethnic position: some parents can anticipate material comfort for their child and themselves, together with the future opportunities which are provided for members of an economically dominant class; others can anticipate only the continued struggle for existence in a context of gender and class oppression, or a future of continuing racial discrimination and exploitation.

Both the parents' (and others') anticipations and their material context mean that there is a sense in which the embryo exists *already in an ideological context and already has the elements of a material future* within the matrix of the expectations and conditions surrounding the impending birth. The child is in effect already being addressed ideologically in *fantasy*, based on the real conditions of the parents' existence. But until the moment of birth there is a most important element missing: the sex of the child. The child's sex will be a most important determinant of its material future and of the specific content of the ideological pressures to which he or she will be subject. Even before the sex of the child is known it may be the focus of gender-specific expectations of the form: 'If it is a boy . . .' or 'If it is a girl . . .' then certain different characteristics may be expected or different futures anticipated.

It is from the point of birth, however, that the child most clearly exists within a specific material and ideological context. Already, the material conditions surrounding the mother, determined primarily by her class position, influence her physical and mental health and may have affected the embryo, quite apart from genetic factors. Such conditions will continue to have a significant effect after birth as the child, 'a mass of struggling id', is ready to begin the process of entering the social order, of becoming human, of constructing a self (see Richards, 1974).

Becoming human depends upon human contact, initially with the mother at least within the first few days or weeks, and later with others including, usually, the father. Other people, so crucial to the baby's physical survival and emotional development, act both as themselves, unique individuals, and also as representatives of the social order, as *bearers* of ideology. Even the youngest infants experience, in verbal and non-verbal communications from their carers, individual responses to them which are shaped by ideological expectations. The most significant of these expectations concern gender, as Eichenbaum and Orbach point out:

> When a baby is born there is a recognition on the part of its family of its place and role in the world based upon its sex. In the most minor and major ways every communication and contact with the baby is imbued with a sense of gender and people have profound different expectations for boys and girls which the child learns . . . For instance 'brave', 'strong', 'rugged', 'capable', 'confident' are examples of valued masculine characteristics while 'petite', 'weak', 'helpless', 'giving', 'pretty', 'dainty', 'demure' are prized feminine ones.
> (Eichenbaum and Orbach, 1982, p. 24)

Whereas sexual category is basic to the identity of every human being, how that sexual identity is socially constructed into gender differences varies according to the social formation, to ethnic origin and, to some degree, to class membership. Eichenbaum and Orbach's list of 'valued characteristics' are specific to certain cultures: the effects of this 'sex-role stereotyping' on the socialisation of children has been discussed in a substantial literature (see, for example, Barrett, 1980; Chetwynd and Hartnett, 1978; Belotti, 1975; Maccoby and Jacklin, 1975). Within this literature there is frequent reference to the fact that female children are not only treated differently but that they are expected to defer to males, to accept the leadership of males, to be, in a word, *subordinate*.

The ideological formation of the female child as subordinate is, however, only the most obvious example of the interpellation of the individual child on the axis subordinate–superordinate. The 'valued characteristics' appropriate to class position are likewise transmitted to the child through a variety of family practices: depending on class membership these are likely to include expectations about intellectual ability, interest in 'high culture', educational achievement, competitiveness, solidarity and – most important – future occupational roles.

Just as patriarchy is committed to the ideological production of gendered subjects, so capitalism must produce class members in order to fill the various roles required for the production and reproduction of capital and labour power: together they lead to the formation of *gendered class subjects*. In general, we can say that in the ideological transmission of subordinacy/superordinacy, gender and class tend to intersect in such a way that, if for simplicity we assume two classes, bourgeois males are considered as superordinate to everyone else, bourgeois females subordinate to bourgeois males but superordinate to working class males and females, working class males superordinate to working class females but subordinate to bourgeois males and females, and working class females subordinate to everyone else. In practice notions of subordinacy and superordinacy in the construction of the personality of the child do not operate in such a clear cut fashion, not least because of the resistance in the child, and to varying degrees the working class mother and family, to internalising subordinacy, and the ambiguities surrounding the intersection of class and gender categories. None the less, a sense of superordinacy or subordinacy is important to the production of class and gendered subjects because it legitimates, in individual consciousness, historically constructed systems of domination and exploitation.

In what ways does the meaning of subordinacy–superordinacy confront the child? Clearly, the growth of language in the child is crucial to the process of the internalisation of ideology: it is by symbolic interaction through language that most dominant meanings are communicated. But it is probably not primarily the direct inculcation of the *idea* that the child is or will be superordinate or subordinate to others that is significant here: the child will be addressed through practices and assumptions in a more indirect way.

Every family will have its own distinctive culture of practices and meanings through which notions of subordinacy and superordinacy are communicated: gestures, tones of voice and silences as well as what is actually said. The activities that families engage in together, including family meals and outings, the rituals of bedtime, what stories are read or told to the child, all provide vehicles for communicating understandings of the social world and the place of family members within it. Some children may be encouraged to see themselves as having many existing or potential abilities and to exercise leadership or dominance in social situations: other children will be regarded as dull, incompetent or 'difficult' in particular ways and be expected to defer to others.

In the case of young female children, we have already noted in Chapter 3 that identification with the mother is a fundamental feature in their development and may possibly, dependent on class, be reciprocated to such a degree by the mother that a very close symbiotic relationship is established. In any case, identification is widely recognised as 'a fundamental mechanism of personality development and socialization' (Mussen, 1973, p. 72) and alongside the imitation of others, especially adult models, and reward and punishment, constitutes the psychological means by which superordinacy and subordinacy are internalised. What messages are transmitted to the child in order to inculcate a sense of superordinacy and subordinacy? To answer this question we can turn again to Therborn's (1980) categorisation of 'three fundamental modes of ideological interpellation' in terms of superordinacy and subordinacy.

First, there is the idea that existing class, gender and ethnic relations are '*natural*'. In so far as superordinacy and subordinacy are perceived as being part of the *natural order of things*, as justified by biological differences and as essential features of human nature, so they have greater penetrating power within the personality of the growing child. Girls identifying with their mothers may come to perceive female submissiveness before males as simply something in nature, symbolised, perhaps, by the possession or absence of certain sexual attributes. For boys, identification with the father will include identification with the father's domination over mother, again a domination which is 'natural'. The interpellation of class and ethnic subordinacy and superordinacy depends also upon legitimating existing forms of oppression in terms of them being 'natural' rather than socially constructed. The white bourgeois child, for example, is, with the support of the media, private education, and other institutional elements, provided with a sense of superordinacy in relation to the working class and the black population. These 'subordinate people' are attributed with characteristics *in their natures* – lack of intelligence, laziness, but with appropriate deference and loyalty if they are 'well led' – which provide a self identity for someone 'destined to lead' subordinates. The domination of the bourgeoisie is *justified to themselves* through the early penetration of the bourgeois male child with a deep-seated confidence in a natural order which places him at or near the top. But because we are considering the ideological penetration of the child within specifically bourgeois society, allowance must be made for limited social mobility. In a feudal society classes are rigidly determined by birth, whereas under capitalism the dominant ideology of equal opportunity in the economic market convinces the growing bourgeois child that those who remain in the working class do so as a result not of lack of opportunity, but because of lack of drive or intelligence.

The bourgeois child witnesses daily the fact that only black, female and working class labour – dustmen, cleaners, performers of all the most menial tasks – undertake certain jobs, a picture which seems to him 'natural'. He neither knows nor can conceive an alternative.

Although the working class child will come to internalise him or herself as subordinate to others as *a fact of life*, the material experiences of lack of opportunity and at least relative deprivation, mean that the consciousness of subordinacy is always especially vulnerable to alternative ideas within the family, the community or the school – ideas which suggest that class, gender and ethnic relations are not 'natural', but historically constructed.

Furthermore, we can see that, even within a general allegiance to a social order based on class domination, many poor working class parents, black and white, have aspired to a better life for their children and sacrificed themselves in order to give them more chances, especially through education. The contradiction they face is that they may accept the ideology of upward mobility whilst experiencing it as impossible in terms of material reality.

Second, is *the notion that, existing class, gender and ethnic relations are right, just and desirable.* The legitimation, at the level of individual psychology, of capitalist social relations requires that, so far as possible, individuals accept the existing social order not simply with resignation before 'natural' hierarchies, but actually embrace them as good and as benefiting themselves. To take one example, the bourgeois male child tends to be inculcated with the superiority of mental compared with manual labour as a preparation for schooling and a class-appropriate occupation. The child's own desires become moulded and structured towards mental labour: what is necessary for the reproduction of his class becomes also what he sees as right for himself. At the furthest end of the class and gender spectrum, many working class girls are subjected to the idea not only that intellectual work is 'not for them', but that the petty manual drudgery of much of domestic labour is what they should wish for, because it will be enjoyable and satisfying to be, eventually, 'a good mother'. For the working class child, pride in achieving certain skills in manual labour often carries with it a contempt for intellectual work which, whilst it is an understandable defence in the face of lack of opportunity, serves the purpose of legitimating mental labour – managing, planning, organising – as the preserve of the bourgeois class (see Willis, 1980).

Third, is *the idea that existing class, gender and ethnic relations are the only possible ones.* Although it is implicit in the notion that because these relations of subordinacy and superordinacy are 'natural', they should not be opposed, the idea that it is *impossible* to have alternative relations deserves separate attention. To 'go against nature' is not only wrong, but not really possible. The acceptance by the child of the surrounding social world, its relationships and hierarchies, as the only possible world is profoundly important to the reproduction of the social order. To take the example of the internalisation of age hierarchies within the family; every parent who has confronted a 'rebellious' small child knows that deferring to parental authority has to be *learned* by the child. The existing family structure of authority is usually seen as the only possible one by the parent and it is this one possibility which is inculcated.

But Poster (1978, p. 149) rightly points out that although to some degree children must be subject to adult authority because they must be socialised to a world they did not choose to be born into and of which they have insufficient knowledge, these facts do not legitimate any particular family structure in history. Echoing Marcuse's references to surplus repression, Poster points out that 'all known family types fall far short of reducing domination [over children] to the base essentials necessary for these requirements'. Furthermore, biological dependence, Poster suggests, 'does not necessarily lead to domination, although it often does'.

THE DIALECTIC RELATIONSHIP BETWEEN PARENT AND CHILD

In our discussion so far about the entry of the child into the social order, we have taken the internalisation of superordinacy and subordinacy as a pre-eminent example of an element in the construction of the self within ideology. We have suggested that self-identity emerges both from ideology transmitted within the culture of the family, and from direct material relations, for example in the distribution of roles in the family between the sexes. Although some reference to 'rebellion' has already been made and will be returned to later, in order to avoid too deterministic a picture of child socialisation it is worth emphasising again that what is internalised by the child contains contradictions and is always to some degree problematic both for the social order and for the individual. But even this recognition of contradictions does not give enough acknowledgement of the essentially *dialectical* relationship between the child and the social order as represented by significant adult figures; the child might still be seen as an entirely passive recipient of contradictory determinations. An over-socialised view of child development serves, in fact, to underscore the futility of resistance.

Whether we draw upon Freud's contention that the newly born baby is 'pure id', or acknowledge, with Mead, that the human subject is active, reflecting 'the insurgent character of the human organism', we must recognise that even the youngest baby is not simply a blank paper upon which is written in miniature the requirements and conflicts of the social order. The baby exhibits in the first weeks of life very distinctive and unique ways of relating to the world which do not appear to be the result of external conditioning. Each baby has, Rayner (1978, p. 31) suggests, 'a particular style of movement, sensitivity and reflex reactivity. No two babies are the same in style . . . Some babies are born very active, others placid.' It is because of this distinctiveness in the baby that the person closest to the baby in the first weeks, usually the mother, *attempts to adjust herself to the baby* as well as adjusting the baby to her. 'If a mother cannot attune to her baby's rhythm', Rayner (1978, p. 33) suggests, 'then distress will result. This in turn stresses the mother, probably upsetting [the baby] more, so that a vicious circle is likely' (see also Rutter, 1980).

So, from the very beginning, significant adults in the child's social world tend to make adjustments in response to the *particular* characteristics of the child. But the form in which these adjustments are made and what is communicated through them may already, as we have seen, be determined by the sex of the child. If, at least amongst bourgeois and petit-bourgeois mothers, identification with their daughters is an important feature in the development of women's personalities, then we can see that this identification process represents a specific kind of adjustment to the female baby which is likely to differ from the form of adjustment to the male baby. Eichenbaum and Orbach provide a striking example of this immediately differential response of mother to baby:

> When my daughter was born each time I looked at her I thought she *was* me; I couldn't tell at all that she was different from me. You know that feeling when you look at yourself in a mirror, well it felt something like that. When my son was born that never crossed my mind. He was different, he was something else (motioning 'out there' and 'away' with her hand). It was completely clear that he was a different person.
>
> (Eichenbaum and Orbach, 1982, p. 32)

The consequences of this differential response to the child's sex together with adjustment to the particular characteristics and qualities of the child, are profound. The mother's response to her daughter is one of identification and projection: she must prepare her daughter to become a woman like herself. The mother's own internal construction of herself, often as a dependent, nurturing and subordinate person in relation to males of her class, acts as the initial source of the ideological penetration of the female baby in preparation for 'appropriate' gender roles. 'Thus when she holds her infant daughter in her arms', Eichenbaum and Orbach (1982, p. 32) maintain, the mother 'reads the various communications of the child in a particular way. She sees a vulnerable, expressive, eager little girl. This in turn reawakens – still at an unconscious level – that part of her that feels needy, wanting to be nurtured, responded to and encouraged.'

The male baby, however, tends to be responded to in a different way. The mother cannot identify with her son in the same manner, though he will, of course, identify with her. Nor can she so easily project upon her son feelings that she has about herself, feelings intricately bound up with sexual identity and her socially constructed gender role. The male baby therefore receives other verbal and non-verbal communications. He is not like her, is going to have a quite different life and different opportunities. Most significantly, the male child can be nurtured and cared for almost unconditionally because in adult life he will continue to be nurtured by women: he is being prepared for his gender-specific role of *being nurtured*. The female child, on the other hand, has to be prepared for the traditional gender role of *providing care and nurturing for others* and therefore cannot be allowed to become too dependent. These primarily unconscious processes involving mother and child are likely to have an effect even upon their physical interaction: male babies may tend to receive more physical contact from their mothers (see Goldberg and Lewis, 1969; Lewis, 1972).

The point that is being made here is that the dialectical relationship between the child and the social order is, even from the very earliest months, a complex one. The child is not entirely predictable in terms of its demands and rhythms and has to be adjusted to by the social order, represented in microcosm by the parents. This adjustment, however, is socially constructed upon certain lines. Even if the process of identification and projection is likely to be more pronounced amongst bourgeois compared with working class mothers, unconscious as well as conscious preparation for gender and class-specific adult roles can be taken to be a necessary feature of all parent–child interaction within a patriarchal and capitalist social formation. Even if under the impact of feminist and socialist politics and other social changes, class and gender-specific interpellations of the most rigid kind are likely to weaken, and to be increasingly resisted at a conscious level, the underlying unconscious tendency to socialise children into class and gender-specific roles will remain until the oppressive structure of class and gender relations is itself swept away.

MATERIAL DETERMINANTS AND USE-TIME

But responses to the child from the social order as represented by the parents are determined not only by the ideologically constructed interactions we have already identified, but also by the actual material relations between the family and the economy as reflected in the parents' distribution of use-time.

If we take the family experience of the working class child as an example, we can see that this experience will be determined to a substantial degree by the precise nature of the wage and domestic labour each parent performs and the extent to which it dominates the use-time available. The most characteristic experience may be of a father who is engaged in wage labour of a most abstract kind with little balance provided through the development of concrete activities which increase his capacities. The same may in general apply to the mother whose personality has been shaped by the drudgery of domestic labour combined with the most unrewarding kind of wage labour. These material relations will tend to be experienced by the parents with resignation as inevitable. In such a context, the child learns something of the harsh reality of the social order, but also of its apparent inevitability. The distribution of the use-time of the parents between abstract and concrete activities determines not only the quantity of interaction between the child and each parent, but also its quality, the extent to which the child has the opportunity to respond to the more concrete, creative aspects of the parents' personalities.

A striking feature of the child's experience within the family in the early years will be, most usually, the relatively limited opportunity he or she will have of interaction with the father. The demands of full-time wage labour alone are likely to restrict severely this interaction, quite apart from the impoverishment of its quality imposed by the psychologically deadening and exhausting effect of the father's work, especially at the end of the working day. The infrequently seen but apparently powerful figure of the father presents a potent symbol of the nature of the class and gender relations inherent in this particular social order. The class-specific nature of the father's wage labour will greatly influence the kind of social world which he brings into the family from outside, its preoccupations and imperatives. Is he carrying into the family the burden of a fiercely individual competitive struggle for survival, or the possibilities of co-operative and collective activity; the desperate fear of redundancy and unemployment or a self-confidence arising from secure and pleasurable work; pride in the skills he has and will develop or an acknowledgement of the unskilled or deskilled nature of his job? For the child, what the father brings into the family from the external economy during their relatively infrequent interaction – in short, what is communicated about the nature of the social order and the family's class position within it – is of decisive importance to the character of this interaction.

Interaction with the frequently absent father also, inevitably, reflects general gender relations. To the small girl, father represents the outside male-dominated world which she can never be fully part of and to which she must defer. Identifying with her mother's role, she sees father as someone to be nurtured. To the small boy, already perceived as *other* by his mother, father's external world is that which he will enter himself in due course: he increasingly identifies with his father's role in this world, including his class position within it. Later, the child comes to realise that the working class father is not, in reality, the powerful figure he seemed; that he is in fact, subordinate to the imperatives of capitalist productive relations. In the older child and the young adult, this realisation leads often to that combination of pity and contempt which characterises much of interaction between 'teenagers' and their fathers.

Interaction with the mother is, in contrast, much more central to the young child's personality development, particularly in those families where the separation of the parents' gender roles is extreme. Most characteristic, especially within the working class family, is the fact that the socially necessary labour which the mother of several young children undertakes almost entirely fills the use-time available. Domestic labour and full- or part-time wage labour dominates her day and the child is likely to experience an interaction with mother which reflects her struggle to manage the interface between two modes of production: domestic and capitalist. The result, for the mother, which we examine in more detail in the next chapter, is frequently depression, guilt and anxiety. From the child's perspective, the mother may be experienced as often angry, inconsistent or withdrawn: in this way the child is affected directly by the very nature of the gender and class-determined division of labour. A depressed and exhausted mother may be unable to provide the stimulus which is necessary to encourage to the full the passive and active learning which is required for the intellectual growth of the young child. Consistent with the dominant ideology of the 'joy of motherhood', the pre-1960s editions of Spock's manuals on child care recommended that depressed and dissatisfied mothers should *seek psychiatric help*.

INSTINCTUAL REPRESSION AND REDIRECTION

What we have described so far in the process of the young child's entry into the social order has centred mainly on external responses to the child and how these are socially constructed. In continuing this description, we need at this point to lay more emphasis on the price the child has to pay in order to gain the most favourable responses. We know that sensual exploration, especially through the mouth, begins very shortly after birth. Erotic pleasure appears to be experienced through sucking either breast, bottle or, later, thumb and usually during this *oral* phase of development the child is allowed or encouraged to pursue instinctual gratification. But gradually the child is expected to learn to renounce or delay certain kinds of gratification. In psychoanalytic terms, the strivings of the id confront first the external demands of the social order represented by the parents, and their internal repression. It is important here to recall the changing historical context of instinctual repression. If we were to follow Marcuse's distinction between basic and surplus repression, we can certainly see the latter as having undergone substantial changes in emphasis during the present century.

Instinctual repression at the *anal* stage, represented by the early demand for bowel and bladder control, whilst it still remains an important part of the child's transition from babyhood to childhood ('only babies wet their pants' is a parental phrase which signifies the social importance of toilet training), is not now usually imposed with the harshness of even fifty years ago. Again, the repression of genital sexuality in the child, such a feature of a Victorian bourgeois family upbringing, is no longer pursued with such terrifying commitment. Whether the instinctual renunciation involved in the anal retention of early toilet training was psychologically functional in preparing the bourgeois child for an adult life devoted to the accumulation of capital remains an interesting speculation. Certainly, the delaying of gratification is on the whole highly dysfunctional for the contemporary capitalist high-technology mass production of commodities. The child must be trained to *consume* rather than *save*.

So, are we in a position to identify the major areas of instinctual repression and especially re-direction which the present-day social order requires of the child? In pointing to these areas we are suggesting that they are clearly 'surplus' to the repression required for human survival and reproduction, and *tend to be functional* to a capitalist social order. But it is important to be cautious about the degree to which a particular aspect of instinctual repression can be claimed to be functional to a historically specific social order; the arena in which early instinctual repression takes place is, after all, the family, a relatively autonomous part of the overall social formation. With these precautions against the dangers of an over functional account, we can proceed to mark out three aspects of instinctual repression and redirection: in relation to *property*, *labour* and *sexual identity*.

First, we must note the encouragement provided to the child in the *accumulation of possessions*. Early oral exploration appears gradually to be directed towards what are considered to be the child's own exclusive possessions. The child is handed her *own* toys to play with and, as she grows, gains more personal property, the amount depending to a major degree on the material circumstances of the parents, and therefore on their class position. Even though some emphasis will be placed upon 'sharing', it is the sharing of the child's own toys; individual ownership remains the central feature of the re-direction of random sensual exploration towards specific objects. Psychoanalytic object relations theory suggests that the baby sees its mother's breast as part of herself, and therefore under her control, an illusion which must subsequently be replaced by disillusionment as the child begins to learn the reality of the mother as a separate person, and substitutes for the breast a possession – the 'transitional object' (a piece of blanket, a soft toy) which enables the child to develop from magical control to manipulation of the environment (see Winnicott, 1958, pp. 229–42).

Although the ferocity of the baby's primitive greed has gradually to be repressed in its original form, it is none the less re-directed not towards a collective ownership of possessions, but towards individual accumulation and competition. In adult life, the working class person can expect only to own his or her labour power, household and leisure commodities and possibly the house itself. The position of the petit-bourgeois middle-strata is in many cases only different in degree, and only the class of high bourgeois capitalists and those who have inherited wealth can expect to own a great deal in terms of possessions, land and property. Across all classes and ethnic groups, however, the reproduction of the social order requires an orientation towards possessions which are the outcome of commodity production. Sensual satisfaction, in short, is directed towards use-values which are abstracted to become exchange-value commodities.

Second, we can see that alongside this orientation to possessions comes the direction of the child towards *wage and domestic labour*. Identification, especially with the same sex parent, is a primary socialising mechanism here: the domestic labour and child care of the mother becomes predominantly the model with which the girl identifies through a range of activities, toys and games. Similarly, the boy tends to identify with 'male' activities: building, fighting, exploring. This quite obviously differential socialisation is very familiar ground within feminist critiques of the family and does not require elaboration here except to point to the debate as to whether gender identity is relatively unproblematic and achieved early because the child *needs* to acquire such identity, or whether it is always problematic, precarious, and only achieved with utmost difficulty (see Mitchell and Rose, 1982, pp. 27–57).

What needs emphasis is that the tendency to gender-specific activities amongst children, varying in intensity due to the differential impact of feminist ideas on different classes and strata of the population, involves gender-specific repression and re-direction. In order to identify with typical gender-specific activities, the girl has to repress her aggressive and exploratory drives and channel her psychic energies into caring for and nurturing others, to being the follower and rarely the leader, to being tender, quiet, patient, feminine, 'motherly'. Likewise, the boy must repress those qualities which might express themselves in nurturing and tenderness, for he is *expected* to be aggressive rather than 'emotional' because 'boys don't cry'. What the long-term consequences for the individual of these repressions are we can consider in the next chapter, at this point simply noting that the taboo on aggression in women may reinforce the tendency for it to turn inwards as self-punishment, guilt and depression, and that the denial of tenderness in men may account for their frequent incapacity to share emotions and to relate deeply and unconditionally to others. Orientation to gender-specific labour involves not only the repression and re-direction of certain drives, but also the achievement of discipline and order. Upon the random explorations and pleasures of early play, the social structure surrounding the child gradually imposes an order. Games have rules and usually involve individual competition: as the attention-span of the child grows, its play gradually becomes more like adult *work*. Ultimately, by the time the child is 'ready' for school, he or she is prepared for the life-long distinction between 'work' and 'play' around which schooling will slowly become organised. The child's 'work' is the precursor for his or her abstract wage labour, 'play' is the forerunner of adult leisure activities, together with, for girls, that domestic labour and child care which is only now becoming recognised as 'real work'.

Third, we must acknowledge that although severe repression of genital sexuality in children is passing, there remains a predominant pressure towards *exogamous heterosexuality*. The incest taboo, symbolised in the resolution of the oedipus complex, remains a powerful regulator of family interaction, though the incidence of incestuous relationships between fathers and daughters appears to be higher than was at one time thought likely. Whilst homosexuality and certain other 'deviant' forms of sexual preference are now more tolerated, the overwhelming effect of the process of the child's entry into the social order is to the construction of a self which is heterosexual. Clearly the social order can contain, without damage to itself, a wide range of *minority* sexual preferences. Sexuality which does not lead to reproduction would only become a problem if it appeared to threaten the future supply of labour power necessary to capitalist production, an unlikely development especially as the newly created forces of micro-technology appear to need a diminishing amount of labour power. Minority sexual preferences may be seen as to some extent successful resistance to the powerful repression and redirection of the 'polymorph perverse' infant. As we have seen, this near-overwhelming pressure towards the most traditional form of heterosexual identity involves the repression in the boy of signs of 'femininity', and in the girl of 'masculinity'.

PROBLEMS AND DEPRIVATIONS

We cannot complete our discussion of the entry process of the young child into the social order without emphasising that the process is problematic for the child and the parents. We have already indicated some of the contradictions involved. For the child's part, he or she must learn to cope with what is experienced as a contradiction between parental love and parental authority. Where love and authority are closely connected in a parent, then identification by the child involves a substantial degree of emotional ambivalence – the continuous struggle between love and hate which characterises much of the interaction between small children and their closest parent, usually the mother. The 'battle of wills' alternates with loving embraces. Where authority and love are more separate, as is sometimes the case with emotionally remote and frequently absent authoritarian fathers, identification is probably not only less ambivalent but also less profound.

The problems which face parents in enabling the child to enter the social order will be discussed in the next chapter. From the child's perspective, we need to note that the material and ideological pressures which parents face are bound to affect profoundly the nature of the child's experience. Poverty, inadequate housing, the loss of social identity through unemployment, depression and guilt resulting from an 'impossible' combination of domestic and wage labour, the stigma of the single poor parent, all have a direct effect upon the child. Especially important to the child will be the experience of separation from the parents, and of the emotional and physical deprivation which may accompany especially adverse material circumstances. As Rayner (1978, p. 46) suggests, we must try to identify those specific functions of which a child seems to be deprived. 'Some children are deprived of nutrition, others of affection, others have plenty of affection but little quiet consistency of stimulation, and yet others may be deprived of variety while experiencing plenty of affection and consistency.' Evidence later than that of Bowlby's (1953) original work on maternal separation (see Rutter, 1980; Clarke and Clarke, 1975) shows that it is discontinuity, unfamiliarity and a chaotic environment which is most likely to produce an adverse affect on a child, rather than simply separation from the mother.

What is especially significant to our materialist understanding is that the deprivations which children experience are profoundly class-linked. In the most general sense, we could argue that *all* children growing up within a capitalist social order are deprived, as are adults, of developing their human potential to a degree which is materially possible given the massive growth of productive forces. So much should be evident from the account so far. But if we give our attention to specific, severe deprivations in childhood which inflict disabling psychological injuries, we can see at once that children of the most impoverished sections of the working class, such as single-parent families, certain ethnic minority groups, and the long-term unemployed, are the most likely victims. As biographies frequently reveal, some bourgeois children may experience a wide range of emotional deprivations such as being sent to boarding schools at an early age, but the massive concentration of severe deprivations are experienced within those sections of the population where the struggle for existence is fought out at its most basic level. In so far as certain sections of the black population share the material circumstances of the most impoverished part of the working class and, in addition, experience the impact of institutionalised racism, the fate of their children is likely to be especially grim.

Such black children often grow up in a context where family resources are minimal because racist employment practices ensure that their parents are only able to obtain the most poorly paid jobs (see Smith, 1976). The impact of the media (Hartmann and Husband, 1974) and of many social interactions outside the home will tend to reinforce the idea that the child is part of a group appropriately subordinate to the dominant white population. Although this may be struggled against, and parents attempt to encourage in the child a pride in black identity and culture, it is a struggle against massive forces, inevitably often frustrating and deeply depressing (see Mullard, 1973).

In outlining a materialist account of the personality development of the child, we are giving most space to the experience of the infant. This is not because of some conviction about the irreversible influence of the early months and years, for adaptation to and resistance against the social order continues throughout life. But examination of the earliest years of life provide us with perhaps the clearest picture of the profound significance of both ideology and material circumstances in the production of personality. The various features we have pointed to, including the internalisation of subordinacy and superordinacy, the mechanisms of identification and repression, the influence of parental abstract labour and the experience of material and emotional deprivation, could all be traced in detail through various stages in childhood. We shall not be able to undertake this task, but will devote the remainder of this chapter to comments first on the role of the state in direct intervention in children's lives, and second on the particular experiences of older children and young adults.

STATE INTERVENTION IN CHILDHOOD

Once the child enters school a new set of determinants act upon the developing personality. In this sense, the state begins its direct intervention early in life, particularly in the case of working class people. The development of compulsory state education for the working class involved the extermination of those indigenous working class experiments in schooling which characterised the early nineteenth century (see McCann, 1979). State education today, although an arena of struggle over gender and class objectives, remains a powerful vehicle for the preparation of children for the labour required of a capitalist social order. The processes of identification and repression act powerfully in the classroom and ideological inculcation, especially of subordinacy and superor-

dinacy, operates through a wide range of routines, pressures
and proceedures (see Sennet and Cobb, 1977; Henry, 1966).
Shipman (1972, p. 49) states with refreshing simplicity the
purpose of the school as 'designed by specially selected adults
to promote forms of behaviour that they see as appropriate in
children'. Although children, both individually and collectively, tend to organise resistance to the most oppressive
aspects of schooling, its general ideological influence over them
remains immensely powerful. It would be an interesting
exercise to trace the distribution of the use-time of school-
children between the development of abstract compared with
concrete capacities. One might expect to find increasing
emphasis on abstract capacities as school-life nears its close,
together with gender-linked differences of balance.

Beyond schooling as a basic area of intervention in childhood, we can identify three further crucial areas of state policy
and practice which especially affect children of the most
impoverished sections of the working class: determining levels
of material subsistence, defining and acting upon working class
deviancy, and discriminating against particular categories of
people.

First, we can see that in the most obviously direct way, state
social security and social insurance benefits and the way they
are administered determine the material level of existence of
children whose parents are unemployed, ill or handicapped, or
managing alone without a partner. The fact that social security
benefit levels represent a bare minimum to sustain life in our
society means that the psychological consequences for the child
(and, of course, the parent) of such a minimal material
existence are profound. Not only is nutrition directly affected,
but because of the general effect of low material resources on
human functioning children become deprived in other specific
areas. Parents who are preoccupied with the daily struggle for
material existence are sometimes unable to provide the affection, the consistency of stimulation or the variety which is
necessary for the development of the child's capacities. The
depression and anxiety of the parents is communicated to the
child both verbally and non-verbally, so that the child may
become also anxious, worried, lethargic.

Second, the state intervenes further in the lives of children who have been affected by poor material circumstances in order to monitor and control their consequences. Families living on social security benefits or low wages are the most vulnerable to the attention of social workers. There is a fundamental contradiction in this social work with poor families which reflects the historic class balance between the objectives of the control and discipline of working class deviance and that of a commitment to caring for children which the labour movement has struggled for. State intervention in this area is not primarily directed towards improving the basic level of material existence of the children within their families, but increasingly to monitoring, controlling and often removing them. The effects upon children's personalities of these state interventions, especially where they result in removal from home, are wide-reaching.

The contradictions experienced by the child as a result of state intervention stem partly from her ambivalence towards the parents. Such ambivalence between love and hate, the strength of which results in part from the particular tensions generated by a nuclear family structure which rests upon a combination of love and authority as its means of socialisation, is seen by Klein as a characteristic of all infants. She writes that

> the newly born baby experiences, both in the process of birth and in the adjustment to the post-natal situation, anxiety of a persecutory nature. This can be explained by the fact that the young infant, without being able to grasp it intellectually, feels unconsciously every discomfort as though it were inflicted on him by hostile forces. If comfort is given to him soon – in particular, warmth, the loving way he is held, the gratification of being fed – this gives rise to happier emotions. Such comfort is felt to come from good forces and, I believe, makes possible the infant's first loving relation to a person. . . . Both the capacity to love and the sense of persecution have deep roots in the infant's earliest mental processes.
>
> (Klein, 1960)

In the case of children subjected to violence or neglect by their parents, the typical ambivalence remains. For the child, to be 'rescued' by the welfare authorities and placed in a children's home or with foster parents is not necessarily an improvement. In spite of the extreme material and ideological pressures to which some parents are subjected and which result in child neglect, the bond between such parents and their children may still be a strong one, one from which the child gains an experience of loving, even if it is erratic and unpredictable.

Although in any society children should be protected from assault or neglect by adults, the lack of satisfactory alternative social and economic strategies which would attempt to *prevent* pressure on parents which most often lies at the root of adverse childhood experiences renders much welfare intervention especially negative. To the original deprivations of living under impoverished and unstimulating circumstances with anxious, depressed or angry parents, may be added the new deprivations and traumas involved in institutional care, court appearances and, above all, separation from parents.

Third, state activities in relation to certain groups of people are especially discriminatory. The most obvious example is the relation of the police to the black population: older children and young adults are the particularly significant targets of policing policy directed to controlling their reactions to institutionalised racism. Although much discriminatory state practice may have the effect of reinforcing the inculcation of subordinacy (for example, amongst the children of stigmatised working class single mothers), its effect can produce a contradictory result: the development amongst an oppressed population (including, eventually, the children) of alternative definitions of their situation which support notions of superordinacy, as Black Power politics illustrate. The growth of alternative ideologies, however, requires the kind of collective consciousness which single working class mothers may find hard to achieve and are therefore unlikely to communicate to their children.

THE OLDER CHILD AND THE YOUNG ADULT

The later years at school coincide with what is considered to be an especially problematic period in the person's life: the period of 'adolescence' or 'youth'. These terms are of Victorian origin and problematic because they are often constructed around ideas about this period of life which a materialist understanding must question. Adolescence is frequently seen primarily and wrongly in terms of the psychological changes which are consequent on puberty. But socially constructed as this period of life is, it has a clear biological and physiological base. Even before 'the 'teens', we can see in children the development of formalised abstract thinking, the ability to manipulate ideas unrelated to the immediate situation in which they are placed. During the teenage period comes the maturation of primary and secondary sexual characteristics and other physical changes. Even these changes appear to vary historically and geographically; menstruation, for example, began on average at 15 years in Britain in 1890, whereas now it begins on average at 13 years.

The construction or reconstruction of the self, and especially the body image, which is a consequence of these physical changes, is very clearly determined by the particular features of the social order in which the person is developing and their class, gender and ethnic position. The concern for a particular body shape, for example, reflects dominant conceptions of female and male roles, with young women being especially at the receiving end of historically specific conceptions of beauty and sexual attractiveness. The media play a significant role here, not least because commodities which are claimed to make a woman more attractive have a ready market amongst older girls. Working class girls, in particular, have realistically low expectations as to their futures: after a period of sexual experimentation and the fun of the 'youth culture', they are generally resigned to marriage (about which they seem to be taking an increasingly less romantic view) and the uncertain pleasures but certain drudgery of 'motherhood'.

Relationships with parents during this period are usually experienced as problematic by all those involved, though differentially according to gender and class. The stimulation of the development of those sexual feelings which have remained relatively dormant since the resolution of the oedipus complex, and the subsequent identification with the parent of the same sex, give rise to two 'problems'. The repression of sexuality is no longer possible and its unmistakable appearance may arouse in the parents feelings of envy, rivalry and anxiety.

Identification with the parents may give way to rejection as their powerlessness and conformity in the face of class and gender relations becomes increasingly obvious to the young person. In any case, the lengthy period of dependency on parents which characterises our social order, and the lack of a clear, unambiguous, culturally recognised point of entry into adulthood, lead to massive contradictions and ambiguities. Both the parents, and their teenage sons and daughters, experience in their own particular ways difficulties over, on the one side, exercising or receiving care and authority and, on the other side, letting go. Most parents and children experience deep ambivalence concerning what they want to happen between them and what should happen during the period of entry into adulthood.

Some psychoanalytic theory suggests that struggles against the authority of the parents and the denigration of their beliefs is essential to the working-out of the young person's own identity and values. Such psychologising of the conflicts of this period should be resisted as reductionist: there are material reasons for many of these conflicts and they often form part of the resistance of the person to a social order perceived within a developing consciousness of its oppressions and exploitations. However, it is important to acknowledge that attacks on parents can be internally problematic to the young person: depression may follow loss of security.

We have suggested that conflict and resistance is especially characteristic of this period of life, but that it contains contradictions. The experience of the 'youth culture' is an example of this contradiction. On the one hand, working class youth culture can represent a real resistance to the dominant bourgeois ideology heavily represented in the cultural media. On the other hand, youth pop culture involves also incorporation into media-managed and highly profitable commodity production and consumption and often reflects deeply sexist and racist ideologies. The separate and subordinate position of girls in relation to youth culture is especially noteworthy (see McRobbie and Garber, 1975).

7
Working in the Social Order

Entering the social order is a long process of preparation for adult roles: direct material experiences combined with what has been internalised from diverse and conflicting ideologies constitute the base of the psychological resources which the young person brings to the socially defined tasks and relationships of adulthood. But childhood, although it is influential, does not finally *determine* the personality characteristics of the adult individual. This is evident from the fact that people who have very similar childhood experiences often exhibit very different personality traits in their adult activities and relationships. Psychoanalytic theories of childhood, especially where they place emphasis on the long-term effects of unresolved unconscious conflicts at oral, anal or genital stages of development, often appear to be highly determinist, not to say pessimistic, concerning the influence of childhood on the adult.

But even within traditional psychoanalysis there is something of a contradiction here, for analytic treatment is based upon the belief that subsequent intervention can have a corrective effect: that an appropriate adult experience can resolve that which was previously unresolved.

From a materialist standpoint the position is even clearer. As an adult, the individual enters into relationships, especially those involved with wage and domestic labour, which are profoundly influential in the construction of the self. But this is not simply a matter of further determinants reinforcing, overlapping or contradicting the determinants of childhood. Central to our thesis has been the conception of the individual as not simply the passive recipient of external determinants, but as actively, dialectically involved in constituting herself within her given social relations. Experiences subsequent to childhood can counteract the ideological penetration of the early years and the individual may construct a self on the basis of alternative ideologies related to alternative material experiences. In this way individual resistances and the struggle against unconscious repression may be transformed into conscious and collective opposition to at least some of the features of the established social order.

The adult personality, then, is a result of an individual history constructed within the ensemble of social relations characteristic of a particular social order. Our approach to the construction of adult personality leads us to give our attention to the activities that adults engage in, the capacities that they develop and the ways in which these activities and capacities are embedded in ideological understandings.

It is the argument of this chapter that the personality of the adult individual is above all determined by the nature of work and the social relations entered into in its performance; secondly, by the ways in which the individual engages in consumption and, in particular, the relationships and structures in which this takes place; and thirdly, by the ideological rationales by which these relationships of work and consumption are given the meanings they hold for the individuals.

PERFORMING SOCIALLY NECESSARY LABOUR

Although economic recession, together with a possibly permanent contraction of the demand for certain kinds of labour power, may lead to a level of unemployment which delays or even prevents the entry into waged labour of many young men and women, for women, especially working class women, domestic labour and the carrying of nurturing roles in relation to children and men is likely to be the dominant experience of their lives. It is appropriate, therefore, that we should begin with this experience and its effects upon individual personality.

We have already pointed to the means by which female children are directed towards gender-specific activities and 'appropriate' ways of feeling and behaving in preparation for their adult female roles. These means are both *external* in that they reflect the imperatives of patriarchal relations generally, but also *internal* in that they are constructed within the individual as the result of identification and the management of repression. The intricate relationship between these external and internal means of constructing the activities and feelings of adult women is such that the internal experiences are already *spoken for* externally. The social construction of gender requires that women (and men, as we shall see later) should not only carry out their roles, but should also experience those roles in particular ways, suppressing the most negative aspects and highlighting their supposed benefits and pleasures. In other words, women often have great difficulty in expressing the reality of their lives because they are *expected* to feel something different from what they often *actually* feel. These expectations stem from the continuous ideological interpellations to which they are exposed from the media, the state, and the immediate interactions within the family and other relationships.

It is the inculcation of subordinacy and its material reality which lies at the centre of women's experience being defined for them from outside. 'Men stand at a centre from which women are surveyed and given determinate being', writes Dorothy Smith (Smith and David, 1976, pp. 3–4). 'Women do not look back at men from a place of their own . . . [they] have learned to subordinate their understanding of themselves and their experience to a conception of who they are that comes from outside. It is one that gives them no alternative to seeing themselves from outside and in terms of their uses to others.'

If it is the case that for women to describe and reflect upon the experience of domestic labour and nurturing requires a considerable struggle to achieve the authenticity of a communication from *within*, then this struggle itself will be experienced as problematic. If women are inculcated from childhood with the desirability, pleasurability and inevitability of their domestic and nurturing tasks, how can they but experience intense conflict if these tasks generally are experienced as undesirable, exhausting and mind-deadening? For many women, the conflict between the internalised dominant ideology of domesticity and motherhood, and the material experience of the actual activities, can only be resolved by *self-blame*.

Self-blame, guilt and ultimately depression are the frequent results of the experience of a certain kind of subordinacy where the subordinate status is perceived not only as existing, but as necessary and even desirable. Where can the anger at an intolerable social reality go, except inwards? Women who must continuously defer to others find it difficult to believe that their own experiences or feelings are of any importance, as Eichenbaum and Orbach point out:

> Women come to feel that they are unworthy, undeserving and unentitled. Women are frequently self-deprecating and hesitant about their own initiatives. They feel reluctant to speak for themselves, to voice their own thoughts and ideas, to act on their own behalf. Being pushed to defer to others means that they come to undervalue and feel insecure about themselves, their wants and their opinions. A recognition of a woman's own needs can therefore be complicated and a process occurs in which women come to hide their desires from themselves.
>
> (Eichenbaum and Orbach, 1982, p. 29)

Although we might see these feelings of inadequacy, lack of confidence and guilt as likely to occur in the experience of all women, class also enters as a factor here, certainly so far as these experiences manifest themselves in the more severe forms of depression. The working class woman's experience of subordinacy in a context of limited material resources is bound to be more stressful than that of most bourgeois women.

Working class women have fewer opportunities to deflect some of the pressure (for example through paying for domestic labour) and so apparently reduce some of the areas of conflict between ideology and material experience. This is perhaps one of the reasons for the high incidence of depression amongst working class women (see Brown and Harris, 1978).

Despite this relative 'silence' of women over the physical and psychological consequences of domestic labour, contemporary feminist work is giving a voice to this experience. Making a home, caring for children, being held responsible for connecting the family to various external organisations – the clinic, the school, the doctor, the shops – and servicing not only men and children, but also the sick, the handicapped and the elderly, are all tasks requiring extremely long hours of work and the massive expenditure of physical and psychological energy. The nurturing, caring role involves an orientation to the world which is dominated by the anticipation of others' needs. This readiness to respond to others and, in the context of the family, to manage the emotional exchanges between family members – facilitating, communicating, placating – is being seen as a social construction which is psychologically seriously unbalancing to the woman. Because, on the whole, her nurturing activities are not reciprocated, she must put her own needs last. She may want to be nurtured herself, and may express it indirectly in dependency on her male partner, but she cannot gain such nurturing: it remains a need which cannot be fulfilled. The more recent voicing of this experience shows us that what was seen within mainstream sociology as a 'functional' division between women's 'expressive' roles and men's 'instrumental' roles (see, for example, Parsons and Bales, 1956) hid from view the deeply oppressive nature of that division.

But in the past women have not, of course, been entirely silent over the experience of domestic labour and child care, especially where an opportunity existed which counteracted the *individualising* of the experience. Without the comparative experience of other women, the individual person may imagine that other women do not face the same problems and this isolation reinforces feelings of inadequacy and guilt. This may be especially the case where little communication takes place between women living isolated lives in housing estates which fragment the possible interactions of those who live there. But where a close community exists, or where a political initiative has been taken to attempt to improve their conditions, working class women have given voice to their experience. The exposure of these experiences, in examples drawn from evidence published in 1915 and 1939, show us that despite the substantial material improvements that have occurred since these times, some of the descriptions of the lives of working class women would strike an echo amongst at least the most impoverished working class women today.

In *Maternity: Letters from Working Women*, edited by Margaret Llewelyn Davies (1978) and first published in 1915, we can see how a campaign aimed at improving maternal and infant care organised by the Women's Co-operative Guild could reveal the actual experience of domestic labour undertaken in a context of extreme poverty, lack of services and subordinacy to a patriarchal husband. One woman writes (pp. 27–9):

> My husband's wages was very unsettled, never exceeded 30s., and was often below the sum. I earned a little all the time by sewing. Did all housework, washing, baking and made all our clothes. But no amount of State help can help the suffering of mothers until men are taught many things in regard to the right to use the organs of reproduction, and until he realizes that the wife's body belongs to herself . . . Very much injury and suffering comes to the mother and child through the father's ignorance and interference. Pain of body and mind, which leaves its mark in many ways on the child. No animal will submit to this: why should the woman?

By the late 1930s, the material position of many working class women had improved, but their experience of domestic labour was still one of drudgery and exhaustion. In *Working Class Wives* by Margery Spring Rice (republished 1981) material collected by the Women's Health Enquiry was used to provide a description of the typical day of the working woman:

> For the majority of the 1,250 women under review the ordinary routine seems as follows. Most of them get up at 6.30 . . . When once she is up there is no rest at all until after dinner. She is on her legs the whole time. She has to get her husband off to work, the children washed, dressed and fed and sent to school . . . When this is done she must clean the house . . . Very often she does not sit down herself to meals. The serving of five or six other people demands so much jumping up and down that she finds it easier to take her meals standing up. Leisure is a comparative term. Anything which is slightly less arduous or gives a change of scene or occupation from active hard work . . . is leisure . . . If she is a good manager she will get [the children] to bed by 8, perhaps even earlier, and then at least, 'a little peace and quietude'! She sits down again, after having been twelve or fourteen hours at work, mostly on her feet (and this means *standing* about not *walking*).

Compare these examples of women's domestic routine in the past with a contemporary account of the typical experience of women in the 'prison' of the family:

> it is 5.45 pm in a block of council flats. In each of fifty boxes a woman is frying the children's fish fingers, bathing the baby, putting its dirty nappies into the washing machine and peeling the potatoes for the husband's tea. All the same, but all in isolation. Even if she goes out to work, a woman must spend many hours on housework, and it is many hours of socially unrewarding work because it is not shared, is unrelieved by companionship . . . Many women will push their toddlers miles to a once-a-week play group just in order to have an hour alone without the child's constant questions and demands.
>
> (Barrett and McIntosh, 1982, p. 58)

There are three points to be made about these accounts of women's domestic labour. First, we must note that the physical strain of long hours of work remains a constant feature of many women's experience of domestic labour. *Second*, the ideological assumptions underlying the work remains largely unchanged within at least some sections of the population, namely that domestic labour is almost exclusively women's work. *Third*, the male partner may still today treat the woman as his property, with rights to sexual assault and battery, as work on marital violence and the provision of hostels for battered women has revealed (see Dobash and Dobash, 1980; Binney, 1981). Domestic labour takes place in a family context of personal interactions; we shall look at these interactions later.

The performance of domestic labour by women, then, because of its gender-specific nature, involves them in predominantly negative experiences which have definite psychological effects. We can summarise these effects by reference to what has to be repressed in women in order that their domestic roles can be performed in a way that is acceptable to dominant ideology. Most basically, women's exclusive role in individualised domestic labour involves the repression of their own needs for nurturing and care in favour of the nurturing and caring of others. The fact that most domestic labour involves the minimal development of capacities, or at least capacities that are socially recognised as such, means that many women have little opportunity for the expanded reproduction of their labour power. Finally, women must often repress their need for autonomy as an adult in favour of subordination to men.

Domestic labour is not the only labour which most women undertake, for they are also involved in wage labour alongside men. We shall refer later to the especially subordinate position of women in relation to wage labour: at this point we need to turn to the experience of wage labour generally by men and women.

THE EXPERIENCE OF WAGE LABOUR

We have already discussed the abstract nature of wage labour under capitalism and the fact that it is a form of labour which stands in essential opposition to the individual, subordinating his or her needs and capacities to the imperatives of capital accumulation and profitability. We must now examine in more detail the actual psychological effect of the wage labour of the worker. Marx identified some of these effects in the *1844 Manuscripts*:

> labour is exterior to the worker, that is, it does not belong to his essence. Therefore he does not confirm himself in his work, he denies himself, feels miserable instead of happy, deploys no free physical and intellectual energy, but mortifies his body and ruins his mind. Thus the worker only feels at home outside his work and in his work he feels a stranger.
> (Marx, 1971, p. 137)

Although it is possible, as Sève suggests, to have 'pride in one's work' because the development of even abstract capacities may involve an expanded reproduction of labour power which unintentionally (so far as capital is concerned) benefits the worker personally, for most workers the experience of wage labour remains as Marx described it. 'Under modern conditions of mass production', Baldamus writes (in Weir, 1973,

p. 79) 'the most pertinent work reality is the high degree of repetitiveness of light work.' He goes on to examine the nature of tedium at work, and the means by which production processes can be devised which 'are likely to overlay, postpone or remove any very acute experience of tedium' (1973, p. 80). He identifies as 'pleasant' the feeling of 'being pulled along by the inertia inherent in a particular activity'. In other words, one abstract alienating aspect of the production process may be used to bring relief from an even more dehumanising aspect. Such an approach, typical of those concerned to ensure the habituation of the worker to the production processes, fails entirely to confront Marx's distinction between mental and manual labour.

For Marx, all human labour involves both a mental and a manual aspect, and in this it distinguishes itself from the activity of animals.

A spider conducts operations that resemble those of a weaver, and a bee puts to shame an architect in the construction of her cells. But what distinguishes the worst architect from the best of bees is this, that the architect raises his structure in imagination before he erects it in reality. At the end of every labour-process, we get a result that already existed in the imagination of the labourer at its commencement. He not only effects a change of form in the material on which he works, but he also realises a purpose of his own.

(Marx 1974, p. 174)

The introduction of mechanisation into the labour process involves the worker in giving increasingly detailed attention to the manual aspect of labour and removing from him or her the mental control, the 'purpose of his own', so that he or she 'becomes transformed into a simple, monotonous productive force'. As automation and capitalist rationalisation develop, this process of stripping the worker of the mental aspects of labour-design, planning and control extends to many 'white-collar' occupations, including clerical workers, technicians, accountants, nurses, social workers, junior supervisors and lower grade managers. Braverman (1974, p. 408) asserts that 'capital, as soon as it disposes of a mass of labour in any speciality – a mass adequate in size to repay the application of its principles of the technical division of labour and hierarchical control over execution by means of a firm grasp on the links of conception – subjects that speciality to some of the forms of "rationalisation" characteristic of the capitalist mode of production'.

The mental aspects of labour, then, are increasingly appropriated by the higher managerial representatives of capital and the worker is thereby de-skilled. His or her abstract labour contains fewer and fewer opportunities to develop capacities and to engage in the extended reproduction of the worker's own labour power. Braverman quotes from a US Government enquiry into work published in 1973 which shows how far mass dissatisfaction with work is viewed with alarm by a state apparatus concerned to maintain stability and the trouble-free reproduction of capital and labour power:

> a growing body of research indicates that, as work problems increase, there may be a consequent decline in physical and mental health, family stability, community participation and cohesiveness, and 'balanced' sociopolitical attitudes, while there is an increase in drug and alcohol addiction, aggression and delinquency . . . Many workers at all levels feel locked-in, their mobility blocked, the opportunity to grow lacking in their jobs, challenge missing from their tasks . . . Women, who are looking to work as an additional source of identity, are being frustrated by an opportunity structure that confines them to jobs damaging to their self-esteem. Older Americans suffer the ultimate in job dissatisfaction: they are denied meaningful jobs even when they have demonstrable skills and are physically capable of being productive.
>
> (Braverman, 1974, pp. 31–2)

The point which Braverman makes most strongly is that the 'rationalisation' process in the factory, whereby jobs are increasingly fragmented and evacuated of many of those intellectual aspects which are inherent in human labour, is being rapidly extended to a wide range of ocupations which were traditionally considered to be 'skilled' or even semi-

professional. Furthermore, many of these occupations undergoing a process of de-skilling are populated predominantly by
women.

What are the psychological consequences for the individual
of engaging in labour processes where conception and execution have been effectively separated, leaving the worker with
only the latter part of labour? Clearly this is the ultimate in
alienated labour, for the worker is reduced to an object – not a
tool-using animal, but a tool. As we have seen, Schneider
considers advanced capitalist labour processes as lying at the
root of a great deal of mental illness: people fall ill from the
ever-present and recurring power of alienating labour. 'The
permanent withdrawal of mental "attention" and cathexic
energy by half-automated work processes', Schneider (1975,
pp. 175–6) writes, 'drives the libido back to regressive levels.
Day-dreaming or dozing during work is an expression of
enforced "regression".' Schneider sees this effect of the most
abstract forms of wage labour as the clue to the higher
incidence of psychosis amongst the working class, compared
with the middle strata and the bourgeoisie. But as the labour
processes of the middle strata of white-collar occupations
become increasingly 'proletarianised', a new contradiction
emerges between what is ideologically accepted within this
stratum and their actual conditions of existence at work. One
result is an increase in white-collar trade unionism which may
to some extent break the individualistic and competitive
ideology of the traditional bourgeoisie. But generally, the
deeper internalisation of bourgeois ideology probably
protects the white-collar worker from the most damaging
psychological effects of de-skilling: clutching at a petit-
bourgeois life style and its attendant values acts as one defence
against consciousness of the extent of dehumanisation at work.

Though de-skilling and the increasing limitation of the
development of capacities is a feature of a wide range of
occupations, it remains the case that it is in working class
occupations that the process has gone furthest. Assembly-line
production is the prime example here but other production
processes are similarly affected, for they all share 'the ultimate
tyranny of forms of social organisation based on "rational
principles" ' (Weir, 1973, p. 245). Capitalist 'rationality'

involves surplus repression and its effects, although they differ in certain respects from those flowing from domestic labour, are similar to those we have already identified: subordination (to management and machines), and the consequent repression of the need for autonomy and creativity in labour.

Grim as the picture of wage labour is, it is important to acknowledge that its detrimental effects upon the individual in anxiety, depression and loss of identity is also resisted. One form of resistance can be seen in industrial deviance and sabotage: the deliberate damage of machinery and products as an individual protest against a dehumanising industrial process. Trade union consciousness also acts as some defence against the fragmenting effect of modern production management: it at least identifies common interests and common enemies. Where such consciousness turns to militancy the psychological effect, as we shall see in Chapter 9, is likely to be even greater.

We have argued that the peformance of wage and domestic labour is a major determinant in the construction of the personality of the individual. But why do women remain locked in domestic labour and in the most subordinate forms of wage labour? How do men become habituated to abstract labour, remaining tied to that which seems both destructive and inevitable? To begin to answer these questions, we must move our attention from the actual material relations involved in performing labour to *ideology*, including in particular the ideology of the family as experienced by adults within this social order.

Individual commitment to wage labour and domestic labour can be seen as a product of both material necessity and ideological internalisation. For Marx, the worker engaged in wage labour in order to achieve a minimal subsistence necessary for existence by the selling of labour power. As women were increasingly excluded from the labour market from the mid-nineteenth century onwards as a result of a coincidence of interests of 'enlightened' capitalists and male trade unionists, they became more economically dependent on their husbands and so their domestic labour role became a matter of necessity. But the *external* constraints which lock people into performing labour may become weakened, as when extensive unemployment and state social security provision combine to make wage labour no longer an absolute necessity for subsistence or even, for many people, a possibility. In any case, the reproduction of the social order demands from the individual an *internal* commitment to labour: the incorporation of ideologies.

PARENTAL ROLES AND FAMILIAL IDEOLOGY

Perhaps the most powerful element of dominant ideology which maintains adults in their labour is that related to the family. It is the ideology of family life experienced through the internal practices of each family and through school, health and welfare services and the law, together with the media, which penetrates the very identities of individuals. As Barrett (1980, pp. 205–6) usefully points out, we are not here referring to the actual relationships within real families, which are remarkably diverse in practice, but to the 'ideology of familialism'. It is within this ideology that gender is socially constructed, and we have already seen in the previous chapter how the child is driven towards the 'appropriate' attributes of 'masculinity' and 'femininity'. This inculcation of gender-specific qualities in childhood is a crucial foundation in the construction of a gendered adult ready to assume his or her family responsibilities. But the internalisation of familial ideology must continue through adult life, otherwise subsequent adverse material experiences, economic changes, or the growth of alternative ideologies might weaken the psychological commitment to labour. As an example of this necessity to continuously reinforce the ideology of familialism, we can point to the current state re-emphasis on the importance of women's family roles now that the economic recession reduces the demand for women's wage labour.

We can select two roles as central examples of the significance of family ideology in the production of personality: *mother* and *male breadwinner*. We will see that the ideology of motherhood and of male economic responsibility together maintain women in domestic labour and especially subordinate low-wage labour, and men in forms of wage labour which might otherwise be rebelled against. These roles are based upon a conception of the ideal nuclear family where the father is the provider and the mother devotes herself full-time to the rearing of children, a conception central to some psychoanalytic writers (see Bowlby, 1953; Winnicott, 1964) and gaining official favour once more (see Kellmer Pringle, 1974).

Although the actual experience of being a mother, of going through the process of pregnancy, giving birth and then caring for the young baby can be a good and satisfying experience, as ideologically constructed, 'motherhood' represents to the woman a deeply contradictory experience. Because motherhood is presented to us from childhood as a highly valued social role with which most women are identified, becoming a mother, especially for the first time, is usually experienced within a context of widespread social approval. This social approval, combined with the personal pleasure which comes from achieving an important individual goal and the emotional significance of a close relationship to the baby, represents some of the positive experience of motherhood. On the other side, however, because 'motherhood' is a feminine role, it involves a set of psychological requirements which are problematic for the woman.

Most important, 'motherhood' involves *subordinacy* to the needs of the child: the mother is expected to place the young child's needs first and her own last (after the needs of her other children, her husband and perhaps dependent relatives too). These child's needs – for love and security, new experiences, innovative play, a good physical environment and diet – often place an immense burden on the mother. To be a 'good mother' is so demanding a role that complete subordination to the child's needs seems often the only way to meet it. In practice, women frequently struggle against this subordinacy of motherhood, seeking some meeting of their own needs; but if they do the result is often guilt and anxiety. 'Can I really be a good mother and pursue a career of my own or enjoy the leisure pursuits in which I am interested?' One way of managing the contradiction between the ideological demands of motherhood and the individual woman's own psychological need to develop her capacities is to deny or repress the latter.

One 'solution' to this problem is to 'live through one's

children'. The psychological limitations of full-time motherhood are such that some women may over-invest in their
children, projecting into them their own needs and thus not
responding to the actual needs of the children (see Philipson, I.,
1982). Another is to accept the kinds of wage labour (part-time,
evening shift or housework) which is very poorly paid, involves
minimal development of capacities but which does not 'inter-
fere' with the mothering role.

This practice of subordinacy in the role of mother involves
other effects upon the development of the personality of the
woman. Subordinacy in the feminine role requires, as we have
seen, an ability to anticipate the needs of others and to act
'expressively' in enabling other people to relate to each other.
Such gender-specific roles frequently place the mother at the
centre of family relationships, carrying the massive emotional
burden of managing conflict, protecting children against
father's anger, attempting to secure peace. Once again, the
mother's own needs may have to be denied, and so she ends up
receiving very little in return for the psychic energy that she has
invested in the family. But above all, subordinacy means that
being a mother is many women's *only status*: once you are a
mother you cannot expect to be autonomous and independent.
Your primary role is as mother rather than woman and so the
construction of the self must centre on the attributes of a
mother, rather than those of a woman who might rebel against
'motherhood'.

The dominant meanings that are attached to motherhood
and which make such oppressive demands on women are
frequently legitimated through a biological reductionist claim
that there is a special biological bond between the baby and the
natural mother upon which infant care must be based. Given
the close and symbiotic relationship which usually exists
between baby and mother and the influence of the ideological
construct of 'maternal instinct', it is not surprising that
biological justifications for the subordinacy of mothers gains
such widespread support and induces such guilt in women who
consider themselves to be acting in a way deviant to the
dominant norms of motherhood. None the less, the work of
Rutter (1980), Clarke and Clarke (1975) and Chodorow
(1978), to which we have already referred, dispels some of the

mystification surrounding motherhood and points to alternative conceptions of mothering. Schaffer (1977), for example,
shows us that young babies can make a number of relationships
and that, therefore, mothering can be shared by several people.
Furthermore, in contrast to the rather depressing implications
of some feminist work on object relations theory which appears,
as we have seen, to invalidate father's increased participation
in infant care, Schaffer suggests that mothering can be
effectively undertaken by a person of either sex and does not
need to involve the biological mother.

What is involved in attempts to redefine mothering in a way
which frees parents to make choices about the distribution of
child care activities is nothing less than an assault on the
gender-based division of labour in the family and, ultimately,
in the economy as well. But to be effective in re-defining
mothering involves also an attack on another powerful element
in the ideology of familialism, that of the *male bread-winner*.

The traditional male role of prime responsibility for the
material base of the family, secured through the sale of his
labour power for wages, can be understood in terms of the
social relations of a patriarchal order. The economic dependence of women and children on the male secures his authority
within the family and enables its material relations to reflect
male rule generally and ensure their ideological reproduction.
So far as the needs of capitalist production are concerned, the
male bread-winner–female home-maker roles are to some
extent experienced as contradictory. On the one hand, the
widespread emulation of the traditional bourgeois family form
secures a certain political stability, but on the other hand
women are frequently needed for full-time wage labour and this
may be an ideologically problematic requirement when it
appears to clash with the female mothering role. One answer to
this problem is to expect women to undertake both roles fully –
to be a full-time wage earner and a full-time mother, working in
total a 14–16 hour day. Even this may be politically difficult
and require substantial state intervention to pick up the
casualties which occur when women are expected to undertake
an impossible set of tasks.

The role of the male as prime bread-winner then, may at
times be problematic to capitalist needs. It is also today often

experienced as problematic by men themselves. Of course, economic dominance in a family with the consequent subordination of the wife and children to the 'bread-winner's needs' produces definite material benefits for the father *within the family*. Others must occupy the servicing role and, psychologically, the man may have the opportunity for compensating for the powerlessness of abstract wage labour by exercising economic power at home. He may not be able to make decisions at work, but at home he can ensure that his word counts for more than anyone else's and so, perhaps, enhance his conception of himself as acting as well as being acted-upon. In a review of family patterns in a number of European countries, Goode concludes that in the division of family power between husband and wife, the husband will tend to dominate:

> In the final analysis, only a few family relations are not determined by the male . . . In reality, in all countries there are many women who manage to dominate the man, but it seems likely that in most countries, when the husband tries to dominate, he can still do this. Even when the husband performs the household chores, his participation means that he gains power – the household becoming a further domain for the exercise of prerogatives for making decisions. Perhaps the crucial qualitative difference is to be found in the extent to which, in one country or another, the male can still dominate *without* a definite effort to do so.
>
> (Goode, 1963, p. 70)

This prerogative in decision-making is traditionally based upon male economic power over family members. In fact, the selection of the male primary bread-winner role as crucial within family ideology, rather than that of *father* which the former incorporates, is designed both to emphasise the material base of family ideology and to begin to point to its contradictions for the individual.

If men gain materially, and to a more limited degree psychologically, from their usual economic dominance within the family, they also pay a substantial price for their 'privileges'. The most obvious cost to the individual working class man is that his family bread-winner role, to which he has been socialised from childhood, effectively locks him into abstract wage labour and often blunts the drive to trade union militancy. The benefits of industrial action, especially strikes, are often counter-balanced against the pressures of 'family responsibilities', with the latter consideration winning in many cases. Furthermore, the ideological interpellation of the 'masculine' qualities required of petit-bourgeois and bourgeois occupations – aggression, competition, deference to authority coupled with the domination of subordinates – may create in the individual a psychological configuration which acts against some of the qualities now expected of a parent. Where the traditional bourgeois father was able to define his role in terms of providing economic security and authority, many fathers today, of all classes, wish to play a more substantial and intimate role within the internal relations of the family. In particular, they may wish to be more closely involved in caring for their children. But the role of *father*, when separated from its previous connection with economic dominance and familial authority, is difficult to specify. Is the father now essentially nothing other than a substitute mother – only second-best at the nurturing and caring tasks, because his securing of masculine identity has been at the cost of repressing, from childhood, the qualities necessary for the effective nurturing of his own children?

In considering gender-typing and its impact upon individual personality the emphasis of most investigation has been its oppressive effect upon women. This has been the right place to start, but to build up a materialist understanding of the individual requires more attention to be given to the detrimental effects upon men of the continuous ideological interpellation of 'masculinity' and of the actual material relations of 'breadwinning'.

CONTRADICTIONS IN FAMILY AND SEXUAL RELATIONS

But the limitation in our account of the production of adult personality so far is that it is too structurally determinist and must be subjected to two qualifications.

First, we can see that each adult individual has a highly

specific biography determined not only by the broader social relations of production and reproduction and the structures of class, gender and ethnicity, but also by the unique contingencies of his or her particular life history. This is why the socialist welfare worker, for example, cannot approach another's problems simply on the basis of *general* theories of personality and social structure: she must often be prepared to explore and exchange the particular experiences which each has had. To be born at a particular time; to experience the distinct interactions within a family of members with specific backgrounds influenced by local cultural practices; to have a specially close and/or antagonistic relationship to a parent as a result of the parent's marital relationship; to be seen as 'taking after' a near or distant relative with the expectations that this involves; to have attended a particular school and later entered a particular occupation with its own history and traditions; to live with another person and attempt to attune oneself to that person whilst maintaining and developing one's own identity – all of these experiences and interactions are unique, whilst at the same time being manifestations of general social forces. The understanding of the personality of a particular individual demands attention to personal biography, to the ways in which individual experiences and intentions within a social order determine what we think and feel, and how we behave. Furthermore, each family incorporates these individual experiences into a specific family cultural system of interactions, traditions and secrets, a deep structure, Seltzer and Seltzer (1982) suggest, containing many contradictions, 'a deep lying underside comprised of elements contrasting to its foreside'.

Second, if we are to acknowledge that *actual* families are relatively autonomous in relation to the economic infrastructure so far as their internal interactions are concerned, we are in a position to note the contradictions within families as experienced by their members. Family life in general cannot be described only in terms of gender oppression and the destructive impact of abstract labour, though for some families, at the extremity, only totally negative pictures can render an authentic account. For most family members, of all classes, life within the family is probably experienced as a set of contradictions: on the one hand a haven of security, an arena of non-instrumental relationships, a place for loving and caring; on the other hand, a prison, an arena for domination, competition, jealousy and hatred. The fact that these contradictions are not simply the product of forces operating within the traditional nuclear family based upon the bourgeois family form is evidenced, perhaps, by the experience of some of these contradictions as existing where people are living together as homosexual couples without children (or with them, as in lesbian adoption). Of course, one might argue that familial ideology, submission to it and resistance against it, still acts as a contradictory factor in most long-term sexual relationships, affecting material exchanges, domestic labour and nurturing roles within them.

A primary area of contradiction lies in the nature of heterosexual relationships themselves. Feminist literature has frequently portrayed such relationships as essentially oppressive to women. But it is important to acknowledge how problematic are some feminist analyses which attempt to account for the interrelation of the social and the biological in sexual relationships. Barrett (1980, p. 67) suggests that 'we should try to distinguish between gender identity and sexual practice; that we should reject any direct link between not only maleness and femaleness and a "natural" orientation to heterosexual genital sexuality, but also between the social constructed identities of masculinity and femininity and their assumed consequences for sexual behaviour'. In other words, the great variety that exists within 'normal sexual behaviour' suggests not only that the ideological interpellation of what is appropriate 'masculine' and 'feminine' sexual behaviour may not be as powerful (or as important) as was once thought, but also that sexual relationships, though they reflect dominant ideologies and meanings, may also be an area where individual intention and choice can play a substantial role.

We must note, however, that dominant ideologies about sexual relations have played a definite part in limiting choice. Within the American bourgeoisie, for example, dominant conceptions of sexuality have suggested that technical competence is of such importance that one might be led to believe that even sexual intercourse, an ostensibly concrete activity, should aspire to some of the characteristics of abstract labour. Lewis and Brissett (1967), in a study of American sex manuals, show that sex came to be seen as work and the orgasm as the product. To the manufacture of the orgasm, immediate pleasure and emotion should be sacrificed it was suggested. Furthermore, gender-stereotyping invariably informed these manuals:

> The female is particularly cautioned to work at sex, for being naturally sexual seems a trait ascribed only to the male. The affinity of sex to her other work activities is here made clear: 'Sex is too important for any wife to give it less call upon her energy than cooking, laundry and a dozen other activities' (Eichenlaub, 1961). To the housewife's burden is added yet another chore.
>
> (Lewis and Brissett, 1967)

Sexual choice may for some only appear possible outside a traditional marriage relationship, for example in relationships with prostitutes (see McLeod, 1982), but this does not weaken the general contention that sexual relationships still contain the opportunity for a substantial exercise of individual choice.

We cannot conclude our comments on the contradictions which exist within family relationships without noting that parents carry their own childhood experiences of interaction with their parents, of distinctive family cultures, into their own parenting. We saw in the last chapter how children are subjected to appropriate gender and class ideologies which prepare them for adult roles in the social order. That the role of mother, for example, is communicated between woman and daughter through processes of identification and modelling. But parents and children also deviate from traditional roles, or consciously resist them.

As we have seen, part of this resistance comes from the ambivalence of the parent–child relationship: an ambivalent struggle between dependence and autonomy in the relationship and between love and hate resulting from the needs of the child and their inevitable frustration. Thus the construction of the adult parent is by no means an unproblematic outcome of smooth socialisation. The psychoanalytic view that we transfer unconsciously to subsequent relationships elements of earlier ones offers a useful insight here provided we do not see the transmission from parents to child in a mechanical way. Parents are not simply the bearers of 'the law' against incest, or of class and gender ideology, but also people living within contradictions and at times struggling against dominant meanings.

The reproduction of parenting and the creation of a family system is not simple then but *contradictory*. There is both *continuity* in the process in so far as parents are models (at a conscious and unconscious level) for their children's own parenting, but also *change and resistance* in that parents are often rejected as models (again at conscious and unconscious levels). Of great significance to internal relationships within a family is the extent to which a parent is able both to identify with the child (through recollection of his or her own childhood) and at the same time see the child as essentially different and separate. It has been suggested as we have seen (see Chodorow, 1978; Eichenbaum and Orbach, 1982) that mothers may find it difficult to see their daughters as separate and that fathers may find close identification with their children problematic. It is partly because of the difficulties which parents experience in maintaining this balance, in one way or another, that parenting is so often an internally conflicting experience, reflecting ultimately external contradictions. The experiences of failure, guilt and pleasure are all usually present in parenting: even the most conscientious socialist feminist parents cannot easily live up to the demands of being a 'progressive parent', if such a thing is possible. The struggle to balance control with freedom, or the attempt to distinguish between necessary and surplus repression, is, in fact, the experience of most contemporary parents.

THE STATE AND THE PARENT

Being a 'good parent' is not however simply the concern of the mother or father but, as we have seen, has become an increasing focus for state intervention since the late nineteenth century. Our interest in state intervention in this area is focused on its *psychological* impact upon the individual and the family as one determinant of the personality structure of adults.

Although the state, through its general education and health services, contributes to the ideological penetration of individuals with notions of 'appropriate' parenting, particular sections of the working class are, in addition, subjected to monitoring and control of a more direct kind.

The most typical target of this direct welfare intervention, usually by social workers, is the working class mother on her own with several children. To the immense material and psychological pressure of struggling to survive as a mother, additional pressures are added. We have noted already that women attempting the impossible tasks involved in their socially necessary labour as mothers often become guilty and depressed at their 'failure'. Such feelings of failure are continuously reinforced by the pressures of consumerism. Women as housewives and sexual objects play a crucial role as consumer for the family unit, but if they are attempting to live on a low income they cannot continue to buy commodities at the level encouraged by the advertising media. For such women, guilt and depression at being 'bad mothers' may be created, at least in part, from the contradiction between a socialisation to consumption and the lack of the material resources necessary to fulfil their socially constructed 'needs'. We can say at once that welfare intervention in the family is unable to overcome the contradiction: suggesting that poor people should budget 'more effectively' or lower their expectations simply reinforces the definition of the problem as an individual one.

Indeed, the idea of budgeting on a low income is especially oppressive for the woman. The low budget 'family meals' presented in the popular women's press often require that for a woman to stay within these budgets – engaging in careful comparative shopping, avoiding expensive 'convenience' foods, spending time in the preparation of vegetables and cheap cuts of meat – demands a 24-hour day. Certainly no wage-earning mother could achieve such economies, though she may feel guilty if she cannot and mutter her 'excuses' to the social worker. Few social workers, health visitors or other 'family advisers' could possibly live within the low incomes of many of their welfare clients.

What is the general effect upon working class mothers,

especially those managing alone, of the additional element of direct welfare intervention in their lives? We can see at once that such intervention is likely to be experienced *as a contradiction*: on the one hand the possibility of material assistance and on the other hand being subjected to close surveillance and checking in relation to domestic labour and child care. Whilst such intervention focuses upon the individual circumstances and capacities of the mother, its psychological effect is likely to be one which simply reinforces the already massive pressure to pathologise parental 'failure' and induce increasing guilt. Because the structural forces (material circumstances and ideologies) which produce 'failure' in mothers cannot be seriously affected by individual welfare intervention, the effect of such intervention on the mother, though oriented to protecting the child, is bound to be at least problematic, at worst, entirely oppressive.

Idealised views of mothering may play an important part not only in inducing guilt in mothers, but also in influencing specific behaviours towards children. In their study of battered children, Kempe and Kempe (1978) suggest that battering mothers often feel that their child's crying, to which they may respond with violence, contradicts their expectation of what it would be like to be a 'good mother'. Similarly, Breen (1975) shows that depression in mothers is also often related to an idealised and romanticised view of mothering – a view which is contradicted by the actual experience of family life. If the social worker or health visitor enters family situations with the avowed objective of 'helping' the woman to become a 'better mother' this simply reinforces the woman's negative image of herself as having failed.

The socially necessary labour of mothers to which, despite its allegedly 'family orientation', welfare intervention devotes its closest attention comprises both abstract and concrete activities. Apart from abstract wage labour (often part-time and usually very low paid) which may be discouraged as an activity undertaken by 'problem mothers', the remaining labour will consist in part of those psuedo-abstract activities where the mother is reduced to performing highly routinised tasks, cooking, washing, cleaning, shopping, where the opportunities to develop capacities appear to be minimal. Other activities, where socially necessary labour and personal pursuits and interest intermingle, will be experienced as concrete, pleasurable and related to some degree to the woman's own intentions.

Interaction with her children is likely to be one such area of concrete activity. But this interaction may be perceived as deviant by the representatives of the state welfare apparatus: too inconsistent, insufficiently stimulating, not providing a sufficiently stable model of 'appropriate' adult behaviour. The effect of close monitoring and control over this interaction, through frequent welfare visits, case conferences and the ever-present threat of the removal of the children, may be to induce some change in the mother's behaviour, if only at the most superficial level.

But the effect upon the mother of this intervention may be at a level more profound than simply a minor modification in behaviour – it will, in effect, *change the distribution of use-time*. This is likely to happen in two ways. *First*, the more routinised socially necessary labour carried out in the home, already experienced as abstract, is under scrutiny inclined to become even *more* abstract. External welfare demands that routine washing, cleaning or cooking tasks be undertaken more 'effectively' or frequently, make such activities even more impersonal, dehumanising and factory-like in their impact upon the woman undertaking them. *Second*, some of the concrete activities which concerned interaction with the children, previously experienced as relatively free and spontaneous, may become, under state welfare surveillance, experienced as more disciplined, calculating, involving increased instinctual surplus repression – in a word, *abstract*. Under the impact of state welfare intervention, the area of concrete personal life shrinks and the externally imposed demands of abstract socially necessary labour increases. The possibilities for psychological growth, especially given the limited opportunities for the development of new capacities within women's domestic labour, are bound thereby to be further restricted.

CONTRADICTORY CONSCIOUSNESS AND ADULT PERSONALITY

We have noted throughout this chapter that the habituation of the adult to the ideologically prescribed roles demanded of the social order is never a simple, trouble-free matter for capital or the state. Avoidance, resistance and dissent are everywhere to be seen in the lives of individuals. Mothers frequently show signs of questioning the gender-specific activities expected of them; male wage earners often acknowledge the psychologically detrimental effects upon them of their abstract labour and strive to develop new capacities; women welfare clients attempt to resist or avoid the more damaging effects of state intervention. The fact that the state and capital may strive to pathologise these resistances as resulting from 'individual problems' is eloquent testimony to the potential danger they might present if they were to be politicised into collective class struggle. We will look at this potential in the final chapter of this book: now we need to emphasise the general point that the production of class and gendered subjects is always problematic.

We have already referred to Therborn's (1980) distinction between ego-ideologies and alter-ideologies. The ideological interpellation of the individual as a subject (in the twin senses of being subjected to and 'qualified' or prepared for the social order) involves developing an awareness of the *differences* between oneself and others. We have used the axis subordinacy–superordinacy as a prime example of this recognition of difference. Those who understand themselves as superordinate have conceptions not only of themselves, but of those who are considered subordinate. Therborn sees in this distinction between ego- and alter-ideologies the source of resistance to domination:

> Male-chauvinist sexist ideology should thus be seen as both an ego-ideology of maleness and an alter-ideology of femaleness . . . In relationships of power and domination, the alter-ideology of the dominating subjects is translated into attempts to mould the dominated according to the rulers' image of them, and into resistance to the opposition of the ruled. It is in this way that domination is ensured. The

alter-ideology of the dominated, on the other hand, while also involving a perception and evaluation of differences between ego and alter, tends towards resistance to the Other rather than towards forming him or her. This difference is inscribed in the asymmetry of domination.

(Therborn, 1980, p. 28)

The importance of this distinction lies in the attention it gives to contradictions in the formation of the consciousness of class and gendered subjects. The ideological interpellation of subordinacy within the working class carries within it a potential for resistance as well as the demand for submission. Women, for example, develop a conception of men as Other, with powerful characteristics but also weaknesses, and it is this overall evaluation upon which is based the possibility of individual resistance. In a similar way, the worker engaged in abstract labour has a conception of the capitalist or managerial Other which generally prevents complete habituation to and acceptance of the exploitive relationships of production. The extent to which individual passive resistance and dissent can be mobilised into an active challenge to domination depends, in part, on whether the existing relations of domination–subjection are seen as immutable or open to the possibility of change. This involves a move in our attention from emphasis on the production of class and gender conscious subjects to the production of subjects of class struggle or gender struggle. As Therborn remarks:

it is, of course, quite possible to be a highly class-conscious member of an exploited class without seeing any concrete possibility of putting an end to one's exploitation. The formation of subjects of class struggle involves, as far as members of the exploited classes are concerned, a process of subjection – qualification such that the tasks of producing surplus labour are performed and the existence of class rule is recognised together with its unjust character and the possibility of resisting it.

(Therborn, 1980, p. 20)

We will turn to precisely these possibilities of collective resistance in the final chapter.

8
Marginality in the Social Order

We have argued in this book that a materialist understanding of the individual must centre upon two aspects of the ensemble of social relations of which the person is constituted: the performance of labour and the incorporation of ideology. Through the economy, the family and the state, the individual is prepared for and maintained in productive and reproductive activity. For the great majority of adults this involves the selling of their labour power and the performance of domestic and nurturing activity which contributes to the reproduction of labour power. For a particular minority of capitalists, and their representatives, personality is formed from the activity of capital accumulation and reproduction and the ideology appropriate to such activity. But there are other minorities which we have not yet considered in our discussions. These minorities (some extremely large and growing) might be characterised as being *outside* the mainstream of productive activity and/or social reproductive activity. We might distinguish two kinds of minority here, both of which are on the margins or periphery of the central imperatives of the social order.

The first group are the *voluntarily marginal*. They do not engage in abstract labour, accumulate capital in any substantial sense, or submit to the mainstream ideological interpellations around work and family: they exist materially and ideologically within a relatively autonomous social world, although always in the last instance subject at least to the repressive state apparatus of law and order and to the material necessity of securing subsistence. Such voluntarily marginal people include members of some minority religious sects, such as the Sufi and the followers of Hare Krishna, members of communes and some artists. Amongst the most interesting work on these minorities has been that undertaken from within the phenomenological and symbolic interactionist perspective (see Berger *et al.*, 1974; and Musgrove, 1977) and it deserves further attention from socialists interested in the problems and possibilities of 'prefigurative' forms of social organisation and interaction in which objectives and relationships are established which prefigure those which might be characteristic of a socialist or communist society.

The second, and by far the largest of groups in the population who find themselves outside the major arena of capitalist productive and reproductive activity can be characterised as experiencing *involuntary subordinate marginality*. It is to these groups that we intend to give attention in this chapter. They are by no means homogeneous, for they contain many diverse characteristics, whilst retaining certain elements in common resulting from their particular relationship to productive and reproductive activity. We shall take as examples of subordinate marginality the experience and personality formation of the *long-term unemployed, people with disabilities and the elderly.*

The problem which we must tackle from a materialist perspective is this: production and social reproduction are central to the social order and to the individual's identity within it. Ideological discourse is directed, from childhood onwards, to the performance of the productive and reproductive roles which gendered class subjects are expected to perform. Familial ideology is especially significant in constructing a self which is congruent with dominant conceptions of the activities and capacities involved in present or future roles: mother, father, bread-winner, 'attractive young woman', 'useful member of society' and others. But what happens to those who do not appear to occupy these central roles? What is the effect of subordinate marginality on personality?

We cannot hope to answer these questions in any comprehensive way in this chapter, but we can point to some of the main experiences of subordinate marginality in terms of material relations, dominant ideological meanings, individual responses and the construction of identity. As we identify some common elements amongst those whose experiences we will draw upon as examples of subordinate marginality – the long-term unemployed, people with handicaps and the elderly – we will need to be aware also of the very different experiences which different kinds of subordinate marginality entail. For example, material poverty is an almost invariable consequence of unemployment and old age within the working class, but not necessarily so amongst handicapped people, depending in part upon the degree of severity of the impairment. Again, some forms of subordinate marginality involve a degree of resocialisation and changes in identity in the adult person, for example among the long-term unemployed, the elderly and those whose handicap occurred in adult life. For others, such as those who have been handicapped from childhood, we are concerned not so much with changes in identity as with the particular problems involved in the developing of a concept of self in a world dominated by the able-bodied.

Some forms of subordinate marginality may be experienced through unexpected events in a person's life: unemployment amongst those who have never previously experienced it, or the sudden onset in adulthood of a severely impairing disease. For those who have been handicapped from childhood, a past genetic or environmental accident or event forms a different context for their experience and how they respond to it. Old age is the expected condition to which all people must eventually orient themselves: for the majority of the working class, however, it is an especially unenviable end result of a lifelong engagement in hard and exploited labour. All the examples of subordinate marginality we will be considering involve, in varying degrees, the experience of stigma expressed through a range of relationships and reflecting dominant ideologies concerning the production of gendered class subjects and their role in the reproduction of the social order.

POVERTY AND THE ABSENCE OF WAGE LABOUR

We are now in a position to begin to identify some of the common processes and experiences involved in subordinate marginality, beginning with an examination of the actual material relations involved. The first point to make is that for the unemployed and the elderly retired, together with those judged by the able-bodied to be too severely handicapped to engage in wage labour, one of the most significant of their experiences is that they do not devote any substantial part of their use-time to the performance of abstract wage labour. Unemployed and retired women will usually continue to undertake domestic labour, though for very elderly handicapped women, especially those living in institutions, even simple domestic tasks come to be considered, correctly or incorrectly, as no longer possible to undertake. The effect of this absence of abstract wage labour from a person's life is determined by a number of factors.

First, we must recognise that, for most people, having no labour power to sell, or having labour power that capitalism does not at present need, means reliance on a level of state benefits which are bound to involve some experience of poverty. As Phillipson points out in relation to the elderly:

> When the older worker steps permanently outside the wage system he or she becomes reliant on personal savings, an occupational pension or the state pension. In fact, most older people (over 70 per cent) rely on the state pension as their main source of income. Yet at the present time this pension (for a married couple) is equivalent to just 50 per cent of the average take-home pay of an industrial worker. For those without significant additions to their income, the most devastating experience can follow.
>
> (Phillipson, C., 1982, pp. 4–5)

For the unemployed, and often for the handicapped person or their families too, poverty is an ever-present experience. 'Certainly, poverty is the greatest nightmare of those who fall out of work', argues Seabrook (1982, p. 24) and quotes in support from Sinfield's study of the effects of unemployment:

> Observing the pressures and strains that poverty and prolonged unemployment place on many families, my own research has made me much more conscious of the many ways the double impact wears them down and turns them in

on themselves. The silent endurance of deprivation and rejection does not make headlines, and is astonishingly often dismissed as apathy or lack of will.

(Sinfield, 1981, p. 18)

But poverty, and its effects on personality and family relation-ships, is not the only possible outcome of living a life without wage labour: how the latter is experienced also depends upon how wage labour is evaluated by the individual and the ensemble of social relations of which the individual is consti-tuted. Let us look at the example of the elderly on this point. The age at which a person is expected to cease to undertake full-time wage labour is an arbitrary one for the individual and related to economic conditions and state policy. This policy tends to be determined by the demand for wage labour at a given time and the cost of pensions and social security provisions generally. In the post-1945 period in Britain, for example, governments have sometimes urged late retirement and sometimes (as when there is an economic recession) encouraged early retirement, linked to redundancy.

Apart from the financial crisis which many people face on retirement, elderly people, especially men, face a crisis of identity too. Men's identity, in particular, is often bound up with their wage labour role: the answer to the questions 'What are you?' or 'What do you do?' lies in describing one's paid work. For many elderly people, at least at the beginning of retirement, there is often an experience which could be described as mourning the loss of a 'productive role'. The neglect of the working class elderly under capitalism, reflecting their exit from production and reproduction, may be seen as the ideological and material base of this sense of loss. Even though the labour which has been lost may have been exceedingly abstract, involving little development of capacities, neverthe-less removal from the social relations of production is often experienced negatively. Only where, as in some petit-bourgeois professional occupations, the abstract capacities developed have a use-value after retirement, may the experience be more likely to be a predominantly positive one (see Phillipson, C., 1982, pp. 47–9).

Class divisions in retirement, in other words, are continuous with class divisions in pre-retirement work conditions. De Beauvoir (1972) argues that the middle classes, in so far as their wage labour is relatively unalienated compared with the working class, have also experienced relatively unalienated leisure. Working class leisure, on the other hand, is often of a passive alienated kind, a continuation of alienated work. As a result, de Beauvoir argues, working class people develop different capacities for using leisure, in that although they may look forward more than middle class people to retirement as an escape from alienated work, they actually experience it more negatively. This is not only because of their poverty, but also because they are less well equipped for it in terms of capacities which can be expanded in their own interests. Whilst de Beauvoir's generalisations, similar to those of Sève, need extensive qualification to take account of the great variations that can be found in leisure pursuits (for example, in the gardening and do-it-yourself activity of working class people and the passive television watching of many middle class people) her argument deserves attention when we look at the retirement experience of any particular individual and its relationship to her or his class position.

For the elderly, the absence of full-time wage labour from their lives may, then, be accompanied by feelings of loss, or relief, or even liberation if the possibility of developing new capacities appears to be present. For the unemployed, the sense of loss may also be experienced by those who were previously in employment, but to this must be added a pervading sense of *guilt* at not being at work. Even when, as now, unemployment levels are so high that individual responsibility can no longer rationally be attached to lack of a job, individual guilt, reflecting the ideological and material significance of wage labour in a capitalist social order, appears to be a widespread experience amongst the unemployed. In an often-quoted passage, George Orwell writes about the experience of unemployment in 1936:

When I first saw unemployed men at close quarters, the thing that horrified and amazed me was to find that many of them were *ashamed* of being unemployed . . . The middle classes were still talking about 'lazy idle loafers on the dole'

and saying that 'these men could all find work if they wanted
to', and naturally these opinions percolated to the working
class themselves. [The unemployed] had been brought up to
work and behold! it seemed as if they were never going to
have the chance of working again. In their circumstances it
was inevitable, at first, that they should be haunted by a
feeling of personal degradation. That was the attitude
towards unemployment in those days: it was a disaster which
happened to *you* as an individual and for which you were to
blame.

(Orwell, The Road to Wigan Pier, 1975)

Here, Orwell describes succinctly what is the predominant
personal experience of unemployment in the 1980s too: despite
its structural causes, it is still experienced as an individual
disaster tied up with the ideology of individual pathology –
'blaming the workless' (see Marsden, 1982, pp. 213ff). The adult
with a severe disability has often to struggle to demonstrate
that he or she can develop the capacities necessary for wage
labour and so secure employment. Loss of employment can
therefore be experienced as shattering by people with disabilities. A 50-year-old wheelchair-bound woman recalls her
experience years before of no longer being able to engage in
wage labour:

When I had to give up work, it was after my pelvis twisted
and it left me with one leg shorter than the other, the doctor
said I would never walk again and they wanted me to go into
care. I felt dreadful when I had to give up work, it was the
most shattering experience I had had, because going out to
work, you felt part of society, you were contributing, you
were earning your money. You also had your friends that you
went to work with, and then suddenly you were cut off, you
were in the house alone. Also of course financially you were
worse off. You were lonely, you felt useless, on the scrap
heap, finished, and it really was a very bad time.

(Campling, 1981, p. 115)

For those experiencing the subordinate marginality of working
class unemployment, handicap or retirement, the absence of

the opportunity to engage in wage labour is most likely to have a negative impact. The consequence of being outside productive activity is likely not only to be poverty, but also, for some, guilt, loneliness and feelings of worthlessness. Only where there have been previous opportunities to engage in the expanded reproduction of labour power is the development of compensating concrete capacities likely to be possible. It is the experience of those who cannot engage in wage labour which demonstrates to us that for all its detrimental effect upon the adult personality, its absence can be even more detrimental. If the use-time normally devoted to abstract activity cannot be replaced by concrete activity which develops capacities, psychological deterioration is a likely result. Seabrook (1982, p. 14) shows us that unemployment means 'the elasticity of time, all those empty hours in the middle of the day, the temptation to sleep more and more as an escape. The fact that employment imposes a time structure on the waking day is the first of the most important "latent functions of work" as identified by Marie Jahoda (1979), as opposed to its manifest functions, pay and conditions.'

THE IDEOLOGICAL CONTEXT OF MARGINALITY

So far we have emphasised the significance of the direct material experiences involved in subordinate marginality: poverty and the absence of wage labour. Already, however, we have begun to indicate the ideological context of these material experiences – the value of work, contributing to society and other dominant elements in ideology. It is to this ideological context that we now give more attention.

A striking feature of the ideological context of marginality is that it provides an illustration of one function of all dominant ideologies – their power to define and characterise a subordinate group of the population *from outside* in the interests of the dominant group. We have already noted the struggle of women to define their own situation themselves, their experiences, feelings, aspirations and capacities, rather than have them defined by men. In an entirely parallel way, we can describe dominant ideologies concerning people considered marginal to the social order as consisting of definitions of the situation of the marginal by powerful others who are not marginal. Within the general context of class, gender and ethnic relations, this means the unemployed being defined by the employed, the elderly by the young and people with disabilities by the able-bodied.

We may take the situation of people with handicaps as a particularly sharp illustration of this point. The lives which those with disabilities can lead, what they are capable of in terms of independent living, wage labour or sexual activity, is invariably defined for them by able-bodied people (see Sutherland, 1981). As part of the dominant ideology about disability, propagated primarily by 'experts' within the state apparatus, is a perspective which can be described as 'the tragedy theory of disability'. Within this perspective able-bodied experts – doctors, teachers, social workers – may feel free to concentrate on explanations of the feelings and aspirations of handicapped people in terms of their supposed psychopathology, 'reactions to personal tragedy' to be understood within a specialised 'psychology of disability'. One result of this powerful external definition of their situation is that it tends to suggest that people with disabilities cannot live worthwhile, active lives and that their capacities can only be defined through medical and social expertise, for their own definitions are bound to be 'subjective'. Pathologising the anger and frustration of people with disabilities diverts attention from the material deprivations and ideological subordination that they suffer continuously: instead of being given proper access to more resources and the opportunity to define their own needs, they are often given only medical, educational and social 'advice and support'.

If dominant ideology acts to perpetuate the position of exploited classes and groups through definitions and meanings which these classes and groups must incorporate into their own thinking and feeling, how is subordinacy ideologically legitimated in the case of those rendered marginal to the social order?

We can see already that such subordinacy is, in part, a consequence of gender and class relations, magnified in respect of those who are marginal to productive activity. But it is not only the person's relationship to the economy which accentuates this subordinacy, but also his or her status in relation to familial ideology. The unemployed, the handicapped and the elderly are all problematic so far as the ideal of the productive and reproductive nuclear family is concerned. Either they are not fulfilling their 'bread-winning' roles, or they are not performing the 'normal and healthy' functions of parents or children, or they are now a redundant appendage to the active family occupying no role except that of dependant. The ideology of familialism, Barrett (1980, p. 225) remarks, 'is centred on the family as the "natural" site for the fulfilment of supposedly "natural" emotional needs. This came about partly through an important process of defining as "marginal" people who did not fall within the confines of immediate nuclear family relations.' With the establishment of the bourgeois family form as hegemonic by the late nineteenth and early twentieth centuries, the construction of the self becomes defined in connection to nuclear family relations. The effective performance of the parent–child relationship becomes central and all other relations and roles become marginalised and subordinate.

We have seen in the previous two chapters how working class men and women are similarly and differentially defined as subordinate. How is that already existing subordinacy is magnified amongst those who are considered marginal to the economy and family? For the unemployed male, the loss of the bread-winner role, if it continues for more than a brief period, exposes him to disapproval and rejection which reflects the dominant condemnation of the unemployed as unproductive and the state's 'scroungerphobia' – the belief that the unemployed are lazy and fraudulent. Most significant, perhaps, is disapproval from relatives: 'My family look at me as if I was a lump of shit', says the wife of an unemployed man condemned by both his and her relatives. 'My father won't speak to me because I'm unemployed' says a young woman. 'He says he won't speak to me until I settle down and have a regular job and marriage and kids' (Marsden, 1982, p. 110).

For people with disabilities the experience of subordinacy is likely to be even more profound, expressing itself through a range of relationships including those within the family. The child with disabilities, for example, especially if she is mentally handicapped, is less likely to be spoken to as less is expected of her (Shakespeare, 1975, p. 19). Thus in their social production as subjects, the two senses of *subject* to which we have previously referred may be profoundly unbalanced in the case of the people with a disability. Ideological inculcation subjects them to the social order, but it frequently does not qualify or prepare them as actors in that order: they may be expected not to act, but only to be acted upon. But even in the case of the most extreme kind of disability, the possibilities of independent living appears to be so great that we can never assume that a person is only capable of being acted upon (see Shearer, 1983; Brechin *et al.*, 1981). We must acknowledge that many children and adults with disabilities receive a degree of support and respect which enables them to act upon their intentions and not simply respond to the actions of others. None the less, the struggle against a magnified subordinacy can be a dominant feature of the life of a person with a handicap (see Finkelstein, 1980; Crossley and MacDonald, 1982). Women with disabilities have discussed this subordinacy with Jo Campling:

> The students did not treat me as a girl with a slight handicap but as a person set apart. I felt I was worthless and very vulnerable every time someone made a personal remark to me or about me.

> Many people have supposed that because I am obviously disabled I am mentally subnormal and have therefore treated me as they would someone of low intelligence or as a child.

> In no time we were thinking of getting married ... My father said we could get engaged but not married and Derek's mother said, 'Why do you want to marry her, she's in a wheelchair?' I was angry. They were both trying to take my rights as a woman away from me.

> (Campling, 1981)

But the treatment of many of those considered to be marginal as if they were children, and had more limited capacities than is objectively the case, is illustrated clearly also in the experience of the elderly. With the deterioration of bodily functioning and the increase in illness and disease which accompanies extreme old age, elderly people are likely to experience growing depression. The general 'slowing down' may be especially significant in producing deep and widespread depressive feelings. Persecutory feelings, reflecting at least in part their objective subordinacy, may accompany this depression as dependency on others, including their own children, increases. In a social order which places so much value on the individual responsibility of adults, dependency is bound to be experienced as failure: 'being a nuisance', including being incontinent, often produces guilt and shame in the old person. Perhaps because dependency is only fully legitimated in the parent–child hierarchy of the nuclear family, dependency in old age (and with handicap) is almost invariably associated with treating the elderly as if they were children. This infantilising process, where the elderly person's rights as an adult are stripped away and he or she is simply *subjected* to the will of others, appears to be widespread, not only among old people's own children, where familial role reversal takes place, but also in the health and welfare interventions of the state. Institutional life is the terminal point of the old person's subordinacy, and women, because of their longevity, are most likely to experience the depersonalisation of the geriatric ward or the authoritarian and infantilising regime of the old people's home. 'The fact that women far outnumber men in old people's homes may itself to some extent explain the low standards of care and privacy', Phillipson, C. (1982, p. 73) suggests; 'degradation on the "inside" reflecting external beliefs about the rights of women in general, and elderly women in particular.' The subordinacy of those considered marginal to the economy or the family is invariably a magnified reflection of gender and class-related subordinacy in general: the wealthy bourgeois elderly male can be seen in dominant positions in industry and politics, reflecting a superordinacy which continues throughout his life.

THE SELF, IDENTIFICATION AND REPRESSION

We have suggested in previous chapters that the ideological production of a gendered class subject involves for the individual the operation of a number of psychological mechanisms whereby the imperatives of the social order are internalised to a greater or lesser degree, depending in part on the level of class and gender struggle and the consequent resistance of the individual to dominant forces. We have pointed particularly to identification and repression as the means by which ideology is both incorporated and resisted. In the case of the subordinate marginal person the effect of being outside production or reproduction can, as we have seen, be all pervasive. But underlying the conscious experiences of anxiety, guilt, or rejection, what are the more profound effects of marginality on the construction of the self? For the long-term unemployed and the working class elderly, marginality may produce a threat to self-identity, a shattering of a previous conception of the self as 'productive', as a 'bread-winner' or as a nurturing mother. A self-image of worthlessness involves at one level an internalisation of an external ideological evaluation, and at another level the turning-in upon oneself of the anger which is experienced at this ideological evaluation. This contradiction may provide the space within which anger can be directed outwards through connection with a counter-ideology which emphasises the structural causes of unemployment, or the worth and status of the elderly or those with handicaps.

The struggle to maintain respect for one's own self may be especially difficult in relation to their body image for people with a physical handicap. For women, in particular, we have already noted the powerful ideological impact of 'appropriate' body images which confirm their status as sexual objects, especially during adolescence. The individual's mental representation of her own body includes both what is considered the desired ideal image and what she sees as her actual body. 'A tendency has been noted for handicapped children to feel that the non-handicapped are perfect', Shakespeare (1975, p. 20) suggests, and points to the risk 'that their ideal body image will be totally different from what they see as themselves.' Such a tendency may well continue in adulthood under the impact of a dominant ideology of female beauty and attractiveness defined in highly conventional terms. A young woman, paralysed from the armpits downwards, confined to a wheelchair and incontinent, describes her own experience of ideal and actual body images in the following terms:

You may compare your body shape with how it was prior to disability and wonder whether your partner is comparing your body with someone else's. The inability of the disabled person to be purely physical, showing body movement, posture, wearing attractive clothes, can be a great disadvantage within the 'market place' of relationships. Seeing such physical abilities in others can result in jealousy which is hard to admit.

(Campling, 1981, p. 18)

Under the impact of subordinate marginality some changes of self-identity will take place. Marsden (1982, p. 155) in reporting his research with the unemployed, suggests that after a long spell of unemployment the individual loses so much self-confidence that 'urgency in looking for work seems to have passed the peak' and that the long-term unemployed 'had begun to feel that their whole identity was changing'. Marsden refers to this process as a *loss of identity*.

Coe's (1965) American study of three homes for the elderly, two for working class residents and one for the retired bourgeoisie showed a 'loss of identity' occurring amongst all the residents, though it was greatest in the institution for the most poor. In this instance we are witnessing the effects of subordinate marginality amongst the elderly being magnified by the characteristic loss of self typical of the inmates of total institutions.

Our materialist approach has involved the contention that because consciousness has a dialectical relationship with material existence, modifications in consciousness, including conceptions of the self, will take place as a result of changes in the ensemble of social relations of which the individual is constituted. Subordinate marginality involves, for most, such a change. But how much change in identity can we expect, and of what kind?

Although we argue that consciousness and the conception of self can and do change, we would be wise to be cautious in our arguments here. Although 'adult resocialisation' does take place, for example under the impact of a 'total institution' as Goffman (1961) has so vividly shown in his studies of the careers of mental patients, there are likely to be limits to the amount of identity change that takes place through the experience of marginality. In his study of a range of marginal experiences, both voluntary and subordinate, Musgrove concludes that even changes of considerable magnitude in the lives of individuals do not necessarily lead to comparable changes in identity.

> The evidence of these studies suggests that adults are capable of more fundamental change than many psychologists will admit; but that 'consciousness', 'identity' and 'the self' are far more resilient and resistant to change than important contemporary schools of sociology and social psychology will concede. We are not, in fact, chameleons.
>
> (Musgrove, 1977, p. 13)

Such a conclusion encourages us to re-emphasise the individuals' resistance and to avoid an over-determinist account of the material basis of individual consciousness. We must see the changes in identity which take place as a result of the experience of subordinate marginality, whether it is unemployment, retirement in old age, or recent disability, as involving struggle and resistance, as well as often submission and self-devaluation. Even more positively, we must recognise that subordinate marginality, if linked to collective action, for example among the militant unemployed or feminists with disabilities, may lead to an enhanced identity.

We have referred, in Chapter 3, to the symbolic interactionist view of the self as socially constructed, the outcome of internalising interactions with others. Furthermore, we have suggested that, following Freud, we can see that these interactions involve both identification and repression. If identification is a fundamental mechanism of personality development, then we need to ask how that mechanism operates amongst the unemployed, the elderly and those with handicaps. If your class, gender and ethnic-related subordinacy is magnified as a result of being *outside* production, or social reproduction, or the conventional nuclear family form and the roles that are entailed, with whom or what do you identify?

For the unemployed man, identification as a child initially with his father and later with other adult males will have invariably involved commitment, however occasionally ambivalent, to the importance of wage labour and of the breadwinner role in the family. Men unemployed for long periods of time cannot easily continue to operate on such identification with those who 'work'. Some men, usually with great ambivalence, may identify with 'housewife' or 'mothering' roles to replace their wage labour (see Marsden, 1982, pp. 119ff). In the deadly boredom and depression of 'hanging about' or 'filling in time', younger working class men may engage in fantasy which reveals how their selves are being shaped by anger at their subordinacy and how they identify with the powerful, the ruthless, and the most chauvinist. Seabrook, in a characteristically depressing account of the destructive effects of unemployment on the working class, reports the fantasies of young unemployed men about what they would do if they had unlimited money:

> I'd go to Canada and build a big house and have a big wall built round it, and electric fences; then I could keep away from all the stupid people in the world . . . I could tell everybody I didn't like to piss off. . . . I'd have all the crumpet I wanted queuing up. I'd never have to take any shit from anybody again. I'd hire a hit man to get rid of anybody who'd ever insulted me or made me look small . . . I'd spend five years just travelling, picking up women on the way . . . I'd just have people round me who'd do everything I told them.
>
> (Seabrook, 1982, p. 59)

Such fantasies are, of course, unlikely to be limited to unemployed youth for they reflect an interaction between elements of dominant ideology and the rage engendered by a material existence of poverty and deprivation, both economic and cultural. Such an existence is not limited to the unemployed, but unemployment may well increase the tendency to fantasy identifications as an escape from an intolerable present which appears to offer no objects of identification in the real world.

For the elderly, the identification available after retirement appear to depend upon a number of circumstances. The most benign view of retirement is that it is a period of liberation during which the individual, freed from wage labour, can assert his or her 'real' self, can at least act upon some of the earliest identifications. Musgrove (1977) describes a man in his late 60s who, after a lifetime as an office worker, has emerged as an artist – the role with which he identified all his life. He had contempt for his wage labour, for 'reality lay elsewhere, and was stored up in abundance awaiting his retirement'. Musgrove concludes from this and other evidence from his research that:

> the post-parental stage of the life-cycle, which is a novelty of our times, clearly does not involve remaking oneself, but subsiding thankfully and comfortably into being one's 'real self' after twenty years of unremitting child care. 'Real selves' may be saved up and carefully maintained for forty years awaiting retirement . . . Retirement is well worth a study as the phase or stage of life when 'real selves' are disinterred after fifty years of camouflage.
>
> (Musgrove, 1977, p. 14)

There can be little doubt that a benign experience of retirement, especially during the early years, is possible. Such an experience depends, however, on the absence of poverty and on the possibility of developing concrete capacities and thus continuing, as in the case of the elderly artist, the expanded reproduction of one's labour power. Benign experiences of retirement, involving the reinforcement of earlier identifications *outside* wage labour and the development of new capacities, are clearly class and gender related. Women appear to be more resistant to retirement from wage labour than men, because full-time domestic labour is a socially isolated occupation which women are reluctant to return to: identification with the 'housewife' role, rooted in childhood, is often experienced as an inadequate basis for women's retirement (see Phillipson, C., 1982, pp. 61–76). Furthermore, the process of identification between mother and daughter may emerge after the mother's retirement as a source of conflict. The retired mother, with no opportunities or preparation to develop her capacities, may continue to see her daughter, now in turn a mother, as an extension of herself and therefore wish to continue her child care role, by proxy, through her daughter, being unable to 'let go'.

For many people with disabilities, even those with severe physical impairments, commitment to a wage labour role is an important aspect of their personalities. Although there is often a struggle involved in training for and entering an occupation, not least against those who infantilise people with handicaps, its achievement is clearly of great significance. Equally important for many people with disabilities is the achievement of sexual and parenting roles, again often in the face of considerable resistance founded on the familial ideology of 'normal' parental and sexual roles. For those, however, who are excluded, because of the severity of their impairment, from achieving either productive or reproductive roles, the sources of identification are more problematic, especially where they are confined to a residential institution. Long-term institutional care, especially of the most severely mentally handicapped, presents a range of familiar problems, the extent depending upon the degree of stimulation provided by the institution. Amongst handicapped children in hospital, for example, compared with those living at home, there is evidence of greater verbal retardation, less developed social behaviour, more emotional passivity and less physical development (see Shakespeare, 1975, pp. 124–9).

Indeed, we can go further and recognise that some residential institutions actually enhance the differences between people with disabilities and the able-bodied, and create handicapping personal attitudes amongst the residents. Segregation of those with disabilities is certainly detrimental to them, as is evidenced by the fact that when mentally handicapped young people mix with able-bodied ones, the former quite quickly begin to lose their shuffling gait, adopt a normal stance and the mannerisms, modes of speech and expectations appropriate to their age. In other words, they drop much of their acquired handicapped identity.

However, for people with disabilities there is a contradiction and dilemma here. Whilst it is important to escape from an externally imposed handicapped identity, it is also important to resist the definitions of normality embedded in the ideologies of the able-bodied. Such definitions put immense pressure on those with disabilities to make themselves acceptable to the able-bodied. The great psychological stress involved in 'passing as able-bodied', and the liberation experienced in claiming one's own identity, including disabilities, is well illustrated in Sutherland (1981). A further illustration of the power of dominant definitions of normality and their resultant material practices can be found in the decision during the 1960s to suppress deaf people's sign language in schools for the deaf in favour of other means of communication. As a result, many deaf children have been further disadvantaged by being denied access to a complex language and culture which had developed within the deaf community.

We have referred earlier (especially in Chapter 6) to the repression that is involved in the construction of the self as a class and gendered subject. In particular, we have pointed to the ways in which, especially through identification with same-sex adults, the child represses those aspects of the developing self which do not conform to the appropriate gender stereotype. Such repression continues throughout life in most cases and maintains itself when the individual is faced with unemployment, retirement or a new experience of handicap. Unemployed and elderly men, for example, may find sharing in, or taking responsibility for domestic labour, or in the former case child care as well, problematic precisely because their nurturing potential has been repressed for a lifetime because it was considered inappropriate to masculine personality.

The repression of genital sexuality was seen by Reich as an important aspect of capitalist oppression of the working class (see Chapter 3). We have suggested, however, that as the bourgeois family form has become adopted by the working class it has also relaxed its control over genital sexuality, though not so much over sexual behaviour considered deviant. The so-called 'permissive society' is not a threat to the capitalist social order but another area into which capital can expand: commercial pornography. Although unemployed men may at times be stigmatised as 'irresponsible parents' who should not procreate children they cannot support through their wage labour, it is the elderly and those with disabilities, especially if they are in institutions, who are still specifically expected to repress their sexuality. Indeed, they are often perceived as non-sexual persons. Noteable as this denial of sexuality is in relation to the elderly (see Comfort, 1963) where the deterioration of body functions is used to legitimate their marginalisation even with respect to their sexual drives, it is with handicapped people that this denial and repression is most evident, though being increasingly struggled against.

In examining social attitudes to the sexuality of people with disabilities, Morgan (1972) suggests that by infantilising the severely handicapped, seeing them as children, institutions and families are able to deny their sexuality. 'People may well have some curiosity about the anatomical and sexual development of physically handicapped people, especially of girls' she writes (p. 91), 'but it is very difficult for many of the "normal" general public to face and accept the mature sexuality of people who are physically damaged in one way or another.' Professional staff in residential institutions for the handicapped may share, at an unrecognised level, this denial, whilst others are striving to assist handicapped people to achieve whatever sexual expression they wish.

But the dominant ideological pressure on those with disabilities is that they should accept an inferior sexual status. This requirement of sexual subordinacy is determined in large measure by the overpowering influence of familial ideology – the severely handicapped person cannot be seen as occupying those stereotypical roles in the nuclear family in the future which still legitimate genital sexuality and account for the continuing stigma which homosexuality attracts.

It is significant to note here that although people with many kinds of disability have experienced sexual subordination, the social order has also responded differentially to those with mental disability, compared with the physically handicapped. The most oppressive controls have historically been those exercised over the mentally handicapped, involving incarceration and sterilisation in the interests of economy, the control of criminality and the prevention of reproduction which would 'damage the racial stock'. The early twentieth century saw the strong emergence of a eugenics movement committed to 'racial purity' and attracting the allegiance of eminent medical experts concerned with mentally handicapped people. Eugenics was a set of ideas and practices which might be said to have reached its zenith with Fascism: Hitler had a solution for the mentally handicapped – extermination. In contrast, the sexuality of the physically handicapped could be denied and state policy directed, where possible, to training for a trade. In any case, the sexuality of those with physical disabilities was not as threatening as that of able-bodied people with mental disabilities; the physically disabled could be left helpless in their beds or wheelchairs, whereas mentally handicapped people could be perceived as clearly able to act upon their sexual drives.

Although oppressed ethnic minority status entails experiences of a different dimension to those of, for example, the white working class poor, the experiences are also similar. Marginality is, however, greatly magnified among the black population: racism ensures that their opportunities are substantially less than others in the working class and so if they are unemployed, or elderly or have disabilities their position is likely to be more depressing, to give rise to more anger and to have therefore a more profoundly detrimental effect upon the personality unless the depression and anger can be released into collective political action.

A clear example of the multiple subordination experienced by members of an oppressed ethnic minority can be seen in the situation of unemployed black youths. The existence of racist employment practices is clearly of increased significance in a situation of mass unemployment; the opportunities to engage in wage labour are even more remote than those of white working class youths. To this we must add two elements. The first is the racism of the repressive state apparatus which results in continuous police harassment of black youth, especially in the inner-city areas. The attempt to develop alternative, non-work activities as some social and psychological compensation for unemployment takes place in a context of increasing state surveillance and control. Second, the overall dominant culture of racism subjects black youths to continuous insult and degradation. It is a context in which injuries to the concept of self, characteristic of the experience of most people relegated to marginality in the social order, may be felt with even greater ferocity. In his classic work on the anti-colonial war in Algeria,

Fanon (1967) describes the psychological and psychiatric consequences of the struggle on both the Europeans and the Algerians. For many black youths in Britain an internal state of war exists between the black population and its white oppressors, with crippling psychological consequences for both sides. The appeal of Fascism to a minority of working class white youths is one example of the devastating consequences which can ensue from an explosive situation of mass unemployment, racist ideology and an increasingly powerful repressive state apparatus.

9
Personality Development and Collective Action

Throughout this book there has existed a crucial *tension* which is characteristic of much of the work which is undertaken within the historical materialist tradition. It is a tension which arises from the balancing act which Marxists must attempt in order to grasp hold of and maintain an understanding of the dialectic between consciousness and material existence. Over-emphasis on consciousness leads to the balance being tipped in the direction of idealism; exclusive concentration on material existence tips the balance towards a mechanical materialism. In this book the tension has revealed itself in the form of continuous attempts to balance an account of the material and ideological production of personality against an acknowledgement of the sources of resistance to the imperatives of the social order. Against the idealism of much of traditional psychological theory has been posed the determining effect of the material relations involved in the performance of wage and domestic labour. Against the determinism of functional accounts of the relationships between individual consciousness and the social order has been posed an emphasis on contradictions which provide the space for individual resistance.

Historical materialism is essentially about movement, about trying to grasp hold of phenomena which are never static but always in a condition of undergoing dialectical change. The social relations which constitute the individual personality are in continuous movement, subject to their contradictions and especially to the impact of struggles between the dominant forces in the social order and the oppressed and subordinate classes and sectors of the population. Although these struggles around gender, class and ethnic divisions are ever-present, their impact upon the construction of personality is determined in part by the extent of the individual's direct involvement in such struggles. In the balance we have tried to hold between the determinism of the social order and the resistance of the individual, the social order has inevitably won and rightly so. Exclusively individual resistance is of limited effect compared with the possibilities and psychological benefits of collective action. It is to these possibilities that we now turn.

PESSIMISM AND THE INCORPORATION OF DOMINANT IDEOLOGY

Although most Left-wing writers and activists would agree that collective struggle will be more effective, even at the level of individual psychological benefit, than atomised personal resistance unconnected to a wider group or movement, it must also be admitted that beneath defiant phrases there frequently lurks considerable pessimism about the real potential of collective action. In Britain, for example, the electoral triumph of the radical Right associated with and followed by an ideological offensive of great effectiveness, has given rise to increased attention being devoted to the problems of the growth of right wing ideology within the working class. The successful management and exploitation by a Rightist government of the Falklands adventure has demonstrated how atavistic and chauvinist appeals to patriotism can have considerable effect. Against an alliance of a radical Right government with a managed mass media the possibilities of even collective ideological resistance seem at times strictly limited.

Such pessimism, springing from a belief that the working class has been so psychically impoverished and incorporated that it can no longer resist, deserves our attention even though we may conclude that such pessimism reflects the incorporation of an element of dominant ideology into the consciousness of some parts of the Left. Its most influential statement in the post-war period comes, as we have mentioned already (Chapter 3) in the later work of Herbert Marcuse. In *One Dimensional Man* (1968) we contemplate a picture of the complete ideological and material incorporation of the working class into advanced capitalist society:

> in which the technical apparatus of production and distribution (with an increasing sector of automation) functions, not as the sum-total of mere instruments which can be isolated from their social and political effects, but rather as a system which determines *a priori* the product of the apparatus as well as the operations of servicing and extending it. In this society, the productive apparatus tends to become totalitarian to the extent to which it determines not only the socially needed occupations, skills and attitudes, but also individual needs and aspirations. It thus obliterates the opposition between the private and public existence, between individual and social needs. Technology serves to institute new, more effective, and more pleasant forms of social control and social cohesion.
>
> (Marcuse, 1968, p. 13)

Thus the working class is, in effect, written off as an agent of change because capitalism has succeeded in 'channelling antagonisms in such a way that it can manipulate them'. 'Materially as well as ideologically,' Marcuse (1965, p. 140) writes, 'the very classes which were once the absolute negation of the capitalist system are now more and more integrated into it.' Such pessimism has been much criticised by the Left (see, for example, Mattick, 1972) and often seen, in part, as the despair generated by contemplating the working class in the United States. But even in a Britain suffering economic recession and mass unemployment a similar account can be given, an account which seems almost to rule out the possibility of socialist collective action emerging from the working class.

In a series of writings, Seabrook argues his thesis that the consciousness of the contemporary British working class has been reduced and neutralised by capitalist ideology and its material relations. The effect has been so to penetrate the construction of individual needs and aspirations that resistance, even at a collective level, becomes increasingly problematic. Concluding his study of unemployment in the 1980s compared with that of the 1930s, Seabrook suggests that the material improvements 'yielded by capitalism' have been used 'as a means of creating a different kind of subordination of the working class'.

> This has been achieved by a series of penalties and forfeits which the working class has paid, the extent and significance of which are only just now being grasped. Among these losses, apart from the damaged sense of function, have been some of the humanizing responses to that older poverty, the solidarity and sharing, the living practice in the daily existence of millions of working people of values – dignity, frugality, stoicism – which offered an alternative to the brutalizing destructive values of capitalism. This has been the greatest loss of all because it means that the option of that alternative as something that could have grown organically out of the way people lived out their lives has been crushed ... In place of those losses, market relationships have encroached as a main determinant on working people's consciousness.
>
> (Seabrook, 1982, p. 221)

Seabrook's view of the destruction of working class values and relationships can be criticised on a number of grounds: it romanticises the working class experience of poverty in the 1930s, it reveals a puritanical attitude to the material improvements achieved since then, and it underestimates the degree of solidarity within working class communities today. However, the problems that he raises cannot easily be dismissed. Our attempt to understand the individual in terms of material relations and ideological domination has underlined how powerful is the effect of the relations of production, reproduction and consumption on the construction of individual consciousness. So we can expect that attempts to change one's orientation from intense atomistic individualism to involvement in socialist collectivity, however psychologically beneficial the change might seem from the point of view of *theory*, is bound in practice to meet many obstacles. The fact that it is possible however to make headway, through collective action, in overcoming some of the psychological obstacles produced by subordinacy – deference, fatalism, self-destructive anger – is surely evidenced in the growth of the Women's Movement and black anti-racist movements. Sensitivity to the oppressions of everyday life and to their effect on personality, from which much feminist work springs, provides a basis for forms of collective action which attempt not only to achieve material results, but to change the consciousness of those involved in the action.

REVOLUTIONARY *PRAXIS*

In arguing that socialist collective action, 'militancy' in Sève's terms, provides a means of personal psychological growth, we are applying to the individual the conception of revolutionary activity formulated by Marx for the working class as a whole. This revolutionary activity always involves, for Marx, both objective and subjective elements: objective material changes accompanied by changes in consciousness. This activity unifies theory and practice into *praxis*, reflecting on the world and changing it within the same process. 'In revolutionary activity', Marx and Engels write, 'the changing of oneself coincides with the changing of circumstances.' Thus the working class must change itself if it is to change society:

> Both for the production on a mass scale of this Communist consciousness, and for the success of the cause itself, the alteration of men on a mass scale is necessary, an alteration which can only take place in a practical movement, in a revolution; this revolution is necessary, therefore, not only because the ruling class cannot be overthrown in any other way, but also because the class overthrowing it can only in a revolution succeed in ridding itself of all the muck of ages and become fitted to found society anew
> (Marx and Engels, 1970, pp. 94–5)

If we conceive of revolutionary activity as a process often taking place over long periods of time involving individuals in collective action, we can see that such activity helps the individual to be rid of the psychological 'muck' (guilt, lack of self-confidence, low self-esteem) which subordinacy to the social order often entails. Marx's formulation of revolutionary praxis emphasises that consciousness cannot change without accompanying action to change the circumstances, the social relations, which ultimately determine that consciousness. If we are not to be bounded forever within ideology, within the 'objective illusion' of the social relations of capitalism, then we must gain knowledge of these social relations and how they are constituted within our own personalities. But only through practice can this theoretical knowledge be developed as Mao Tsetung argues in his 1937 paper *On Practice*:

If you want to know a certain thing or a certain class of things directly, you must personally participate in the practical struggle to change reality, to change that thing or class of things, for only thus can you come into contact with them as phenomena; only through personal participation in the practical struggle to change reality can you uncover the essence of that thing or class of things and comprehend them.

(Mao Tsetung, 1971, p. 71)

Such a conception of the relationship between consciousness, practice and change must underly a materialist understanding of the place of collective action in the psychological development of the individual. Increased understanding of oneself involves, within psychoanalysis, participation in a process (analytic treatment) directed towards change. But the idealist basis of traditional psychoanalytic theory assumes that change in the person's life can come about simply as a result of changes in consciousness. Indeed, Freud made it a condition of therapy that his patients should make no major changes in their lives whilst they were in treatment. Our materialist approach maintains that greater self-knowledge is dependent on engaging in the struggle, along with others, to change some aspect of the social relations through which the self is constructed. The relationship between feminist psychotherapy and collective consciousness-raising provides an illustration, as we shall see later, of the importance of connecting individual change to collective experience.

CONSCIOUSNESS-RAISING

Although the conception of revolutionary *praxis* as involving
both subjective and objective elements was formulated by
Marx, the more recent versions of this *praxis* have been
outlined in the work of Paulo Freire (1970) and in the
contemporary Women's Movement. Freire describes the radical literacy programme in Latin America as involving a process
of *conscientisation* whereby an oppressive social order is revealed
as connected to the misery and fatalism of the peasants' lives.
Thus the attainment of literacy involves both changes in
consciousness and participation in action to overcome an
oppressive material existence as elements of a single process of
praxis: reflection/action. With a similar set of ideas and
intentions, consciousness-raising has been a powerful base in
the development of the Women's Movement. Mitchell sees
this consciousness raising as a

> process of transforming the hidden, individual fears of people
> into a shared awareness of the meaning of them as social
> problems, the release of anger, anxiety, the struggle of
> proclaiming the painful and transforming it into the politi-
> cal.
>
> (Mitchell, 1975, p. 61)

Thus through the practice of collective consciousness-raising,
the individual's experience is contextualised by an understanding of the social order which *stands against* the dominant
messages contained in the ideological inculcation of subordinate people. In the Women's Movement, this resistance and
the development of alternative understandings of the self came
through a process whereby

> the threads of common experience in the family, at school,
> with sex, at work, in the medical system and elsewhere began
> to knit together a picture of women's lives and of women's
> oppression. Women discovered that they shared feelings of
> powerlessness and rage, a sense of themselves as less than
> whole people, of frustration and under-development.
>
> (Eichenbaum and Orbach, 1982, p. 11)

In sharing and revealing to themselves the real experience of their existence, an experience which was largely and systematically denied by the dominant forces in the social order, a basis was established for the formulation of alternative explanations of women's subordinate position.

VARIETIES OF POLITICAL PRACTICE

Although those engaged in political activity on the Left would all place emphasis on the close connection between changes in consciousness and effective collective action, the differences that exist concerning how this connection is established and in what priority is of relevance to our discussion on collective action as means of personality development. The theory of consciousness-raising, because it rests ultimately on a conception of praxis (reflection/action), maintains that 'consciousness-raising is action aimed at altering societal conditions' (Longres and McLeod, 1980, p. 268). Thus consciousness-raising is seen as already being action because it is bound, if it is truly consciousness-raising, to accompany practical struggle for change. But despite such statements, we can see that political practices of the Left vary greatly in their emphases on either action or consciousness. A full discussion would necessitate the identification of a variety of political practices, but for our purposes we can point to two models of practice, that which is action-oriented and that which is consciousness-oriented.

The first, *action-oriented practice*, lays great emphasis on the achievement of material changes through collective action. Focus centres on the common material interests and concerns of those involved and the practical means by which material improvements can be obtained. The process of identifying and realising common material interests may lead to such changes in consciousness as are likely to accompany the necessity for moving from narrow individualism to some conception of collective needs. Within this form of practice, substantial changes in consciousness are a possible outcome, but are not a primary objective of the practice. Much trade union activity can be seen as an example of practice which does not aim primarily to develop a critical consciousness of an oppressive social order, but to gain material benefits for its members. Those living on social security benefits who organised themselves into Claimants Unions placed more emphasis than trade unions do on developing overall critiques of the social order which ensured their poverty, but still identified their starting point as the practical struggle for improved state benefits.

The second, *consciousness-oriented practice*, although it sees practical action as an outcome, places its initial emphasis on the changes in consciousness which are necessary before effective action can take place. Here, understanding of oneself in the context of the social order is the first priority, rather than the immediate identification of (possibly superficial) material interests. Women's consciousness-raising groups, and those men's groups which are concerned with combating gender oppression, are prime examples of this kind of practice.

Although the two kinds of practice we have identified are presented in extremely simplified terms and do not reflect the complexities which exist in all practices, the two models can be used as a device for exploring the ideological and material conditions under which collective action takes place.

At the level of theory, or what might be described as alternative political positions within the Left, it is possible to see action-oriented practice as reflecting an emphasis on material relations and consciousness-oriented practice as placing its focus on ideological struggle. Such theoretical differences can be seen, on the one hand, in Sève's argument that as the prime determinants of consciousness are the actual material relations of production, such relationships must be transformed before we can expect to move out of the illusions resulting from 'positive lack of awareness' of exploitive class relations (see Chapter 4, p. 97). The active struggle to transform these relations through revolutionary practice is the means by which changes in consciousness takes place, culminating in the altruism of the militant. On the other hand, Freire and others, following Gramsci (1971; 1977) place more emphasis on the ideological side of the dialectic between consciousness and action. The hegemony of the ruling class involves the domination of its world view, a view which drenches individual consciousness and which must therefore be actively struggled against *at the level of consciousness*. Changes of consciousness (especially concerning class, gender and ethnic relations) can take place prior to a revolutionary change in social relations and are indeed a precondition of the transformation of social relations.

Although, at the level of theory, we are identifying differences in models of practice which stem from differences about whether material relations or ideology constitute the more significant element in the dynamics of the social formation, there is also considerable overlap between the two positions as can be seen in the black civil rights movements in the USA. Both, after all, must give attention to material relations and ideology: it is the priority that they accord one or the other which differs. But variations of emphasis may stem from a range of factors alongside theoretical/political differences. Strategic and tactical considerations are of great significance when engaging in any political practice. Whether to emphasise either immediate material benefits or the need for changes in consciousness must depend upon (a) the degree of mystification surrounding that element in the ensemble of social relations against which struggle takes place, (b) the degree of ideological and material homogeneity amongst the participants, and (c) how pressing are the material needs of the participants.

PSYCHOLOGICAL BENEFITS OF COLLECTIVE ACTION

This preceding discussion on varieties of political practice has been a necessary part of our account of the relationship between personality development and collective action. Sève's emphasis on action-oriented struggle results in his identifying the development of concrete capacities as the psychological product of participation in collective action. The argument of Mitchell and others concerning the priority of consciousness-oriented struggle suggests that it is change in the conception of the self which is the main psychological benefit of collective action. Although expressed in the very different terms which reflect their different theoretical origins, 'the development of concrete capacities' and 'changes in the conception of the self' may be seen as the complementary and overlapping psychological benefits of collective action.

The most crucial benefit is, perhaps, that it enables those involved to begin to move away from the cult of individualism which dominates people's lives within capitalist societies. Individualism is especially strong amongst 'professionalised' workers – it requires them to remain fragmented from each other, encourages competition and envy and enables state managements to exercise control in a way which would be much more difficult in the face of collectivity. The authors of *In and Against the State* give an example of this benefit:

> The teachers we talked to, particularly Mary, had found that when they organized collectively it was possible to give each other support to work in a way which challenged prevailing attitudes in the school. Teachers of different subjects started using their free periods to sit in the classroom for each other's lessons, so that they could discuss problems together afterwards. This was done without the knowledge of the school authorities. The arrangement helped the teachers to develop socialist ideas about their work and to combat the isolation they otherwise felt.
>
> Mary also worked in a department with a number of other socialist teachers. Collective commitment to certain activities like showing films about racism enabled them to widen the scope of what they were able to do. 'Because the whole department decide to do something, there is no way they can stop us doing it'.
>
> (London–Edinburgh Weekend Return Group, 1980, p. 93)

Changes in the conception of the self centre, at their most powerful, on the gendered class subject becoming substantially more aware of the ensemble of social relations of which she is constituted. Such changes in the individual are especially directed against those 'common sense' meanings and understandings which render subordinacy as *natural* rather than as historically constructed, and see no alternative to the existing social order. Where the social order is fetishised as natural, then changes in the conception of self involve a struggle within the individual and alongside others against particular effects: a sense of inevitability, of deference and of resignation (see Therborn, 1980, p. 95). Such struggles are at the centre of the experiences of women's groups and of the work described by Freire with Latin American peasants.

A more specific example of such struggle can be seen in the developing collective practice of people with disabilities. In Britain, through a number of organisations, including the Liberation Network of People with Disabilities and the Union of the Physically Impaired Against Segregation, people with handicaps are fighting to escape from the domination of the able-bodied. Such escape involves a raising of consciousness amongst those with disabilities in order to resist the identities imposed upon them. This includes resistance to their politicisation being controlled by able-bodied people.

Changes in the conceptions of the self also involve, where the collective experience becomes penetrating enough, a recognition of that which has been repressed in the individual in the interests of the social order. In the Women's Movement, those interested in uncovering the unconscious legitimation of subordinacy have ventured into group psychotherapy as a form of collective practice which takes the consciousness-raising group a step further in the exploration and reconstruction of female personality. Eichenbaum and Orbach describe the work of the Theme-centred workshops of the London Women's Therapy Centre as aimed at learning about women's psychology.

> The topics [of the workshops] themselves range from dependency, competition, sexuality, mothers and daughters, anger, and jealousy, to issues around power, difficulties in intimate relationships, giving and receiving, compulsive eating and anorexia. In all these workshops emphasis has been on exploring painful and complicated themes with a view to enriching one's understanding of the underlying dynamics of each woman's individual psychology as well as opening up space for a new relationship to the issue to emerge.
>
> (Eichenbaum and Orbach, 1982, p. 71)

The development of the changed conceptions of self which such experiences provide are not, however, considered as ends in themselves, but as one part of a praxis of political struggle against women's subordinacy. Similarly, where Left political parties concentrate on the political self-education of their members, the very process often reveals to the individual the taken-for-granted assumptions about the social order which lie at the root of incapacitating emotions: despair and cynicism. The consciousness-oriented practice of Left-wing parties and groups is frequently directed in effect to confronting and attempting to resolve the contradiction in the individual between a revolutionary optimism based upon a theoretical understanding of the social order and a deep-seated pessimism which comes from the unrecognised incorporation of dominant ideology. To acknowledge that pessimism *and its origins* is an important step in the struggle to overcome the despondency which, in effect, affirms the dominant idea that socialist transformation of society is impossible.

Changes in consciousness are clearly necessary to the development of collective resistance and the growth of alternative socialist practices within state services:

> The only realistic socialist practice is that of building a *culture of opposition*. By culture of opposition we do not mean culture in the narrow sense to do with people's forms of recreation, or indeed in the sense of 'alternative culture' of a few years ago. It is about infusing all aspects of everyday life, from work and health to child care and personal relationships, with oppositional practice.
> (London–Edinburgh Weekly Return Group, 1980, p. 132)

Alongside changes in the conception of self which reflective political action can involve, there emerges the development of new capacities. We have suggested already that participation in a consciousness-raising process entails the development of important capacities: communicating one's experiences and feelings, overcoming the fear of isolation and rejection, developing the skills necessary to enable others to share experiences and feelings and to relate changes in consciousness to practical political objectives. The development of such capacities through the experience of consciousness-oriented practice involves considerable interactional skills and is likely to enable the individual to become more reflective and to direct anger about subordinacy outwards, rather than inwards as depression.

Some state workers within the social services and health fields have shown an increased interest, in recent years, in working alongside groups of service consumers in developing a critical consciousness of the nature of the services and how they define both the recipient of the service and the state worker within it. In hospital out-patient departments, for example, social workers have been able to assist in the development amongst patients diagnosed as depressed of an increased understanding of the material and ideological basis of their depression – its roots in gender, class and ethnic minority relations. Such work is exceptionally difficult to undertake, for the depression which many people experience is not an illusion but a reality which penetrates the person as guilt and self-loathing. The medicalisation of these experiences through drug treatments and 'support' does little to shift a person's understanding from an individual pathology explanation to perceptions of the structural determinants of his or her condition. But in a group committed to sharing experiences and perceptions, and building upon these an understanding of the social origins of depression as a step towards exploring practical solutions, it is possible to make progress (see Partner, 1979; Goy, 1980).

Action-oriented practice places great emphasis on the development of individual capacities which are seen as beneficial to the group's objectives. Community action at the neighbourhood or city-wide level, for example, involves a range of people developing new skills: public speaking, organising meetings, taking notes, writing letters, making alliances, negotiating with state officials, and so on. The specific issues around which community action frequently revolves – housing, planning, transport, employment, education – increase the knowledge of the participants of the complexities and contradictions of the social order and of the range of strategies by which it legitimates and defends itself. The development of these and other concrete capacities can have a profound effect on the individual. The person who previously had a distribution of use-time dominated by abstract labour and the passive consumption of commodities comes to have a use-time more balanced in the direction of concrete capacities. The effect of this expanded reproduction of the individual's labour power can be profound. As many community activists are women, we can see the transformation in their consciousness which is brought about through entry into the arena of community politics. When a working-class woman is elected to the chair of a community group of which her husband is a 'rank and file' member, certain changes in consciousness and in family practices are likely to occur and to result in personal struggles which can more readily be seen as essentially political (see Bradley, 1980).

Although we have sought to show that collective action can bring definite psychological benefits to the individual, we must also acknowledge that collective action can be experienced as disturbing and depressing. Eisenbaum and Orbach (1982, p. 14) suggest that one of the reasons for developing feminist psychotherapy was to try to uncover the social and psychological roots of the difficulties which were encountered in women's consciousness-raising groups. They suggest that 'feelings of envy, competition, anger and love emerged and were so powerful that the groups could sometimes neither contain or cope with them'. The problems encountered by the individual within collective political practice are rooted, of course, in the ensemble of social relations which constitute the individual and the group. The power of dominant ideology in producing competitiveness, the desire for prestige and supremacy, the feelings of hopelessness and other emotions, must be recognised and analysed if the individual is to gain psychologically from collective action. In the absence of such recognition, those powerful emotions and behaviours which are perceived as detrimental to effective collective activity will tend to be pathologised as the sole responsibility of the individual, and so bourgeois ideology will have triumphed in the very core of revolutionary activity.

CONCLUSION

The aim of this final chapter has been to suggest that despite the massive power of an advanced capitalist society, it is possible to resist its penetration into the very core of our personalities. We cannot of course avoid being subjected to and prepared for our various positions in the social order. But both dominant ideology and the material relations which it legitimates contain contradictions and are continuously struggled against, sometimes more overtly, sometimes more covertly. It is these contradictions and these struggles which provide the space for individual and – more importantly – collective resistance. But engaging in this resistance and, more positively, taking the offensive in demanding a social order which no longer deforms and limits the potential of human personality, requires us to understand how the present order constructs our consciousness. If we are to help ourselves and others to work for an alternative society, then we must try to grasp more fully what we have been required to repress in ourselves in order to be gendered class subjects properly prepared for labour. Understanding ourselves and changing ourselves are parts of a single process: a materialist approach to this process of reflection/action shows us that such understanding and change requires us to direct our attention to the ensemble of social relations of which we are constituted.

References

Althusser, L. (1971) *Lenin and Philosophy and Other Essays* (London: New Left Books).

Ariès, P. (1973) *Centuries of Childhood: A Social History of Family Life*, trans. R. Baldick (Harmondsworth: Penguin).

Barker, M. (1981) *The New Racism: Conservatives and the Ideology of the Tribe* (London: Junction Books).

Barrett, M. (1980) *Women's Oppression Today: Problems in Marxist Feminist Analysis* (London: Verso).

Barrett, M. (1983) 'Marxist–Feminism and the Work of Karl Marx' in Matthews, B. (ed.), *Marx: A Hundred Years On* (London: Lawrence & Wishart).

Barrett, M. & McIntosh, M. (1982) *The Anti-social Family* (London: Verso).

Beauvoir de, S. (1972) *Old Age* (London: Weidenfeld & Nicolson).

Beechey, V. (1977) 'Female Wage Labour in Capitalist Production', *Capital and Class*, no. 3.

Belotti, E. G. (1975) *Little Girls: social conditioning and its effects on the stereotyped role of women during infancy* (London: Writers & Readers Publishing Co-operative).

Benjamin, J. (1978) 'Authority and the Family Revisited; or, a World Without Fathers?', *New German Critique*, no. 13, pp. 35–37.

Berger, P. L. *et al.* (1974) *The Homeless Mind* (Harmondsworth: Penguin).

Binney, V. (1981) 'Domestic Violence: Battered Women in Britain in the 1970s', *Women in Society: Interdisciplinary Essays* (Cambridge Women's Studies Group).

Blackman, D. (1974) *Operant Conditioning: an Experimental Analysis of Behaviour* (London: Methuen).

Bowlby, J. (1953) *Child Care and the Growth of Love* (Harmondsworth: Penguin).

Bradley, J. (1980) 'Housing vs. Housework: a study of women community activists on housing issues in Coventry' (unpublished dissertation: University of Warwick).

Braverman, H. (1974) *Labour and Monopoly Capital: The Degradation of Work in the Twentieth Century* (New York: Monthly Review Press).

Brechin, A. *et al.* (1981) *Handicap in a Social World* (Oxford University Press).

Breen, D. (1975) *Birth of the First Child* (London: Tavistock).

Brenner, M. (ed.) (1980) *The Structure of Action* (Oxford: Basil Blackwell).

Brooks, K. (1973) 'Freudianism is not a basis for Marxist Psychology' in Brown P. (ed.), *Radical Psychology* (New York: Harper & Row).

Brown, G. W. & Harris, T. (1978) *The Social Origins of Depression: A Study of psychiatric disorder in women* (London: Tavistock).

Brown, P. (1974) *Toward a Marxist Psychology* (New York: Harper & Row).

Campling, J. (ed.) (1981) *Images of Ourselves: Women with Disabilities Talking* (London: Routledge & Kegan Paul).

Chetwynd, J. and Harnett, O. (eds) (1978) *The Sex Role System: Psychological and Sociological Perspectives* (London: Routledge & Kegan Paul).

Chodorow, N. (1978) *The Reproduction of Mothering* (Berkley: University of California Press).

Clarke, A. M. and Clarke, A. D. (1975) *Early Experience, Myth and Evidence* (London: Open Books).

Coe, R. M. (1965) 'Self-conception and Institutionalization' in *Older People and their Social World*, ed. Rose, A. M. and Peterson, W. A. (Philadelphia: W. A. Davis).

Cohen, S. (1975) 'Its All Right for You to Talk: Political and Sociological Manifestos for Social Work Action' in Bailey, R. and Brake, M. (eds) *Radical Social Work* (London: Edward Arnold).

Comfort, A. (1963) *Sex in Society* (London: Duckworth).

Corrigan, P. (1979) 'Popular Consciousness and Social Democracy', *Marxism Today*, vol. 23, no. 12.

Crossley, R. and MacDonald, A. (1982) *Annie's Coming Out* (Harmondsworth: Penguin).

Dale, R. (1976) *Schooling and Capitalism* (London: Routledge & Kegan Paul).

Dally, A. (1982) *Inventing Motherhood: Consequences of an Ideal* (London: Hutchinson).

Dobash, R. E. and Dobash, R. P. (1980) *Violence Against Wives* (London: Open Books).

Eichenbaum, L. and Orbach, S. (1982) *Outside In Inside Out: Women's Psychology. A Feminist Psychoanalytic Approach.* (Harmondsworth: Penguin Books).

Eichenlaub, J. E. (1961) *The Marriage Art* (New York: Dell).

Engels, F. (1955) *Anti-Dühring* (London: Lawrence & Wishart).

Engels, F. (1968) 'Origins of the Family, Private Property and the State', in *Marx and Engels Selected Works* (London: Lawrence & Wishart).

Engels, F. (1968) Letter to J. Bloch, in *Marx Engels Selected Works* (London: Lawrence & Wishart).

Eysenck, H. J. (1971) *Race, Intelligence and Education* (London: Temple Smith).

Fanon, F. (1967) *The Wretched of the Earth* (Harmondsworth: Penguin).

Finkelstein, V. (1980) 'Attitudes and Disabled People': *World Rehabilitation Fund Monograph No. 5.*

Firestone, S. (1979) *The Dialectic of Sex* (London: Paladin).

Foreman, A. (1977) *Femininity as Alienation: Women and the Family in Marxism and Psychoanalysis* (London: Pluto Press).

Freire, P. (1970) *Pedagogy of the Oppressed* (Harmondsworth: Penguin).

Freud, S. (1927) *The Future of an Illusion* (London: Hogarth Press).

Freud, S. (1963) *The Standard Edition of the Complete Psychological Works* (London: Hogarth Press).

Fromm, E. (1971) *The Crisis of Psychoanalysis* (London: Jonathan Cape).

Fromm, E. (1973) *Marx's Concept of Man* (New York: Ungar).

Geras, N. (1983) *Marx and Human Nature: Refutation of a Legend* (London: Verso).

Ginsburg, N. (1980) *Class, Capital and Social Policy* (London: Macmillan).

Goffman, E. (1961) *Asylums* (New York: Doubleday).

Goldberg, S. and Lewis, M. (1978) 'Play behaviour in the year-old infant: Early sex differences', *Child Development* 40: pp. 21–23, 1969, quoted in Chetwynd, J. and Hartnett, O. (eds) *The Sex Role System* (London: Routledge & Kegan Paul).

Goode, W. (1963) *World Revolution and Family Patterns* (New York: Free Press).

Goy, S. (1980) 'Group Work with Depressed Women' (Unpublished Dissertation: University of Warwick).

Gramsci, A. (1971) *Selections from the Prison Notebooks* (London: Lawrence & Wishart).

Gramsci, A. (1977) *Selections from Political Writings* (London: Lawrence & Wishart).

Hall, S. (1979) 'The Great Moving Right Show', *Marxism Today*, vol. 23, no. 1.

Hall, S. (1983) 'The Problem of Ideology' in Matthews, B. (ed.) *Marx: A Hundred Years On* (London: Lawrence & Wishart).

Hall, S., Critcher, C., Jefferson, T., Clarke, J. and Roberts, B. (1978) *Policing the Crisis: Mugging, the State, and Law and Order* (London: Macmillan).

Harré, R. (1979) *Social Being, A Theory for Social Psychology*. (Oxford: Blackwell).

Harré, R. and Secord, P. F. (1972) *The Explanation of Social Behaviour* (Oxford: Basil Blackwell).

Hartmann, P. and Husband, C. (1974) *Racism and the Mass Media* (London: Davis-Poynter).

Henry, J. (1966) *Culture Against Man* (London: Tavistock).

Hewitt, J. P. (1979) *Self and Society: A Symbolic Interactionist Social Psychology*, 2nd edn (Boston: Allyn and Bacon).

Hollingshead, A. and Redlich, F. (1958) *Social Class and Mental Illness* (New York: Wiley).

Jahoda, M. (1979) 'The Latent Functions of Work', *Bulletins of the British Psychological Society*, 32, pp. 309–14.

Jay, M. (1973) *The Dialectical Imagination: A History of the Frankfurt School of the Institute of Social Research 1923–50* (London: Heinemann).

Jones, C. (1983) *State Social Work and the Working Class* (London: Macmillan).

Kellmer Pringle, M. (1974) *The Needs of Children* (London: Hutchinson).

Kelly, G. A. (1955) *The Psychology of Personal Constructs* (New York: Norton).

Kempe, R. S. and Kempe, C. H. (1978) *Child Abuse* (London: Open Books).

Klein, M. (1960) *Our Adult World and its Roots in Infancy* (London: Tavistock).

Kuhn, A. and Wolpe, A. M. (eds) (1978) *Feminism and Materialism: women and modes of production* (London: Routledge & Kegan Paul).

Laing, R. D. (1959) *The Divided Self* (Harmondsworth: Penguin).

Laing, R. D. (1971) *The Politics of the Family* (London: Tavistock Publications).

Laing, R. D. and Cooper, D. (1964) *Reason and Violence* (London: Tavistock).

Lasch, C. (1981) 'The Freudian Left and Cultural Revolution' *New Left Review 129*, Sept–Oct.

Leonard, P. (1979) 'Restructuring the Welfare State', *Marxism Today* vol. 23, no. 12.

Lewis, L. S. and Brissett, D. (1967) 'Sex as Work: A Study of Advocational Counselling', *Social Problems*, 15.

Lewis, M. (1978) 'State as an infant – environment interaction: an analysis of mother – infant behaviour as a function of sex', *Merrill-Palmer Quarterly*, 18, pp. 95–121 (1972) quoted in Chetwynd, J. and Hartnett, O. (eds) *The Sex Role System* (London: Routledge & Kegan Paul).

Llewelyn Davies, M. (1978) *Maternity: Letters from working class women* (London: Virago; reprinted from 1915).

Löfgren, O. (1982) 'The Swedish Family: a study of privatisation and social change since 1880', in Thompson P. (ed.) *Common History: The Transformation of Europe* (London: Pluto).

London–Edinburgh Weekend Return Group (1980) *In and Against the State* (London: Pluto).

Longres, J. F. and McLeod, E. (1980) 'Consciousness Raising and Social Work Practice', *Social Casework*, May.

McCann, P. (ed.) (1979) *Popular Education and Socialization in the nineteenth century* (London: Methuen).

McLeish, J. (1975) *Soviet Psychology* (London: Methuen).

McLellan, David (1971) *The Thought of Karl Marx* (London: Macmillan).

McLeod, E. (1982) *Women Working: Prostitution Now* (London: Croom Helm).

McRobbie, A. and Garber, J. (1975) 'Girls and Subcultures', in Jefferson, T. (ed.) *Resistance through Rituals* (Working Papers in Cultural Studies 7 & 8, Centre for Contemporary Cultural Studies, Birmingham).

Maccoby, E. and Jacklin, C. N. (1975) *The Psychology of Sex Differences* (Oxford University Press).

Mao Tsetung (1971) 'On Practice', in *Selected Readings from the Works of Mao Tsetung* (Peking: Foreign Languages Press).

Marcuse, H. (1965) 'Socialism in the Developed Countries', *International Socialist Journal* (Rome: April).

Marcuse, H. (1968) *One Dimensional Man* (London: Sphere Books).

Marcuse, H. (1969) *Eros and Civilization* (London: Sphere Books).

Marsden, D. (1982) *Workless*, 2nd edn (London: Croom Helm).

Marx, K. (1971) *The Early Texts* D. McLellan (ed.) (Oxford University Press).

Marx, K. (1974) *Capital* Vol. I. (London: Lawrence & Wishart).

Marx, K. and Engels, F. (1970) *The German Ideology* C. J. Arthur (ed.) (London: Lawrence & Wishart).

Marx, K. and Engels, F. (1968) *Selected Works* (London: Lawrence & Wishart).

Mattick, P. (1972) *Critique of Marcuse* (London: Merlin Press).

Mead, G. H. (1964) *On Social Psychology* (Chicago University Press).

Mead, G. H. (1962) *Mind Self and Society* (Chicago University Press).

Memmi, A. (1965) *The Colonizer and the Colonized* (London: Souvenir Press).

Mészáros, I. (1972) *Marx's Theory of Alienation*, 3rd edn (London: Merlin Press).

Mischel, W. (1973) 'Toward a cognitive social learning reconceptualization of personality', *Psychological Review 80*: pp. 252–83.

Mitchell, J. (1975) *Psychoanalysis and Feminism* (Harmondsworth: Penguin).

Mitchell, J. and Rose, J. (eds) (1982) *Feminine Sexuality: Jacques Lacan and the école freudienne* (London: Macmillan).

Mooreland, N. (1982) 'Petit-Bourgeois Hegemony in Nineteenth Century Birmingham' (University of Warwick: Unpublished Ph.D. Thesis).

Morgan, M. R. (1972) 'Attitudes of Society towards sex and the handicapped', in D. Lancaster-Gaye (ed.) *Personal Relations, the Handicapped and the Community* (London: Routledge & Kegan Paul).

Mullard, C. (1973) *Black Britain* (London: Allen & Unwin).

Musgrove, F. (1977) *Margins of the Mind* (London: Methuen).

Mussen, P. (1973) *The Psychological Development of the Child 2nd Edition* (New Jersey: Prentice Hall).

Orwell, G. (1975) *The Road to Wigan Pier* (Harmondsworth: Penguin).

Parry, N., Rustin, M. and Satyamurti, C. (eds) (1979) *Social Work, Welfare and the State* (London: Edward Arnold).

Parsons, T. and Bales, R. (1956) *Family, Socialization and Interaction Process.* (London: Routledge & Kegan Paul).

Partner, M. (1979) 'Depression in Women' (unpublished dissertation, University of Warwick).

Philipson, I. (1982) 'Heterosexual Antagonisms and the Politics of Mothering', *Socialist Review*, no. 66.

Phillipson, C. (1982) *Capitalism and the Construction of Old Age* (London: Macmillan).

Platt, A. M. (1969) *The Child Savers: The Invention of Delinquency* (University of Chicago).

Poster, M. (1978) *Critical Theory of the Family* (London: Pluto Press).

Poster, M. (1979) *Sartre's Marxism* (London: Pluto Press).

Rayner, E. (1978) *Human Development*, 2nd edn (London: Allen & Unwin).

Red Collective (1978) *The Politics of Sexuality in Capitalism* (London: Red Collective and Publications Distribution Co-op).

Reich, W. (1970) *The Mass Psychology of Fascism* (New York: Farras, Straies & Giroux).

Reich, W. (1972) *Dialectical Materialism and Psychoanalysis* (London: Socialist Reproduction).

Rice, M. S. (1981) *Working-Class Wives: Their Health and Conditions* (London: Virago; first published Penguin, 1939).

Richards, M. (ed.) (1974) *The Integration of the Child into a Social World* (London: Cambridge University Press).

Roberts, L. (Aut. 1977) 'George Herbert Mead: the theory and practice of his social philosophy'. *Ideology and Consciousness* no. 2.

Rogers, C. R. (1951) *Client-centred Therapy* (Boston: Houghton).

Rowbotham, S., Segal, L. and Wainwright, H. (1979) *Beyond the Fragments: Feminism and the Making of Socialism* (London: Merlin Press).

Rutter, M. (1980) *Maternal Deprivation Reassessed* (Harmondsworth: Penguin).

Sampton, H., Messinger, S. L. and Towne, R. D. (1964) *Schizophrenic Women: Studies in Material Crisis* (New York: Atherton Press).

Sartre, J.-P. (1963) *Search for a Method* (New York: Vintage).

Sayers, J. (1982) 'Psychoanalysis and Feminism Revisited' (Mimeographed paper: University of Kent).

Schaffer, R. (1977) *Mothering* (London: Fontana).

Schneider, M. (1975) *Neurosis and Civilization* (New York: Seabury).

Seabrook, J. (1982) *Unemployment* (London: Quartet Books).

Sedgewick, P. (1982) *Psychopolitics* (New York: Harper & Row).

Seltzer, W. J. and Seltzer, M. R. (1982) 'Material, Myth and Magic: A Cultural Approach to Family Therapy', *Family Process*, September.

Sennett, R. and Cobb, J. (1977) *The Hidden Injuries of Class* (Cambridge University Press).

Sève, L. (1975) *Marxism and the Theory of Human Personality* (London: Lawrence & Wishart).

Sève, L. (1978) *Man in Marxist Theory and the Psychology of Personality* (Brighton: Harvester Press).

Shakespeare, R. (1975) *The Psychology of Handicap* (London: Methuen).

Shearer, A. (1983) *Living Independently* (Oxford University Press).

Shipman, M. (1972) *Childhood: a sociological perspective* (London: NFER).

Sinfield, A. (1981) *What Unemployment Means* (Oxford: Martin Robertson).

Skinner, B. F. (1964) 'Behaviourism at Fifty', in Wann, T. W. (ed.) *Behaviourism and Phenomenology* (University of Chicago Press).

Skinner, B. F. (1974) *About Behaviourism* (London: Jonathan Cape).

Smart, C. and Smart, B. (eds) (1978) *Women, Sexuality and Social Control* (London: Routledge & Kegan Paul).

Smith, D. (1976) *The Facts of Racial Disadvantage: A National Survey* (London: PEP).

Smith, P. (1978) 'Domestic Labour and Marx's Theory of Value', in Kuhn A and Wolpe, A. M. (eds) *Feminism and Materialism* (London: Routledge & Kegan Paul).

Smith, D. E. and David, S. J. (eds) (1976) *Women Look at Psychiatry* (Vancouver: Press Gang Publishers).

Stedman Jones, G. (1971) *Outcast London* (Oxford: The Clarendon Press).

Strauss, A. L. (ed.) (1956) *The Social Psychology of George Herbert Mead* (University of Chicago Press).

Sutherland, A. T. (1981) *Disabled We Stand* (London: Souvenir Press).

Therborn, G. (1980) *The Ideology of Power and the Power of Ideology* (London: Verso).

Timpanaro, S. (1980) *On Materialism* (London: Verso).

Weir, D. (ed.) (1973) *Men and Work in Modern Britain* (London: Fontana).

Williams, R. (1978) 'Problems of Materialism' (*New Left Review* 109).

Willis, P. (1980) *Learning to Labour: How Working Kids get Working Class Jobs* (London: Gower).

Wilson, E. (1977) *Women and the Welfare State* (London: Tavistock).

Wilson, E. (1983) *Only Halfway to Paradise: Women in Post War Britain 1945–1968* (London: Tavistock).

Winnicott, D. W. (1958) *Collected Papers: Through Paediatrics to Psychoanalysis* (London: Tavistock).

Winnicott, D. W. (1964) *The Child, The Family and the Outside World* (Harmondsworth: Penguin).

Winnicott, D. W. (1965) *The Maturational Process and the Facilitating Environment* (London: Hogarth Press).

Zaretsky, E. (1976) *Capitalism, the Family and Personal Life* (London: Pluto Press).

Zegiob, L. E. and Forehand, R. (1975) 'Maternal Interactive behaviour as a Function of Race, Socioeconomic Status and Sex of the Child', *Child Development* 46, pp. 564–68.

Zeitlin, I. M. (1974) *Rethinking Sociology* (New York: Appleton-Century-Crofts).

Index

acts 87, 90
alienation theory 77–83
Althusser, L. 48, 100, 103, 104, 218
Ariès, P. 121, 218

Baldamus, G. 160
Bales, R. 157, 222
Barker, M. 66, 218
Barrett, M. 3, 6, 7, 48, 50, 65, 67–8, 105, 131, 159, 165, 172, 189, 218
Beauvoir, S. de 185, 218
Beechey, V. 105, 218
behaviourism 12–14, 20, 80
Benjamin, J. 61, 218
Berger, P. 181, 218
Belotti, E. G. 131, 218
Binney, V. 159, 218
biology
  as a determinant 64–70, 109, 121, 167
  differences 51, 52, 65, 133
  needs coming from 89
Blackman, D. 13, 218
Bowlby, J. 146, 166, 218
Bradley, J. 216, 218
Braverman, H. 59, 161, 162, 218
Brechin, A. 190, 218
Breen, D. 176, 218
Brenner, M. 15, 219
Brissett, D. 172–3, 221
Brooks, K. 33, 219
Brown, G. W. 63, 156, 219
Brown, P. 32, 33, 42, 219

Campling, J. 186, 190, 193, 219
capacities, development of 87–90, 111, 117, 162, 185, 211, 214–16
capitalism, capitalist production and reproduction
  adult labour within 153–79
  childhood as preparation for 121–52
  its economy as a major determinant 110–111
  marginality within 180–201
  its nature 26–28
  and personality development 57–62
  its relation to individual labour and capacities 85–99
Charity Organisation Society 127
Chetwynd, J. 131, 219

childhood 37, 50, 52–4, 91, 100, 115, 121–52
  deprivation in 145–7
  ideology of 121–2, 128
Chodorow, N. 52–4, 167, 174, 219
Clarke, A. M. and A. D. 146, 167, 219
Clarke, J. 107, 220
class 109, 131, 149
  bourgeois 58, 60, 122–9, 133
  struggle 42, 43, 74, 97, 112, 202–6
  working 58, 60, 107, 126–9, 134, 138–41, 169–70, 203–6
Cobb, J. 148, 223
Coe, R. M. 193, 219
Cohen, S. 4, 219
collective action 118, 202–17
Comfort, A. 199, 219
commodity fetishism 28, 62, 63, 77, 82, 97
consciousness 2, 25, 29, 47, 60, 83, 97, 132, 152, 205, 206–7
  contradictory 116, 117, 178–9
  riasing of 118, 208–11
consumption 62, 63, 111
contradiction 27, 28, 75, 79, 83, 84, 87–8, 91, 112, 115, 116, 136, 145, 149, 152, 166, 170–4, 176, 192, 197
Cooper, D. 61, 221
Corrigan, P. 3, 219
Critcher, C. 107, 220
Crossley, R. 190, 219

Dale, R. 107, 219
Dally, A. 126, 219
David, S. J. 63, 155, 224
deviance as resistance 116–7, 164
  and the state 113, 149
disability see under marginality
Dobash, R. E. and R. P. 159

ego 16, 17, 58, 59, 60
ego psychology 18
Eichenbaum, I. L. 52, 53, 54, 130, 137, 156, 174, 208, 213, 216, 219
Eichenlaub, J. E. 173, 219
Engels, F. 22, 24, 26, 42, 44, 88, 206, 219
ethnic minorities 108, 109, 146–7, 150, 200–1
eugenics 199–200
Eysenck, H. J. 12, 66, 219

family 43, 44, 46, 47, 61, 64, 86, 100,
106, 111–12, 127–8, 157, 165–78
bourgeois form of 122–9
culture of 123, 132
ideology of 3, 111, 112, 113, 165–70,
189–91, 199
Fanon, F. 24, 201, 219
Fascism 40, 43, 44, 200, 201
fathers 44, 53, 139–40, 168–70
their authority 51, 126, 133, 145,
168
in bourgeois family 124–6
in working-class family 127,
139–140
feminism 3, 6, 7, 33
and biology 65, 67
and collective action 208, 213, 214,
216
its critique of Marxism 40, 105
and domestic labour dispute 101
its emphasis on ideology 104
and psychoanalysis 47–55
Finkelstein, V. 190, 219
Firestone, S. 67, 220
Forehand, R. 61, 224
Foreman, A. 34, 42, 47, 50, 75
Freire, P. 208, 220
Freud, S. 16, 18, 34, 35, 41–4, 46,
48–51, 54, 56, 58, 64, 220
Freudianism see psychoanalytic theory
Fromm, E. 18, 79–81, 220

Garber, J. 152, 221
gender 63, 100–1, 109, 130–2, 165–70
differences 47, 48, 50–4, 124, 129,
130, 134, 137–8, 143–4, 151, 154
Geras, N. 68–9, 220
Ginsburg, N. 107, 220
Goffman, E. 193, 220
Goldberg, S. 138, 220
Goode, W. 169, 220
Goy, S. 215, 220
Gramsci, A. 104, 210, 220

Hall, S. 3, 11, 107, 220
Harré, R. 14, 15, 220
Harris, T. 63, 156, 219
Hartmann, P. 146, 220
Hartnett, O. 131, 219
Henry, J. 148, 220
Hewitt, J. P. 72, 220
historical materialism 19–23, 24–9,
103, 202–3

and the individual 23–9, 39, 40
'human nature' 29–32, 36, 64–70
humanism 77–82, 103
Husband, C. 146, 220

id 16–17, 59, 60, 141
identification 115–6, 132, 136–8, 140,
143, 145, 152, 174, 194–8
ideology 11, 28, 32, 49, 52, 54–5, 74–5,
97, 100, 103–4, 106–7, 109, 115,
129, 135, 148, 187–8, 203–5
its interpellation 106, 108, 115, 131,
132–5, 138, 178–9
individual biography 170–1
individualism 212
instincts 35, 37, 44, 45, 49, 56
see also under repression

Jacklin, C. N. 131, 221
Jahoda, M. 187, 220
Jay, M. 42, 220
Jefferson, T. 107, 220
Jones, C. 107, 127, 221

Kellmer Pringle, M. 166, 221
Kelly, G. A. 15, 16, 221
Kempe R. S. and C. H. 176, 221
Klein, M. 52, 149
Kuhn, A. 101, 221

labour
abstract and concrete 84, 90, 92–6,
98, 99, 111, 148, 160–3, 176–7, 187
domestic 85, 86, 99, 100, 101, 110,
134, 143, 154–60, 176
and marginality 182–7
theory of 37, 45, 46, 57, 59, 78, 82,
83–90, 160–2
wage 85, 99, 100, 101, 110, 134,
143, 160–5
Laing, R. D. 61, 70, 221
Lasch, C. 41, 48, 55–6, 221
Lenin, V. I. 86
Leonard, P. 2, 221
Lévi-Strauss, C. 51
Lewis, L. S. 172–3, 221
Lewis, M. 138, 220
libido theory 49, 50, 54
Llewelyn Davis, M. 157, 221
Löfgren, O. 124, 221
London–Edinburgh Weekend Return
Group 2, 212, 214, 221

Longres, J. F. 209

McCann, P. 147, 221
Maccoby, E. 131, 221
MacDonald, A. 190, 219
McIntosh, M. 3, 159, 218
McLeish, J. 20, 221McLellan, D. 77, 78, 82, 221
McLeod, E. 173, 209, 221
McRobbie, A. 152, 221
Mao Tsetung 207, 221
Marcuse, H. 44–7, 57, 203–4, 221–2
marginality 114, 180–201
    as affecting the elderly 183, 184–5, 190–1, 195–6
    as affecting the handicapped 186, 188–9, 192–3, 197–8, 199, 213
    as affecting the unemployed 183, 185–6, 189, 193, 195, 200
Marsden, D. 186, 189, 193, 195, 222
Marx, K. 21, 23, 26, 28, 42, 56, 57, 77, 78, 79–82, 84–5, 94, 97, 160, 161, 206, 222
Marxism
    absence of a theory of the individual in 5, 6, 7, 40
    critiques of 40, 56
    see also under historical materialism
Mattick, P. 204, 222
Mead, G. H. 14, 31, 70, 71, 73, 222
Memmi, A. 24, 222
mental illness 59–62, 70, 117, 163, 215
Messinger, S. L. 63, 223
Mészáros, I. 30, 77, 78, 222
Mischel, W. 13, 222
Mitchell, J. 19, 20, 33, 42, 48–52, 68, 92, 103–4, 143, 208, 222
Mooreland, N. 127, 222
mothers, motherhood 44, 48, 68, 107, 130, 166–8, 176–7
    in bourgeois family 124–6
    relationship with child 52–4, 68, 124–5, 130, 132, 136–8, 173, 177
    in working-class family 126–7, 128, 175–6
Morgan, M. R. 199, 222
Mullard, C. 147, 222
Musgrove, F. 181, 194, 196, 222
Mussen, P. 132, 222

needs 88–90
neurosis 59, 60, 61, 117, 12

Oedipus complex 17, 48, 50, 51, 106, 144, 151
old age see under marginality
Orbach, S. 52, 53, 54, 130, 137, 156, 174, 208, 213, 216, 219
Orwell, G. 185–6, 222

Parry, N. 107, 222
Parsons, T. 157, 222
Partner, M. 215, 222
patriarchal relations 41, 43, 47, 154
patriarchy 51, 131, 168
performance principle 45, 46
personality, major theories of 12–19
pessimism 203–5, 214
phenomenological approaches 14–16
Philipson, I. 167, 222
Phillipson, C. 183, 184, 191, 196, 222
philosophies of science 14
Platt, A. M. 128, 222
Poor Law 127
Poster, M. 6, 64, 106, 124, 125–6, 128, 135, 223
poverty
    and child deprivation 145–6
    and consumption 111
    in nineteenth-century family 126–8
    and marginality 182–4
    and state intervention 114, 148–9, 174–6
praxis 206–7
production 26, 37, 45, 56–62, 100, 103–4, 109, 110, 161–2
property 142–3
psychoanalytic theory 16–18, 32, 33–8, 141, 142, 152–3, 173, 207
    in relation to Marxism 19, 40–64, 105
psychology, major trends in 12–19
psychosis 60, 61, 117

racism 24, 108, 146, 147, 150, 200–1
Rayner, E. 136, 145–6
Red Collective 33, 223
Reich, W. 42–3, 44, 46, 106
repression
    instinctual 58, 59, 116, 117, 141–5, 213
    surplus 45, 135, 141, 177
    see also under instincts
resistance 98, 108, 111, 112, 116–18, 136, 152, 153–4, 164, 173–4, 178–9, 194

through collective action 118, 164, 202–17
unconscious 117, 125
see also under deviance
revolutionary practice 206–8
Rice, M. S. 158, 223
Richards, M. 130, 223
right-wing ideology 1, 2, 203
Roberts, B. 107, 220
Roberts, L. 20, 223
Rogers, C. R. 15, 16, 223
Rose, J. 143, 222
Rowbotham, S. 104, 223
Rustin, M. 107, 222
Rutter, M. 136, 146, 167, 223

Sampton, H. 63, 223
Sartre, J.-P. 5, 6, 223
Satyamurti, C. 107, 222
Sayers, J. 52, 54, 55, 61, 223
Schaffer, R. 168, 223
schizophrenia 61–2, 63, 64
Schneider, M. 21, 22, 35, 36–7, 56–64, 76, 163, 223
Seabrook, J. 183, 187, 195, 204–5, 223
Secord, P. F. 14, 15, 220
Sedgewick, P. 62, 223
Segal, L. 104, 223
self, construction of 16, 31, 71, 72, 73, 115, 118, 144, 151, 167, 189, 191–4, 200
changing concept of 211–13, 214
Seltzer, W. J. and M. R. 123, 171, 223
Sennett, R. 148, 223
Sève, L. 31, 32, 37, 81, 82, 83–101, 103–4, 106, 223
sexuality 17, 35, 49, 172–3
preferences in relation to 145–6
repression of 35, 42–7, 124–5, 198–200
Shakespeare, R. 190, 192, 197, 223
Shearer, A. 190, 223
Shipman, M. 148, 223
Shotter, J. 15
Sinfield, A. 184, 223
Skinner, B. F. 12, 13, 223
Smith, D. 146, 224
Smith, D. E. 63, 155, 224
Smith, P. 101, 224
social learning theories 12–14
social psychology 14–15
social security 148

social work
and consciousness-raising 215
intervention in working-class families 149–50, 175–8
origins 127–8
socialist practice 2, 209–11
state
as determinant of the individual 112, 113, 114
intervention 107, 113, 114, 122, 127–8, 147–50, 174–8, 191
Stedman Jones, G. 107, 127, 224
Strauss, A. L. 72, 224
subordinacy, inculcation of 108, 114, 115, 131–5, 146, 150, 155–6, 166–7, 178–9, 205–6
as part of marginality 180–201
superego 16, 17, 60, 106
superordinacy, inculcation of 115, 131–5, 150, 178–9
Sutherland, A. T. 188, 198, 224
symbolic interactionism 14, 70–4, 181
in relation to Marxism 20, 72, 73, 74–5

Therborn, G. 106–7, 108, 132–3, 178–9, 213, 224
Timpanaro, S. 66, 67, 224
Towne, R. D. 63, 223

unconscious 16–18, 35, 43, 49, 52, 117, 137–8, 173
unemployment see under marginality
use-time 90–6, 111, 115, 126, 138–41, 148, 177, 187, 216
use-value 57, 62, 85, 143

Wainwright, H. 104, 223
Weber, M. 14
Weir, D. 161, 163, 224
Williams, R. 67, 224
Willism, P. 134, 224
Wilson, E. 107, 129, 224
Winnicott, D. W. xi, 52, 142, 166, 224
Wolpe, A. M. 101, 221
women see under gender, mothers
Women's Movement 29, 208, 213
see also under feminism
work see under labour

Zaretsky, E. 58, 128, 224
Zegiob, L. E. 61, 224
Zeitlin, I. M. 72, 73, 224